THE ACCELERATION CURE

28
BIBLICAL PRINCIPLES
TO GET UNSTUCK IN LIFE AND BUSINESS NOW

LATANYA R. QUINN

The Acceleration Cure

Copyright © 2024 by LaTanya R. Quinn

Published by Cure 4 the Soul, Frisco, Texas

Cover Design: LaTanya R. Quinn

Headshots: C Squared Media Group

Photo Credits: Front Cover Stock DNY59 Getty Images

All Rights Reserved. No part of this publication may be reproduced, stored on a retrieval system, or transmitted in any form or by any means, electronic, mechanical, photocopying, recording, scanning, or otherwise, except as permitted under Section 107 or 108 of the 1976 United States Copyright Act without prior written permission of the publisher. The copyright owner retains reproduction rights, and reselling in any capacity is prohibited.

Scripture quotations are taken from King James Version KJV.

Scriptures from the New King James Version® NKJV Copyright © 1982 by Thomas Nelson. Used with permission. All rights reserved.

Scriptures from The Holy Bible, New International Version® NIV® Copyright © 1973, 1978, 1984, 2011 by Biblica, Inc. Used with permission. All rights reserved worldwide.

Scriptures from Amplified Bible (AMP) Copyright © 2015 by The Lockman Foundation. Used by permission. All rights reserved.

Limit of Liability Disclaimer: This book is for educational purposes, not financial, business, medical, or legal advice. Its content does not guarantee success in any area and is not meant to replace sound professional advice.

If you would like to incorporate The Acceleration Cure into a group, class, training, or program, don't hesitate to contact us at info@cure4thesoul.com.

ISBN 979-8-9917122-1-7 (ebook)
ISBN 979-8-9917122-0-0 (Paperback)

Library of Congress Control Number 2024923561

Printed in the United States of America

DEDICATION

GOD

I dedicate this book to the eternal Triune Godhead—God the Father, the Son Jesus Christ, and the Holy Spirit. I can do nothing without your love, redemption, forgiveness, mercy, sanctification, purposes, discipline, guidance, wisdom, knowledge, and faithfulness. I look forward to the joy set before me.

PARENTS

My parents, George and Lynette Quinn, thank you for loving, caring for, and sharing Christ with me. You taught me how to depend on God and His Word. I'm forever grateful to you two for providing the space and environment to exercise my gifts and talents and supporting my dreams.

CONTENTS

INTRODUCTION		IX
PART 1 THE ACCELERATION CURE - FOUNDATION		**1**
CHAPTER 1	THE ACCELERATION SHIFT - MY STORY	3
CHAPTER 2	WHY CHRISTIANS ARE STUCK	15
CHAPTER 3	IDENTITY BLINDNESS	27
PART 2 BIBLICAL ACCELERATION PRINCIPLES		**41**
PART 3 EMOTIONAL ACCELERATION		**43**
DAY 1	PUT OFF ANGER	45
DAY 2	RELEASE ANGER TOWARD GOD	53
DAY 3	PRACTICE FORGIVENESS	59
DAY 4	CONQUER DEPRESSION	65
DAY 5	DESTROY JEALOUSY AND COMPETITION	73
PART 4 SPIRITUAL AND PHYSICAL ACCELERATION		**81**
DAY 6	UNLOCK THE VISION	83
DAY 7	USE WISDOM AND DISCERNMENT	93
DAY 8	DON'T TRUST THE FLESH	103
DAY 9	VALUE YOUR HEALTH	111
PART 5 FINANCIAL ACCELERATION		**121**
DAY 10	MASTER YOUR FINANCES	123
DAY 11	LOOK AT YOUR FINANCES	131
DAY 12	OVERCOME FINANCIAL EMERGENCIES	141
PART 6 MINDSET ACCELERATION		**151**
DAY 13	RENEW YOUR MIND	153
DAY 14	MOVE FORWARD FROM THE PAST	163
DAY 15	PRACTICE SELF-DISCIPLINE	173
DAY 16	COMMIT TO CONSISTENCY	183
DAY 17	PRODUCTIVELY PRODUCE	191
DAY 18	FOCUS AND PERSIST	201
DAY 19	ELIMINATE DISTRACTIONS	209
DAY 20	OVERCOME OBSTACLES	219
DAY 21	FIND YOUR MOTIVATION	227

| DAY 22 | CONVEY AN ATTITUDE OF GRATITUDE | 235 |

PART 7 EXECUTION ACCELERATION — **243**

DAY 23	CREATE AND INNOVATE	245
DAY 24	TELL IT	253
DAY 25	SELL IT	265
DAY 26	DETERMINE YOUR LOCATION	275
DAY 27	ROOT FOR THEIR SUCCESS	283
DAY 28	FINISH STRONG	289

NOTES — 297

ABOUT THE AUTHOR — 299

INTRODUCTION

Do you feel stuck in life, as if something is missing? Is it challenging for you to gain momentum in your pursuits and move forward? Even though you know and love the Lord, do you find yourself constantly struggling or going around the mountain year after year? As soon as you progress, it seems like a regression hits. You're not alone. Many of God's children feel stuck but are unaware of the reasons behind it. Although it can feel like you're not progressing, you are as long as you haven't given up the fight of faith. As we dive deeper into this topic, let's consider how understanding the concept of acceleration can bring clarity and assistance to our concerns. As we flesh out its meaning, I hope you'll discover solutions and triumph to these questions.

My acceleration started early in life as it symbolizes the ordering of steps God ordained for my feet—spiritually speaking. My mom, Lynette Quinn, reminds me of how I learned to start walking at *seven* months and then independently by *eight*. Sounds unheard of—I know, but anything is possible if the Lord wills it. If you ask, she'll give you a play-by-play of that moment with passion and conviction. My father, George Quinn, a minister, shared the gospel with me at *seven* (but closer to *eight*), and I believed and placed my faith in Christ Jesus for salvation. I finished this book at forty-*seven*, two weeks shy of my big forty-*eight*, and I'm holding on closer to my God than ever before because He's a faithful keeper.

So why am I telling you this and why did I pose those entry questions? Over twenty-five years ago, I embarked on a faith journey to achieve my dream big goals. As a fast mover, I had great successes but got stuck and decelerated. At a point, nothing I did in my life and businesses worked consistently or long-term. The stagnation frustrated me because I'd been learning to set and accomplish goals for years and knew how to achieve them. Why wasn't this proven process working anymore? Something was missing!

SUCCESS

I used to think implementing the world's strategies for goals and success was okay because of the proven results. Then, I realized that no matter how much I pushed to attain, some serious roadblocks made it impossible to accelerate. Thirteen years ago, God began slowing me down, shredding my inaccurate beliefs, and holding me in the valley with His mighty hand. God destroyed my faux foundation and the success pathway I erected. The Holy Spirit showed me how my original ideas of winning were incompatible with God's revealed truth, ways, and methods. He wouldn't let me go the route everyone else went, and that always worked because He has a purpose, design, and standard for my life. Therefore, He took me the long way to get the *ME* out of me.

Jesus took me away from all that business book learning and hustling for a decade and had me become a student of His Word. During those years, I felt like a kid learning to read, write, and do math for the first time. It was uncomfortable, and I wanted out of feeling stuck as He uncovered my sins and hidden wounds by holding a mirror to my heart and soul. I wish I could say it was easy—nope, far from it!

As visionaries, we all must endure this testing in God's unique way at some point, as the Father's goal is always to conform us to the image of His Son, Jesus Christ. The victory I've always wanted arrived from dealing with my heart through the experiences on these pages of soul-transforming biblical principles and lessons I learned since growing up in a Christian household and beyond. I will continue to use these principles for the rest of my life. Fortunately, I learned a thing or two between starting, stopping, slowing down, and settling for less than God's best for me. I've unpacked the meaning of acceleration and identified what's causing so many of God's children to remain stuck.

WELCOME

Welcome to **The Acceleration Cure28 Biblical Principles to Get Unstuck in Life and Business Now**. You didn't pick up this book by happenstance. God ordained this moment in your life for me to serve you through the text on these pages. As your sister in Christ, I desire to help you live the abundant life Christ promised to all who believe and place their faith in Him. Jesus says, "The thief comes only to steal and kill and destroy; I have come that they may have life, and have it to the full" **John 10:10 NIV**. I'm dedicated to seeing you—visionary, dreamer, leader, high achiever, and creative soul, break free from stagnation and become a spiritually healthy believer and leader. I encourage you to maximize your life and relationship with Christ on a firm foundation to create profitable, purpose-driven businesses.

As Christ's daughter, I aim to obey God's instruction to encourage, inspire, teach, and motivate you to reach your destination while successfully sharing the truth in love. I promise always to point you towards God. The twenty-eight-day lessons highlighted in this book never wavered from the time the Holy Spirit downloaded this concept and manuscript thesis in my spirit in 2017. This book will help you face obstacles and fears, guiding you to work through them and experience spiritual growth and joy in the Lord daily. While unpacking this book's depth, I realized the story began in my mother's womb. The inspiration for authoring this first title for the *Cure Collection* of books comes from my walk with God and my journey in business, ministry, and sales, which collectively span over twenty-five years. My experience has been humbling, challenging, complex, rewarding, transformational, and life-changing.

SOUL-TRANSFORMING

In 2018, God appointed me to teach His Word and provide commentary through a biblical lens using my writing and media skills. Cure 4 the Soul Ministries (C4tS) came from my prompt obedience to that calling. The name I received for C4tS from the Holy Spirit changed my outlook on spiritual growth and caused me to explore why the words *cure* and *soul*. With the name came a great responsibility to study and elevate. I had to become familiar with the soul's purpose in sanctification and transformation. This mission led me to my purpose of becoming *The Soul Coach*.

BRAVE FAITH

I've always enjoyed learning about business owners' success. But I wondered why we never hear too much about their day-to-day struggles and how they overcame them. How did they deal with anger, depression, money issues, leadership, inconsistency, disappointments, and failure? Starting and running a business (especially full-time) is a brave walk of faith. It takes spiritual, physical, emotional, financial, time preparation, discipline, and stability. As a Christian, it takes humility and spiritual endurance to run an enterprise purposed for you by the King of kings since before the foundation of the world. You're set apart—sanctified and holy. So, the assignment in your life is higher than you think because you're a servant and child of the Most High God, and you must advance to fulfill your purpose. Therefore, you can't just jump into the success pool like everyone else because you're not everyone else.

With your brave faith, you'll need to learn survival in the marketplace and how to persevere beyond places unbelievers can't go. You'll need to work smart and wisely. For instance, sacrificing your nights and weekends for some years to study *and* work on the vision to be who God designed you to become is necessary. Work six days and rest on the seventh.

HOW TO READ THIS BOOK

Before you get into this book, defining what it's about and what it isn't is essential. First, **The Acceleration Cure** is a resource to aid your spiritual growth but isn't written to replace reading and studying the Bible. Second, this book doesn't replace professional business, medical, legal, or financial advice. It's written only for educational and informational purposes, and I'm not guaranteeing any results. Third, it's divided into consumable parts. I recommend reading one chapter daily and, if possible, reading it with a friend. The goal is to deal with the hard things so you can spend more time enjoying your life instead of stressing about your needs and finances.

- **Part 1** The Acceleration Cure - Foundation
- **Part 2** Biblical Acceleration Principles
- **Part 3** Emotional Acceleration
- **Part 4** Spiritual and Physical Acceleration
- **Part 5** Financial Acceleration
- **Part 6** Mindset Acceleration
- **Part 7** Execution Acceleration

KEY TERMS

The terms herein are unique to my writing style and creative projects. They share practical ways of seeing things but aren't meant to replace biblical or doctrinal definitions and standards.

The Acceleration Cure—involves living purposefully and trusting God to guide your steps toward succeeding in what truly matters and counts for eternity.

The Acceleration Principle—synchronizes prayer with obedience, faith-driven action, and God's wisdom for acceleration. An easy way to remember the formula is to pray + obey + faith + wisdom = accelerate. It's the difference between trying to succeed in life and business with the Holy Spirit versus without Him.

Dream Big Goals—dreams and goals that align with God's will and purpose for your life. Dreaming big is not about becoming wealthy with money. It's about successfully completing the assignment you're called to by God.

The Gap—the opening that separates where you are now and where you want to be.

Identity Blindness—is the failure to authenticate, approve, validate, and confidently live one's identity as a new creation in Christ.

Purpose-Driven Business—is a venture God created and anoints you to build that aligns with His will and purpose for your life. It connects your gifts, talents, skills, testimony, story, background, passion, loss, triumphs, and interests to serve others for His glory.

Soul—the mind, will, and emotions.

Soul Work—is submission and co-laboring with the Holy Spirit's sanctification to remove unaligned habits and strongholds plaguing the soul for transformation.

THE CURE PILLARS

Acceleration CURE actions and prayer are included at the end of every daily devotional. The CURE pillars help link practical actions with the daily biblical principles.

- **Pillar 1:** **C**larify and **C**ommit
- **Pillar 2:** **U**nshackle and **U**nstuck
- **Pillar 3**: **R**eignite and **R**ewrite
- **Pillar 4:** **E**nrich and **E**ndure

The Acceleration Cure will reveal blind spots and hindrances to your success. Here, you'll find a holistic view of biblical and practical insights to help you get unstuck, grow spiritually, and align your priorities for transformation, acceleration, and abundance in Christ. If you've yet to start your endeavor, this book equips you for the preparation phase. If you're already on a mission, the book can open fresh insights and perspectives to strengthen your focus and add to your learnings. I hope you thrive all for the glory of God. I want you to reach the destination God has designed exclusively for you. I pray that your soul prospers and you'll be a stronger believer and leader as you embark on the acceleration path. "Beloved, I wish above all things that thou mayest prosper and be in health, even as thy soul prospereth" **3 John 1:2 KJV.**

Soulfully,
LaTanya R. Quinn | The Soul Coach

Part 1

THE ACCELERATION CURE

Chapter 1
THE ACCELERATION SHIFT – MY STORY

I finished that year's first quarter with the highest sales ever in business. Praise God! New Year FI—NA—LEE! Finally, I'm off the struggle bus. Just a year prior, I wasn't concerned about creating because of the depressing hardship I experienced with needing to put artistry to the side. It felt like every time I'd get excited about my dreams, dashed hopes followed, and I'd have to pick up the pieces from failures alone. But this time was different. People started reaching out about art again, and God inspired me to rebuild. Regardless of prior failures, my desire to win wouldn't end.

MONTHS EARLIER

Months earlier, while at my job, I knew God was stirring my heart to leave. There was no way I could continue working in that role because it consumed my soul's energy. Being in those cold buildings in corporate spaces always left me desiring and yearning to operate in my gifts. So, in May 2017, I trusted God's leading. I took a leap of faith and exited the 9-to-5. Cautious and wiser, I wasn't trying to jump out and lean on my own understanding because I knew how it felt to fail in business prior. Nevertheless, I was excited and planned for a successful year, trusting God for each step and the outcome. I evaluated the weak areas from prior experiences that prevented me from growing and made it a point to use them as lessons for progression. I rebranded Art by LaTanya Renee, converting it to Cure For Bare Walls. I knew that my commissioned work was my biggest income driver, but I didn't always want to paint on command for hire. I passionately created new art lines and options for various price points. I upgraded my inspirational/gift art and set up future revenue streams to roll out months later, such as mobile art classes, curated home packages, and prints from my originals. I also painted a new luxury collection called *Fresh*! Finally, I located a commercial space to service clients when they needed to use the local pick-up option, view art, or come in for a consultation.

I worked forty-plus hours on a strict schedule of themed days and rhythms. I dedicated Mondays to admin and planning. Tuesdays and Thursdays to door-to-door business and cold calls and field meetings. On Wednesdays, I'd work on digital marketing and YouTube videos and conduct business from my office. Fridays were my home studio paint days, while on Saturdays, I caught up on orders, photography, graphic design, website updates, preparing for classes, shipping, and other business-related tasks.

CRICKETS

The first ninety days were incredible. That's why I was shocked when I could only hear the piercing sound of crickets at the 120-day marker. Before I could launch my other income streams, everything suddenly dried up! There were no more interested art collectors in sight. The phone wasn't ringing, the email marketing wasn't working, and the momentum halted. The silence and the backdrop of crickets were too much. The sudden struggle and shrinkage were unreal! I questioned whether I heard God correctly to jump all in *again*, but to this day, I know I heard Him say—GO!

STUCK AND HEARTBROKEN

Unfortunately, the story didn't pan out as I had anticipated. It was a case of grand opening—grand closing. I was heartbroken and had to close the doors to my physical location just six months after renting the space. I continued with most of the business from home and booked a few mobile classes, which helped tremendously. I also created a last-ditch marketing campaign aimed at new homeowners—I only needed to sell one home package to stay afloat. However, during that sixth month, as I closed down shop, I felt a strong nudge from the Holy Spirit to start writing this book. The request felt strange, and I tried to move on, believing I had somehow conceived the idea. I wondered, "What kind of advice would I offer a business owner since I just shut my doors?" "Why would anyone listen to me?" But I began penning this book when I didn't understand its purpose. When I didn't even understand the delivery vessel—*me*—I still wrote what I was told.

Seeing my business crumble again, I felt lost while becoming an author. As my funds dwindled, I threw myself at the mercy of Corporate America. I worked full-time as a temp. In desperation, I didn't have time to negotiate my skill set and pay rate. I had to take whatever was available to keep from drowning financially.

This pivot was a gloomy time for me. I took a bold leap of faith—and now this? I couldn't process my life clearly and wondered why God would allow me to suffer on this level again when my God-given gifts and passion were in the knowledge and creative industries.

Despite my financial wins, I couldn't accelerate in business consistently. I thought God didn't want me to succeed as a business owner, and I was worn out striving to move ahead, only to hit brick walls and constantly fall flat on my face. My thoughts were, "Why am I the losing Christian who always embarrasses God?" "What's wrong with me, Lord?" "What do you want from me?" "Why can't I figure this business thing out when I always excel at everything I learn?"

BELONGING

My love for spiritual, personal, and business growth, goals, and learning has always kept me moving on in life. Of course, God is always first, but I felt unfulfilled without an aim. I needed love, acceptance, and belonging. So, I clung closer to my ex-husband because I loved him. Even though our previous marriage was unhealthy, this bond was better, but it was still unfavorable. I thought I could still be a mom and wife, so I was willing to work through things. I figured I'd continue helping him build the trucking company while learning to overcome the consistent relational breakdowns. My self-worth was hanging on by a thread, and I couldn't see who I was. Whenever he came back around, my foundation in Christ veered off track, and I'd transport into endless distractions and a ball of confusion. I was losing traction.

THE ACCELERATED SHIFT

In February 2018, I experienced an accelerated shift. God showed me several signs that my season was up in Atlanta. It felt too saturated, and the environment didn't feel the same as when I moved there from Detroit, MI, seventeen years earlier. One sign was how frustrating and limited opportunities were for me with my skill set in sales. I felt picked over and of little use. I needed to get back into corporate consultative selling quickly to rebuild my finances, but options were few. My ex moved to Dallas a year prior during our on-and-off again connection and wanted me to see if I liked it. And I did.

So, I sold most of my belongings to relocate there in April. On the morning of my move, I filled up my car and took a lot of artwork to my friend Amina Gillespie's house about thirty-five miles away. Since I'd be sharing a trucking load, I wanted to ensure that my ex had no issues adding all my stuff to his eighteen-wheeler. Despite two months of meticulous organizing and planning for my move, I was utterly shocked by the unfolding disaster. After leaving Mina's, I drove nearly an hour to the south side to check on my ex's *light load*, and I learned the trailer was full. Like that, my original relocation plans fell apart on the day of the move. He had no room in his truck to add my things, and he tried distancing himself from the mess and catastrophe it caused instead of taking accountability. Instantly, I had to make a new moving plan.

DESPERATION

Silly me. I was getting off track again. As I grew in Christ and moved on, my ex always had a way of pulling me back when I thought I'd never return. I had a vulnerable area that would eventually bend to let my ex back. I was in a toxic cycle that was desensitizing me from different vantage points. In those areas, I wasn't rooted within Christ enough to get out of it. There was an opening in my soul—a foothold—a raw and wounded part that needed healing. God wanted to shake me from mindlessly submitting to my ex as an idol again and the plans to remarry.

However, I'm responsible for my decisions. I allowed the man I once married to continue draining and trampling me underfoot and extracting every inch of my purpose, time, attention, financial and emotional resources, and proficiency. I was beyond angry but livid with myself for allowing me to be used and fooled, but I had no time to cry. I belted out words. I pray you'll never hear from my tongue again. Movers were arriving, and I knew the company's foreman—Arnold. He had assisted me with prior moves. I had to think fast and secure a storage unit because I had to leave my apartment that day. I was embarrassed and in disarray.

That night, after getting most things into storage, I lay on the apartment floor with a blanket, seething with the raw emotions of rage and anger. My ex had been calling me consistently to see if I calmed down so we could continue the journey to Dallas. "I told him, NO!" Why would I plan a long-distance move only to put everything in storage?

While talking to my mom, Lynette, who was hurt and upset, she asked me, "What are you gonna do now, baby?"

In my response, I felt a burning fire rise in me from the Holy Spirit, and my mouth said, "I'm gonna go anyway!" I knew that the power of God was shifting within me because I felt supernatural emboldened strength.

I turned in my keys the following morning after packing my remaining boxes alone in the car in the pouring rain. I stayed in a hotel room. My friend Amina was at work on Sunday, so I had her help me research some stuff online for my journey. It poured rain all that day, and my soul resonated with the atmosphere.

The next day, I checked out of the hotel and pressed forward. I turned into the mighty version of ambitious Tanya as I felt the acceleration of God's power press the supernatural speed velocity button. I was in the faith-speed adrenaline zone with tunnel vision as the Holy Ghost's GPS led and protected me. After driving for about twelve hours, I arrived in Dallas's fertile soil, and the next seven days were a whirlwind. Reality kicked in—I had just moved across the country without a job or apartment.

FERTILE SOIL

I arrived in Texas on Monday, April 16. I stayed in a hotel that evening and had the keys to a new apartment the next day before noon. I got settled in and prepared for the two interviews I had previously arranged. The opportunities weren't a good fit. I needed to make money now, and sitting around was too risky. I needed to produce income. By Sunday, the start of next week, I drove back to Atlanta to work sixty-plus hours. I resumed temp work, Monday through Friday, and drove for Uber.

I experienced many emotions, and tears always flow when I reflect on that week. My friend Kim Briggs allowed me to stay with her for seven days while in Atlanta during my work week. While on my lunch breaks, I set up and attended phone interviews. I was offered a few roles and accepted an offer through a temp agency. The following Sunday, April 29, I spent the day driving back to Texas. The 14-day nonstop hustle and faith flow were a lot on me. However, I started my new job that week. After about six weeks of learning the role, I asked my boss, Sonja Moss, if they could open up overtime for me. I obtained favor, and she granted my request. I took as much overtime as possible—glory to God!

FAVOR OVERLOAD

In August, while dining with my longtime friend and colleague, Jessica Williams, I casually said, "I need to get back in sales." She said, "You wouldn't believe this, but yesterday, my boss announced they're splitting my territory." She didn't know if they had filled the position internally, but she recommended I give her my resume. She submitted it directly to the hiring manager, Lindsey Hankinson.

After the interview, I cried for hours, telling God I wanted the job, but I didn't think He would let me have it. I named all the reasons I thought this and laid them before His throne. My sincere asking and reasoning with all my heart opened my faith because I began to believe the job was mine. And it was! I was offered the God-customized remote Healthcare Field Account Representative (FAR) position based in my city's location. The job was a consistent and financially stable blessing. The position allowed me to learn the DFW as a newbie and meet new people.

During my first six months of arrival, the Lord secured my foundation in Him with more vigorous and deeper roots. He kept me safe and prospered me spiritually and financially.

I slept on an air mattress for a year because it kept me humble, and I wasn't sure if I wanted to return to Atlanta. I slept that way until my brother in Christ, minister and businessman Terence "TJ" Davis, and his twelve-year-old son Kamen offered to bring the things I placed in storage from Georgia. Mendy gave her blessing so that her husband and son could serve me. They picked up the U-Haul in College Park, loaded my stored items in Roswell, drove my belongings to DFW, and packed most of them into a new storage unit.

I became debt-free within two years of moving to Dallas, arriving with only about $1600 in cash. God used the work of my hands to pay off the $25K in debt (which included my car) I accumulated to stay in business and live off of before my relocation.

CLOSED DOORS

I needed strong roots, spiritual restoration, and freedom from the years of manipulation, devaluing, and gas-lighting I sat in. I also was my worst enemy in some ways. I needed to see myself as God sees me—complete in Him. **Colossians 2:10 KJV** says, "And ye are complete in him, which is the head of all principality and power." The enemy planted so many traps in my life since childhood, and God moved me away from everything and everyone to cure my soul. Thank God for shutting down the original plan. I had a severely shattered view of myself, and I wasn't fit to run a thriving God-aligned enterprise or remarry my ex if I was looking elsewhere for my sufficiency, identity, and acceptance. All who choose a godly life in Christ must have their work tested in some form for His sake. "The fining pot is for silver, and the furnace for gold: but the LORD trieth the hearts" **Proverbs 17:3 KJV**.

Since I set foot on Texas soil, Jehovah has pointed out many landmines and schemes of the enemy. He's highlighted many character issues. I never would have gotten to my purpose if God hadn't intervened like He did on the day of my move. Finally, my spiritual eyes and ears opened. It was time to accelerate.

CALLED OUT

I didn't have peace during my house searches in 2020 and 2022 due to the limited options and the impact of COVID on the housing market. Additionally, God started to shake the foundation of my FAR role with several significant issues and incidents. So, I inclined my ear to the Almighty to listen to His instructions. I asked Him if He wanted me to stay and faith it out. His response was—NO! After three and a half years, God called me out. I resigned from my role on March 7, 2022.

As much success as I enjoyed, I pondered why God only allowed me to succeed in my corporate roles as a sales professional but not in any of the dreams and desires within my heart. After all, many artsy, creative people aren't interested much in selling or business. They hire agents, publishers, editors, and producers to free up that side of the brain so they can create more, so who did I think I was?

The truth is that somehow, I hoped business success would rescue me from the valley of despair. I subconsciously believed I could work and paint my way out of my issues. I didn't know I was functioning in survival mode. I didn't realize I was displeasing and dishonoring God. I had no life plan when I resigned because I didn't know what God wanted me to do next. I continued video content and writing for Cure 4 the Soul Ministries. But I sensed the Lord wanted me to rest in Him. I shifted to growing in the knowledge of God by reading through the Holy Bible from cover to cover a few times, books about hermeneutics, theology, systematic theology, and other Christian living books. I did all of these things, not knowing what was next. However, my desire for business success never left me, and I needed to learn how to generate income as I knew art wasn't the focus. That dream was officially stripped—at least for a season!

THE DEATH OF YOUR DREAMS

Did you stop dreaming because the promise is taking too long? Do you wonder if you'll ever see it become your reality? Did you settle for some other life because the path was too hard? Do you feel God doesn't want you to succeed in your dreams? The answers are more profound than you think. I shared my story for God's glory. Embracing obedience and nurturing a dream in your heart comes with a steep price. You must be willing to die to yourself, take up your cross, and follow Christ for your soul's sake. **Matthew 16:24-26 KJV,** "Then said Jesus unto his disciples, 'If any man will come after me, let him deny himself, and take up his cross, and follow me. [25] For whosoever will save his life shall lose it: and whosoever will lose his life for my sake shall find it. [26] For what is a man profited, if he shall gain the whole world, and lose his own soul? or what shall a man give in exchange for his soul?'" Jesus Christ is our great reward; anything lost for His sake is always a gain.

A seed must die for it to live. I later had a heart-to-heart with God, with tears flowing. I surrendered my life to His will. I also submitted my love and passion for a successful business since I was content with the ministry. I asked Him to take away my desire if I shouldn't have one. He, in return, answered my prayer by reigniting my dreams and blessed me to start using my gifts with a new business. Jesus says in **John 12:24 KJV**, "Verily, verily, I say unto you, Except a corn of wheat fall into the ground and die, it abideth alone: but if it die, it bringeth forth much fruit." The old, you must die for God's dream to live and multiply! In Genesis 37, Joseph dreamed prophetic dreams. **Genesis 37:9 KJV** says, "And he dreamed yet another dream, and told it his brethren, and said, Behold, I have dreamed a dream more; and, behold, the sun and the moon and the eleven stars made obeisance to me."

After Joseph shared his dreams with his brothers, the life he knew instantly died and changed. He went from having a home to the pit, then to slavery. "And they took him, and cast him into a pit: and the pit was empty, there was no water in it. Then there passed by Midianites merchantmen; and they drew and lifted up Joseph out of the pit, and sold Joseph to the Ishmeelites for twenty pieces of silver: and they brought Joseph into Egypt" **verses 24, 28 KJV**.

Along Joseph's journey, he grew into someone who could fulfill God's purpose. After being falsely accused and spending years in prison, after Potiphar's wife's accusations, the former prisoner recalled him to interpret Pharaoh's dream. Instantly, Joseph got unstuck, became second in command of the Pharaoh, and began accelerating into fulfilling God's prophetic reality.

Joseph was a type of Christ. Types are prophetic symbols, behaviors, qualities, and representations in the Old Testament that link to Christ in the New Testament. [1] Joseph's life events led to him becoming a savior during a severe famine. His preparation period lasted for thirteen years.

You may have or are experiencing severe similar ups and downs. Through these experiences, God is working to prepare you for acceleration and multiplication. He must destroy what's not of Him to renew you for an instrument of His glory. God is always concerned about your sanctification and transformation before the destination. He must make sure you're equipped to handle the call. The Lord uses us as vessels for His work and purifies us for His glory until the job is complete. God wants to use your former years and testimony to help others get unstuck, move forward, and accelerate into a life of service and purpose. With each step forward comes testing. A dreamer goes through the death valley of breaking and refining, which can take decades. You must be examined, refined, and purified to represent God well as He advances you. His priority is holiness and building Christlike character. **Philippians 1:6 NIV** says, "Being confident of this, that he who began a good work in you will carry it on to completion until the day of Christ Jesus."

Business owners and purpose chasers must be willing to abandon a bi-weekly pay schedule and mindset when God calls them from a 9-to-5.

THE PAST LIMITS FUTURE PROGRESS

You know you're stuck when you're wedged in one place and want to get to another. The best example of stuckness is the Hebrew slaves from their past.

- They were **stuck** in slavery in Egypt for 430 years.
- They were **stuck** during God's plan to free them through Moses and Aaron during the Ten Plagues.
- When Pharaoh finally let them go, he came after them, and they had to flee. They were **stuck**—but God parted the Red Sea.
- Once they walked across the Red Sea on dry ground, they got **stuck** in the desert (worshiping false gods, afraid, complaining, disobeying, and doubting God). They believed they couldn't conquer the Promised Land because of the giants and lacked faith. So, they stayed stuck for forty years, and a generation died off until God raised a new one.
- Another gap of **stuckness** existed between the Jordan—and the Promised Land.

However, their mindset was the most prominent stuckness. Although they were free physically, they were shackled in their thinking. Many believers wrestle with some areas of bondage. Most of the time, we're trying to escape things that traumatized us in the past. Instead of healing and progressing, we've bandaged up our lives to *adjust to the scars* of abuse, rape, molestation, rejection, loss, grief, health diagnosis, disaster, PTSD, heartbreak, divorce, abandonment, and many other painful experiences.

We set up idols such as success, achievements, relationships, marriage, our children, indulgences, sex, drugs, pornography, sports, and vices to escape and cope while compartmentalizing inner agony. We display multiple faces, masks, characters, disguises, cover ups, and facades depending on who we're talking to and what we're going through. Our actions are inconsistent and don't align with our identity because we've gotten so far away from our foundation in Christ. When we function as double-minded agents parading as Christians, we can't go far in life or business until these partitions and fragilities are acknowledged, broken, and dealt with.

However, God will never leave you fractured. He will take all the lacerations, gashes, wounds, injuries, damages, breaks, and cracks and paint a beautiful masterpiece of your life for His glory. He will cure your soul. The Holy Spirit is our Counselor, Schoolmaster, Teacher, Coach, Trainer, and Confidant. You can't lose with Him. He will guide you into all truth by penetrating your heart's deep, dark crevices with His healing balm, light, and water. God's repairing reaches your spirit to purify you.

HIS SOVEREIGNTY

Truthfully, I wasn't ready then for the kind of work God had planned for me. God's dominion and purposes work in His perfect timing and providence. I journeyed through a thirty-year obstacle course to arrive at my purpose. When I was unaware of God's sovereignty, He came bursting through with His mighty right hand and snatched me out of my ten-year valley to get me unstuck. In this new season, I wasn't going to cure any bare walls, but it was time to submit to His remedy and assist Him in curing my soul and others for His glory. **Matthew 4:19-20 NIV** says, "'Come, follow me,' Jesus said, 'and I will send you out to fish for people.' [20] At once they left their nets and followed him." They left behind everything for Jesus.

I thought my struggle was business growth or money, but because my entire life and being matters to the Almighty God, there's pain embedded in gain. He was transitioning me into a purpose greater than ministering through paintings. Since I wrote the foundation of this book during a drought, it can help you in your lowest valley. I completed the manuscript in 2024, still with life's obstacles but far removed from stagnation. I want to support you as you strive for greater heights. God is sovereign, and His Holy Word will lift you from inertia and accelerate you if you stake your expectations in Him.

If you believe in new possibilities, there's still time to fulfill what you've been assigned. "Now may the God of hope fill you with all joy and peace in believing, that you may abound in hope by the power of the Holy Spirit" **Romans 15:13 NKJV**. If you place your future in the LORD's hands and relinquish your grip and expectations about how things will turn out, do not doubt—He will give you a new song to shout about. "The LORD is my strength and my shield; My heart trusted in Him, and I am helped; Therefore my heart greatly rejoices, And with my song I will praise Him" **Psalm 28:7 NKJV.** Your better and happier days are on the way, no matter what anyone has to say. God wants to give you His plans, bless the work of your hands, and maximize your remaining time in the land. You are the sheep of the Good Shepherd's pasture, and you get to work with Him to recapture His divine intentions here and thereafter. But before you can carry out His purposes, the next chapter will highlight why most Christians are stuck.

Chapter 2
WHY CHRISTIANS ARE STUCK

Why do Christians struggle to succeed as business owners? Why is it challenging to hit goals and gain the momentum to move forward? Why do so few thrive financially? These questions have been the focus of my reasoning, analysis, and research. I've spent much time discerning and examining why Christians trail behind in life and business when grafted into an eternal life-altering relationship with the true and living God of heaven and earth.

Over the past twenty-five plus years, I've ventured into various business endeavors. From my early days in the cosmetology industry to my exploration of songwriting, print and digital publishing, artistry, sales, ministry, and coaching. I know what it's like to believe I'm doing things right but still be on the struggle bus and stuck in the gap. **The gap** is the opening that separates where you are now and where you want to be.

I realized that I neglected crucial biblical principles while writing this manuscript, which kept me stagnant and unable to achieve some desired outcomes and goals. I usually kept or returned to a 9-to-5 job for financial stability during my business pursuits before discovering the insights here. After overcoming failed businesses, divorce, bankruptcy, depression, anxiety, and the loss of everything I had worked for, I've found joy in faithfully walking with and serving the Lord and restarting my business journey.

The psalmist expresses, "But the plans of the Lord stand firm forever, the purposes of his heart through all generations" **Psalm 33:11 NIV**. It can be frustrating when trying to reach your destination while encountering constant personal and financial setbacks. Nonetheless, overcoming obstacles makes you stronger if you don't give up. Learning the lessons and passing the tests will root you firmly in God and make you more like Christ if you allow them to. When you trust and surrender to the transformative power of the Holy Spirit, your life can look different a year from now.

ALWAYS SEARCHING BUT NEVER FINDING

I searched for the formula to crack the success code for decades but never found it. I used to cry to build a business with consistent profits. I stepped out on faith, set goals, made plans, memorized Bible verses, read tons of books, bought courses and coaching, and researched to uncover solutions for profitability. I even thought God was against me. I was wrong and needed to slow down and find footing within His pace.

Suppose you blaze through these teachings without getting to the root of the problem. In that case, stuckness is inevitable regardless of how much you love the Lord, how many Scriptures you journal, books you read, podcasts you listen to, courses and workshops you buy, or how much random advice you acquire from conferences, coaches, friends, search engines, and social platforms. No matter how much money you throw at the condition, it won't work if you miss this book's biblical principles.

You'll keep returning to the 9-to-5 grind, falling short of truly living your purpose. You'll remain stuck on a hamster wheel of starting, stopping, and restarting. The constant disposition of defeat and discouragement will hinder your progress. I'm sharing this to grab your attention, not to frighten you. I want you to understand that being a well-intentioned Christian alone doesn't move God; there are specific actions that do. Everything else is a band-aid fix until you prioritize your spiritual life and soul's condition. Why? Because God is more concerned about your holiness than your business success. What good is it to succeed in business by vision boards, manifestation, and the world's ways but miss the mark of God's standards?

Paul shares in his letter to Timothy how many women burdened with sins and unfocused on God's values were allowing anyone to worm into their homes and minds and keep them baffled. **2 Timothy 3:7 AMP** "[These weak women will listen to anybody who will teach them]; they are forever inquiring *and* getting information, but are never able to arrive at a recognition *and* knowledge of the Truth." But God is the Truth! He doesn't want His children running around looking to psychics, gurus, false prophets, ancestor worship, secret societies, word of faith prosperity preachers, self-help books, positive thinking and manifesting coaches, and everyone else for solutions—the Creator is the solution! He wants you to get your truth directly from Him. Because God has a solid design for your life, there is no other way for you to succeed, void of it. "Jesus answered, 'I am the way and the truth and the life'" **John 14:6 NIV**.

It's imperative not to miss why you're here and what God wants to teach you so your efforts aren't in vain. There's no need to be puzzled about how to live a good life and run a successful business because God is the originator of both. God's wisdom doesn't need reinvention or additions; you can follow proven blueprints and the first laws in God's Word, which start in Genesis.

You no longer have to leap into entrepreneurship, skipping critical components and fundamentals because you're in a hurry to get money. Authentically growing your relationship with God is your best life, ultimate priority, and the joy you've been ultimately seeking. As His children, we have access to hidden wisdom, which is greater than money, which the world knows nothing about, and it starts with our fear of the Lord. The insight in **Proverbs 16:16 NIV** teaches, "How much better to get wisdom than gold, to get insight rather than silver." **Proverbs 1:7 NIV** teaches, "The fear of the LORD is the beginning of knowledge, but fools despise wisdom and instruction."

WHY CHRISTIANS ARE STUCK

Here, I'll begin sharing why most Christians are stuck in life and unable to grow thriving, profitable businesses. This list isn't exhaustive because the remaining chapters and the devotionals will highlight other reasons. However, I want to emphasize the five listed here to prepare you for the journey ahead. And although this book is about acceleration, it's vital to slow down initially. So, by the end of the next chapter, you'll have an understanding of the acceleration cure. Take a break wherever you need to pause and let the Spirit of God work through whatever you read that caused you to ponder. I believe the reason for being stuck as a child of God is always rooted in a spiritual problem. I pray that you're in a space where your heart is open for understanding and you can accept total responsibility for where you are, your past actions, and your decisions moving forward.

1. **Fear**—Some people want to do, be, and have more but struggle with trusting God. They fear failure before they step beyond their comfort zone. So they give up on life and settle, shrink back, and wait to get to heaven to start living. They say, "The last time I tried, this happened." "I always wanted to do that." "I don't have enough money." "Everyone isn't meant to succeed." "I'll never be able to build that." Therefore, they sit by watching others live and pursue their dreams and purpose.

2. **Excuses**—Many Christians say, "I already prayed about it." "I'm waiting on the Lord." "The doctor says there is no cure." "I'm not good at that." "I'm a procrastinator." "It's too far." "I don't like reading." Sadly, many of God's children make excuses because they feel unworthy and unmotivated to find a way out of their life trajectory. Instead, they settle and park at the busy intersection of Poor Me St. and No Way Out Blvd. They develop excusitis to protect themselves from loss and personal responsibility for their decisions.

3. **Blame**—Christians can also blame and play the victim. They blame God for not answering their prayers, their employer for not paying them enough, and their parents for not doing a good job raising them. They blame their spouse, kids, ex, dogs, neighbors, and the devil for why they aren't progressing in life and business. They also say phrases like, "The man is keeping me down." "They won't let me in." "They should help me out."

I hope you're picking up what I'm putting down. Believers hibernating in the place of being stuck isn't God's fault. These rationales are symptoms of a spiritual problem. In Christ, we're free, not victims, no matter the circumstances. The valley is the place where the real you shines through. What emerges from someone during discomfort and difficulties reflects their identity and character. These are the things God sees and wants them to flee. Unfortunately, they're unaware that they're the common denominator. Most of God's people are stuck because it's where they want to be.

4. **Preparation**—Sometimes, they're in the gap because they're training

for the calling and assignment God destined them for—purpose. Here, they may work on various jobs and businesses that aren't meant to be the breakout company. In those seasons, God's hand of mercy may develop obedience, work ethic, patience, faith, knowledge, wisdom, healing, and dealing with character flaws, pride, and unconfessed sins. My brother TJ Davis says, "Hide me, heal me until you're ready to reveal me." Therefore, we must endure God's training, sanctification, and discipline to stretch, strengthen, and humble us until He presents us for His glory. We must learn to trust Him and pass the tests to level up. "Thus, don't despise the discipline and humbling of God. Remember how the LORD your God led you all the way in the wilderness these forty years, to humble and test you in order to know what was in your heart, whether or not you would keep his commands" **Deuteronomy 8:2 NIV**.

5. **Timing**—Sometimes, it's just not our time. Some things don't come full circle until the appointment is ready and the Most High God calls your name to move forward. The big picture of how God wants to use and position you in life and business isn't prepared, as it involves divine events, connections, and specific prerequisites. Therefore, we often take on our seasonal purpose and actively wait in a holding training facility serving the Lord until opportunity knocks.

Now that we've identified some reasons for being stuck, returning to the root cause is vital to laying the foundation for a fresh start.

BUILD WISELY

Imagine investing in your custom dream home. Two years after moving in, you discover cracked walls and shifting floors. You call the builder. They found the root cause was the faulty foundation due to inadequate digging. You request an immediate resolution so they can make things right. After all this back and forth with engineers, construction, and lawyers, you learn they can't fix it because they'd need to tear the house down.

Similarly, we must examine our spiritual problems to understand how to move about when God reveals setbacks in our lives. Who do you call first when your life and business aren't working? Sadly, most Christians do not call God. They bypass the Manufacturer because they don't want to hear anything that will cause them to slow down. So, they seek alternative methods to circumvent challenges and avoid responsibility and the core cause.

However, a wise builder seeks God first, obtains knowledge, listens to truth, hears for understanding, obeys instructions, and puts faith into action. A reckless builder listens to the parts they want to hear, lean on their knowledge, and executes their perceived understanding. **James 1:22 NIV** teaches, "Do not merely listen to the word, and so deceive yourselves. Do what it says."

For this cause, numerous entrepreneurs within the Christian community are running disjointed and inconsistent businesses. This happens when they imitate and extract what seems good from others and alternative methods. Hurriedness often results in launching new companies without proper planning, believing they'll work out successfully because they're Christian-owned. However, we failed to consult the Owner for help or a diagnosis. But patience is a virtue of God's Spirit.

In **Matthew 7:26-27 NKJV** Jesus says, "But everyone who hears these sayings of Mine, and does not do them, will be like a foolish man who built his house on the sand: [27] and the rain descended, the floods came, and the winds blew and beat on that house; and it fell. And great was its fall."

People assume they know more than the manufacturer, servicer, or the teacher. So, they start construction with no guidance. They aim to minimize effort without committing to learning the recommended approach to achieve the desired outcomes. For instance, most people skip reading introductions in books, bypass instruction manuals for new products, and look for quick solutions in health, finances, marriage, relationships, parenting, and everything. They run to a psychologist before digging into the Scriptures. They become frustrated and upset with God when their relationships don't work, and enterprises don't attract investments. But what about building the foundation? Remember, without the Rock, we can't withstand the storms and challenges that come our way. Like we'd soon discover the dream house isn't built right—since God loves us, He isn't slapping the signature of approval on the things we rush into or are aligned with alternative means. He keeps people at a distance until we decide to get things right by coming to and waiting on Him.

How can we aim to excel in the market despite things reflecting God's excellence? We can find solutions to improve when we revere, start, and solve problems in God's way. Our Holy Manufacturer is our only hope for assembly, repair, and restoration. Whatever He destroys, He will build back more marvelous. Our life and business are outlets for God's mission. Since our life is our ministry, it first starts with personal stability at home before we can lead others. We can't depend on unreliable, faulty foundations, blueprints, and structures to serve the souls God wants to send our way.

God knows you need to make money. Yes, you must eventually jump out and start with what you have and where you are and dodging perfection, but skipping steps, rushing, taking shortcuts, half-finishing, and throwing anything into the marketplace to check it off your to-do list won't get you where you desire to go long-term. Knowing the season, order, and timing in which you apply the wisdom and tools is just as vital. Our God has a standard and principles. You'll still have to do it over—the right way—because we serve a God of planning, structure, and order. Our businesses should always set the criterion that others want to follow, not the other way around.

ACCESS YOUR FOUNDATIONAL FAITH

I believe you have faith, but the problem isn't necessarily that you have faith—but do you have foundational faith? What if Christ, the Solid Rock and source of our substance, didn't keep His Word and reneged on His promises of salvation and eternal life? What if our holy and righteous Father changed His mind about sending His Son? Who's promises could we trust and depend on? Where would we go? How would we stand? How would we know right from wrong?

Thankfully, our Lord and Savior Jesus Christ resolved those worries because our faith is in Him—the Stone the builders rejected. Therefore, we retain objective truth and faithfulness to stand on. God's promises never fail. "Haven't you read this passage of Scripture: 'The stone the builders rejected has become the cornerstone'" **Mark 12:10 NIV**.

Cornerstones are the largest foundational stone of any building structure. The enormous stones are perfectly crafted and constructed with significant planning, time, and care. Their size and settings determine how the remaining rocks for the building are measured and serve as a guide for the workers [3][4]. Without them, everything else built on them will collapse. If master builders lay the stone slightly slanted or angled, the building will rotate slightly or tilt, eventually leading to failure. That's why master masonry craftsmen pick these base stones and lay the rocks perfectly. [5]

We who placed our faith and trust in Christ Jesus are living stones built upon the establishment of Christ by the prophets and apostles. **Ephesians 2:19-20 NIV** says, "Consequently, you are no longer foreigners and strangers, but fellow citizens with God's people and also members of his household, [20] built on the foundation of the apostles and prophets, with Christ Jesus himself as the chief cornerstone." Christ is the head and the temple, and He made us living stones that contribute to the building of His holy temple. The Apostle Peter writes in **1 Peter 2:4-5 NIV**, "As you come to him, the living Stone—rejected by humans but chosen by God and precious to him— [5] you also, like living stones, are being built into a spiritual house."

The faith our Father God gives us (through trusting in Jesus Christ as our sin-bearer and redeemer) is unique from the ordinary faith we hear people talk about who don't know Christ as Savior and Lord. Our faith is eternal and unbreakable because it's the pillar of our relationship with God. Our eternity is imperishable, incorruptible, and indestructible. It doesn't rot, spoil, or fade (1 Peter 1:3-9). It's rooted in Jesus' resurrection. It's seeped in the gory, bloody sacrifice of our Risen Savior. Our faith is a gift from Almighty God. Paul expresses in **Ephesians 2:4-5 NIV**, "But because of his great love for us, God, who is rich in mercy, [5] made us alive with Christ even when we were dead in transgressions—it is by grace you have been saved." God saved us and gave us the right to be called His children.

Our foundational saving faith is embedded in the God who designed and created us in His image for His purpose. "For the wages of sin is death; but the gift of God is eternal life through Jesus Christ our Lord" **Romans 6:23 KJV**. We trespassed against God in our sins, had nothing of value to offer, and couldn't pay the debt we racked up. Our works of righteousness compare to filthy menstrual cloths. "But we are all as an unclean thing, and all our righteousnesses are as filthy rags; and we all do fade as a leaf; and our iniquities, like the wind, have taken us away" **Isaiah 64:6 KJV**. Yet, God bestowed many blessings upon us and loves us unconditionally. He rescued us from the auction block of darkness. Without Jesus' redemption from the penalty of sin and death, we wouldn't have eternal life or anything worth claiming as good. Our structures would consistently breach, cave, rupture, and crumble. Now that we're grafted into God's holy temple as living stones of the body of Christ—we can confidently build everything we touch from this point forward on a solid foundation. I'll touch on salvation more on *Day 13, Renew Your Mind.*

Hebrews 11:8-10 NKJV says, "By faith Abraham obeyed when he was called to go out to the place which he would receive as an inheritance. And he went out, not knowing where he was going. ⁹ By faith he dwelt in the land of promise as *in* a foreign country, dwelling in tents with Isaac and Jacob, the heirs with him of the same promise; ¹⁰ for he waited for the city which has foundations, whose builder and maker *is* God."

See, Abram believed in the Constructor and Architect of the promise and took faithful actions. Likewise, our calling is about going out by faith, not knowing what it looks like or where we will end up because we trust God's plan. Faith pleases the Lord and helps us abide regardless of obstacles or warfare.

ABIDE IN THE VINE

There's good news! Father God predestined you to abide in Christ because He's given you the power to do so. You're never stuck as long as you're enduring in the Vine, and God is in you. Dr. Tony Evans calls abiding *hanging out.* Your continuous feeding off Christ's living roots is an abundant transformative fruit-bearing life. When you *choose* to abide, success is inevitable because you're becoming more like Christ. Apart from God's life and power, you can't accelerate. Jesus says in **John 15:5 NIV**, "I am the vine; you are the branches. If you remain in me and I in you, you will bear much fruit; apart from me, you can do nothing."

It's easy to fall into the trap of complacency and settle for a mundane existence due to fear, but you must fight from victory for God's vision for your life. God's soul has no pleasure in those who shrink back because "the righteous live by faith" (Hebrews 10:38). We're called to a life of impact—not to detract.

Have you disconnected from the Vine somewhere in your journey? You may have strayed from the flock into sinful patterns and habits. Possibly, you're in survival mode, numb, and navigating traumatic experiences or a recent disaster. Perhaps you've shrunk back along the way and stopped trusting the Lord's plans. Maybe you've wandered far into the world's philosophies, psychology, science, new age, new thought, prosperity, and self-help teachings and can't find clarity.

As believers, we have direct access to God. We don't need to submit and fall victim to the devil's alternatives, narratives, plots, schemes, antics, and tactics. We can access principles and wisdom anyone could only dream of having to build successful marriages, relationships, businesses, ministries, organizations, and alliances. If you've strayed away, God will redeem the wasted time once you get back on course because it's never too late to accelerate. Just as Moses got on God's agenda and led the Israelites out of 430 years of slavery, Joshua commanded Israel into conquering nations, Daniel survived the lion's den, and Jesus, the God-man, accomplished and finished so much in just three years of His earthly ministry. These events happened suddenly and supernaturally.

SLOW DOWN

The Lord God will test everything to prove its authenticity and stability. Constructing from the middle out instead of the bottom up leads to frustration because you can never identify the cause. So, destroying to rebuild and returning to the beginning is best, starting with your spiritual life. We must go back to the basics and the introduction. When you inspect and diagnose the root of the fruit, you'll see how some of your structures survived—while others didn't. You'll explore how *seemingly small matters* are why you trail behind.

In many instances, Satan has done such work in our hearts and souls over the years that kept us blocked from the truth. He battered, distracted, bruised us, and stuffed so many lies into our minds that we're now learning to get back to God first. So, don't beat yourself up for not applying many of these principles sooner. Nothing in your life is wasted! Whatever is crooked, God will straighten it out. God can use every test, trial, failure, success, and experience you've undergone into a vision for His glory, more beautiful than anything you could've dreamt. You have a message to get to the world, and the devil has worked non-stop since your mother's womb to keep your light from shining on a hill. But that stops today!

ACCESS YOUR HABITS

God created a sophisticated system of habits in our brains to conserve energy for physical and mental activities. Habits are the programmed automatic behaviors we perform on cue or when triggered to take action. Our routines started in childhood. We picked up good ones according to our parents' or guardians' instructions. We also learned bad ones by mimicking people. We also develop beliefs linked to how we see ourselves. If we see ourselves as successful and happy, our habits correlate with these views. If we've been taught to fear, blame, make excuses, or see ourselves as victims, we will behave in such a manner to validate our reality. We'll fight for our reasons, defenses, and low requirements because we believe they are the best we can do.

God wants us to be conscientious and develop good habits that build up our essential spiritual disciplines. Let's take learning and education, for instance. We're never supposed to stop learning and studying—never! But many believers have never read the entire Bible cover to cover or studied any of its books verse by verse. And because we don't know the Word of God in context, we don't know the God of the Word. Therefore, we're building our spiritual lives from what we *think* God is saying and are learning from teachers who share this allegory of distributing the unsound doctrine.

We rush to success without knowing God's heart about a matter. Developing the habit of reading, studying, meditation, and Scripture memory is a God-given gift and privilege to help us. Our God wrote and gave us His Word (spiritual food) to live by daily. Many of our ancestors weren't allowed to learn how to read. When we dismiss the ability to read, we leave blessings behind and room for error on the table. This consistency of learning strengthens our faith muscles and discernment. Additionally, we become better, well-read leaders and discover things we'd never find outside of learning about them in books.

Dr. Ben Carson saw a transformation from quick, angry outbursts as a teen to developing a relationship with Jesus Christ, learning His Word, reading two books per week, and writing a report about them. His passion for reading, sparked by his mother, made him one of the world's most sought-after neurosurgeons.[1] Pastor Paul Washer mentioned that he could easily spend four to ten hours a day studying.[2] My dad put a book about motivation and goals in my hands at seventeen, which sparked my ambition.

What do your daily habits look like? Good habits start with delighting in the Lord. Scheduled, planned, and intentional spiritual and personal development practices are vital to rebuilding. Habits can either trap or advance us. It's up to us to implement thriving practices.

THE ACCELERATION PRINCIPLE

The **acceleration principle** synchronizes prayer with obedience, faith-driven action, and God's wisdom for acceleration. An easy way to remember the formula is to **pray + obey + faith + wisdom = accelerate**. It's the difference between trying to succeed with the Holy Spirit versus without Him.

- **Prayer** is constant communication, reasoning, asking, seeking, knocking, questioning, honoring, and listening to God.
- **Obedience** is reverence, surrender, and following the Holy Spirit's leading and instructions when He gives them.
- **Faith** is believing the evidence of what you hope, think, pray for, and spiritually see while acting towards it until you realize it naturally.
- **Wisdom** is learning, discerning, and applying God's knowledge, understanding, and truths He teaches, illuminates, reveals, and shares.

Accelerate, defined by Oxford, is to make something happen faster or earlier to move more quickly, increase in amount or extent, and undergo a change in velocity. [6] Suppose you must reach a desired destination 100 miles away. First, you'll need a clear start and end point. You can walk or drive. When driving, you build acceleration as you co-work with the vehicle's motor and fuel power sources. That's what this book is all about. Co-working with the Holy Spirit to get your life in step.

You would never travel from the United States to Europe without a plan. A sculptor has an image in mind before they spend years molding the work of art. Everything we do begins with fundamentals. The key to movement in life and business is knowing and implementing them. Acceleration starts with a foundation in Christ, reliance on His guidance and speed, and a solid plan. Therefore, acceleration is rightly getting there instead of *quickly* reaching your destination faster while missing all the mandatory stops and milestones. The firmer we're embedded in the Vine of Christ, the Father positions us for use. So, let's move forward, as tomorrow isn't promised. Walk by faith, not by sight, and see your life and business turn around and mountains move and cast into the sea. The Holy Spirit will take your commitment and obedience and press the supernatural power supply to lead you into fulfilling your call. Are you ready?

Chapter 3

IDENTITY BLINDNESS

I remember hip-hop's influence on me when I was a kid. Shy and quiet, my love for music, arts, culture, and expression was how I fit in with my peers. The songs seemed to be more light-hearted and fun. Later, the lyrics slowly became brazen. The explicitness, raunchiness, and harshness slowly increased. By then, I was becoming desensitized and addicted because I had to sneak and listen to it. I didn't realize that what started as fun times, rapping to melodic hooks and dope beats, would make me a willing agent of chaos.

    The music became my minister, shaped my identity, and had its hooks in me until my early thirties. It set up strongholds and rhythmic patterns in my brain that bypassed my frontal lobes and went right to my subconscious mind. I let it in, and it took over, rewiring my brain and programming my soul (mind, will, and emotions). I was a professing Christian caught in a sinful stranglehold—bound in enslavement through imagery, rhythms, words, melodies, harmony, rim taps, 808s, and DJ scratching. My bad habit of listening to ungodly songs made me ungodly. The mindset taught overrode the Holy Spirit's influence because the composition's effect outweighed my biblical life. Hip-hop and certain R&B records influenced how I sought and behaved in relationships. They affected my attitude, thoughts, and the type of woman I was becoming. I was bold inside the church but a scared hypocrite outside.

    It took me years to unlearn those destructive teachings. I allowed the lost's mouthpiece to speak death into me because those artists have broken and shattered souls. I picked up and quoted their lyrics through good-sounding frequencies and knew them more than life-giving Bible verses. "The tongue has the power of life and death, and those who love it will eat its fruit" **Proverbs 18:21 NIV**. These artists weren't Holy Spirit-filled. Therefore, they didn't have the responsibility to obey and reverence God like I did, so I was in sin. I had eaten this rotten fruit too long.

IDENTITY BLINDNESS

I got sucked into the devil's nihilistic agenda through raunchy tunes because I was identity blind. **Identity blindness** is the failure to authenticate, approve, validate, and confidently live one's identity as a new creation in Christ. It's when you live below God's standards. I morphed into a blind-blown, unidentifiable character far from the vision God had in mind. The holy version of me was unsighted because it hid under layers of pride and destructive thoughts and actions.

Success will evade anyone unable to live boldly and authentically. Ask yourself: Am I trapped in an artificial identity by failing to live fully as a new creation in Christ? Is the truth I accept and believe about God and myself genuine? We cannot live our purpose when uncertain about who and Whose we are. Therefore, we remain in soul-sucking lifestyles, jobs, relationships, and cycles that enslave and shackle us. When we pick and choose what we prefer to obey, we believe in a false gospel and seek another Jesus. Without direction, we fail to build our life on the precious Cornerstone of Christ. There's no more time to be identity blind. Ask God to open your spiritual eyes to see and ears to hear.

Establishing the spiritual discipline of studying God's truth will transform your thinking so your mind aligns. Remember the acceleration principle? The **acceleration principle** synchronizes prayer with obedience, faith-driven action, and God's wisdom for acceleration. **Pray + obey + faith + wisdom = accelerate**. Your life changes when you demolish your old ways and take on new ones.

WHO YOU ARE NOT

Identifying who you are is as essential as knowing who you're not. You're not the lies Satan planted in your thoughts. You're not your past, pain, trauma, sickness, disease, or health diagnosis. You can come out of hiding behind the superficial definition of the world's success and beauty standards. The Bachelors, Masters, or PHD isn't who you are. The police badge and awards aren't you. Fraternities, sororities, or secret societies are not your keys to connections. You're not the rejected one. You're not the criminal they named you out to be. You don't have to shack up to feel acceptance and love. That homosexual lifestyle is not the real you. Sisters, the banging body, makeup, acrylics, weaves, lashes, and revealing clothes aren't who you are. Brothers, your buff chest, groomed beard, six-pack, and massive biceps don't make you. Your identity isn't in the alcohol bottles. Your creativity isn't discovered through smoking weed or popping pills. Your *who* is not found in your *do*—nor is the past your future you!

The authentic you divorced from all the titles, work, and accolades hides in Christ's finished work. You discover *you* and your purpose in Jesus Christ alone! He's calling you out of hiding behind the identity crisis and iron walls you built up over time to fit in and protect yourself from pain, abandonment, and rejection. The Father will use your experiences to help shape and mold you into the image of His Son.

IDENTITY IN CHRIST

- **You Belong to God – John 1:12 KJV**, "But as many as received him, to them gave he power to become the sons of God, even to them that believe on his name:"
- **You're Predestined – Ephesians 1:5 KJV**, "Having predestinated us unto the adoption of children by Jesus Christ to himself, according to the good pleasure of his will."
- **You're God's Workmanship – Ephesians 2:10 KJV**, "For we are his workmanship, created in Christ Jesus unto good works, which God hath before ordained that we should walk in them."
- **Your Body is The Temple – 1 Corinthians 6:17, 19-20 KJV**, "But he that is joined unto the Lord is one spirit. [19] What? know ye not that your body is the temple of the Holy Ghost which is in you, which ye have of God, and ye are not your own? [20] For ye are bought with a price: therefore glorify God in your body, and in your spirit, which are God's."

- **You're a New Creation – 2 Corinthians 5:17 KJV**, "Therefore if any man be in Christ, he is a new creature: old things are passed away; behold, all things are become new."
- **You're Crucified With Christ – Galatians 2:20 KJV**, "I am crucified with Christ: nevertheless I live; yet not I, but Christ liveth in me: and the life which I now live in the flesh I live by the faith of the Son of God, who loved me, and gave himself for me."
- **You're Hidden in Christ – Colossians 3:1, 3 KJV**, "If ye then be risen with Christ, seek those things which are above, where Christ sitteth on the right hand of God. ³ For ye are dead, and your life is hid with Christ in God."
- **You Have Eternal Life – 1 John 5:13 KJV**, "These things have I written unto you that believe on the name of the Son of God; that ye may know that ye have eternal life, and that ye may believe on the name of the Son of God."

The list of blessings goes further than this shortlist. However, if you believe you can lose your salvation, you'll have trouble living in your identity because you'll be working to save yourself and maintain it. Jesus says in **John 10:27-28 NIV**, "My sheep listen to my voice; I know them, and they follow me. I give them eternal life, and they shall never perish; no one will snatch them out of my hand." He also exclaims, "So if the Son sets you free, you will be free indeed" **John 8:36 NIV**. And as Paul writes to the church at Galatia, "It is for freedom that Christ has set us free. Stand firm, then, and do not let yourselves be burdened again by a yoke of slavery" **Galatians 5:1 NIV**.

As salt, light, and the aroma of Christ, we have to represent Him well. Acceleration requires living as freedmen. From now on, you believe what God says about you. The actions, lifestyles, habits, patterns, thoughts, and people you entertain and establish today reflect your future.

FAMILY AND IDENTITY

Authenticity is realness that produces joy, support, and alignment. There's no way to live out your purpose in a false identity or alone. You're a living stone—a part of God's building. You have many siblings you've yet to meet. You're in the royal family because you're the King's child. Royal kids behave and present differently from the world because they're set apart.

The King sets the regulations and standards for us to live by. We build the legacy and fulfill His intentions. Your identity connects to building up and serving the family of believers for God's purposes. Although you may not know or see all the members, they play their position and are fighting the good fight of faith and praying for you.

ONE TEAM – ONE MISSION

I remember how I felt when the Detroit Pistons won the back-to-back NBA Championships in 1989 and 1990. Watching the playoff games with my family was exciting. The Pistons' dominance and wins were the talk of the town. The celebratory energy and feeling brought such happiness and smiles being on the winning side. My residency and citizenship automatically made me a part of the victorious home team. Rick Mahorn even visited our home that summer because my sister Shenetta Quinn wrote him a letter.

The team's success was built on the leader's vision and trickled down to every coach and player. However, the team's championship goal was accomplished by following the core fundamentals to compete at a high level, starting with their foundation and strategy. Everything they did had to align with the team whose jersey they wore and the leader's vision on and off the court. They didn't support the other side—because their loyalty lay with the Pistons. If they veered off the track and failed to follow the rules established by the league, management, and coaches—they'd be disqualified.

They trained, practiced, studied, listened, followed, implemented, and prepared tirelessly. The dream worked due to discipline, consistency, and teamwork! When the individual players work harmoniously as a team, their skills and gifts harmonize to create unmatched synergy.

If any individual works within their own rules or the ego of selfish ambitions—it harms the whole. When a squad member gets prideful and runs his plays in the clutch, it dismantles the morale and gives a win to the opposing team. Therefore, as God's family, we rest in God's pacing. We never impatiently outpace God and jerk away to build our version of a Tower of Babel as it will surely fail. As God's representatives, we declare what He decides. Anything beyond that is pride.

So, the accelerated life is living and applying the foundational principles and building blocks of the God we serve and the family we're a part of. Team Jesus, all day, every day! As Christians, we have one Lord and Master—one Sovereign. When we run the plays He calls, we succeed with the family of believers against our enemies. The Pistons had to play to the end to claim their victory, and although we know it's ours, we still must finish successfully.

IDENTITY, PURPOSE, AND ALIGNMENT

No different than an NBA team, every believer has a God-created purpose and a role to play. First, we're to grow the family of Christ by sharing the gospel and using our spiritual gifts, resources, and time to advance the body through service. Second, glorify God in whatever our role is in various seasons.

According to Oxford, purpose is the intention, aim, or function of something; the thing that something is supposed to achieve. Purpose is the reason for which something is done or created or for which something exists. [1] Our purpose is *why* God created us to be here at this time. The *why* helps to define the *what, when, where, and how.* Seasonal purposefulness is whatever you're supposed to be doing *now*. It can be working at a job or building a business. For instance, when I moved to Atlanta to pursue my magazine publishing and songwriting dreams, I was in newness and exploration, so God didn't plant me with a permanent employer. Instead, I worked on long-term contracts through temp agencies while exploring the ATL landscape and building my business in the evenings. I met people I never would've met had I been stuck and assigned to one job location.

You'll never *find* your purpose, but you'll *discover* it when you obey God and take faith-driven action in all you do because it's concealed until revealed. So, if you feel you're in a business, job, or career that doesn't align with where you want to be, don't panic and jump ship just yet. Persist in training and continue building the King's vision wherever you are because God will providentially and sovereignly move you at the appointed time. Your persistence, patience, abiding, and enduring unlock blessings and rewards. **Jeremiah 32:18-19 AMP** says, "O great and mighty God; the LORD of hosts is His name; [19] great [are You] in counsel and mighty in deed, whose eyes are open to all the ways of the sons of men, to reward *or* repay each one according to his ways and according to the fruit of his deeds."

FOCUS AND STAY IN YOUR LANE

When the Pistons won their championship titles, each squad member played an assigned position and stayed in their lane. They focused and maximized that role no matter how uncomfortable or challenging because they discovered growth during discomfort.

The time here is short, and we can't continue believing we're only here to pay bills, take what people hand to us, suffer in the corner of the roof, live for the weekends, and die. God put a dream in your heart for a reason. Yes, failure and loss at some parts of the journey are unavoidable. That's a part of our walk of faith. But God set you apart, and you'll one day see the promise if you keep getting back up when you fall. God wants to extend the territory of those who live by faith and trust Him. He wants to increase their position on Team Jesus.

Operating within your lane helps you focus on God's call for *you* while at the same time considering the needs of others. Although many vehicles are on the road, everyone isn't going to the same destination. That's why highway lanes are marked with lines on the road so you can stay in them safely as you drive to your destination marked with the assigned exit. God created you to live fully and dream big with all your needs supplied instead of merely scraping by and existing. Staying in your lane is discovering your uniqueness and genuineness. God made you to do what you're good at. If you copy everyone else, you'll struggle with growth, profitability, and authenticity.

4 PILLARS OF ACCELERATION

The Acceleration CURE pillars help you ditch your comfort zone, eliminate identity blindness, and move through the gap. **The gap** is the opening that separates where you are now and where you want to be.

The CURE Framework Pillars

- **C**—Clarify and Commit
- **U**—Unshackle and Unstuck
- **R**—Reignite and Rewrite
- **E**—Enrich and Endure

PILLAR 1: CLARIFY AND COMMIT

C pillar: Clarify and commit. Clarifying and refining identity, purpose, and messaging grants the confidence to follow God faithfully. Good fruit comes from the evident ability to flow in our God-given abilities. Until we have the assurance of identity in Christ, clarity, and purposefulness for living, communicating the message of the cross, and articulating our values, we will struggle with commitment if we're confused about who we are and why we wake up each morning.

We discover *life's purpose* predominantly later in life. This gift is an enormous blessing because you'll see how God uniquely and custom-tailored it to you. You've triumphed over much and see God's hand of providence and faithfulness going back decades. You'll spiritually reflect on how multiple events show you God's fingerprints through various experiences, fragments, and unexplained incidents in your life. These puzzle pieces and threads slowly connect, wove, build, and draw you into your purpose.

Although you can get there independently, discovering purpose is a gift and skill everyone can't assist with. It involves knowledge of the intricacies of the spirit and soul to lead one to that illumination through the Holy Spirit. Purpose contains decades of life experiences, stories, skills, and gifts. That person of God must also know how to extract the best to encourage the seeking soul to walk out their purpose boldly and understand the business landscape. Serving multi-passionate and multi-skilled (modern-day Renaissance) believers in this area as the soul coach and creative entrepreneur is a part of my call. In turn, I assist believers in arriving at their purpose-driven business venture.

A **purpose-driven** business is a venture God created and anoints you to build that aligns with His will and purpose for your life. It connects your gifts, talents, skills, testimony, story, background, passion, loss, triumphs, and interests to serve others for His glory. **Proverbs 21:5 AMP** expresses, "A plan (motive, wise counsel) in the heart of a man is like water in a deep well, But a man of understanding draws it out."

Nonetheless, clarify what you want to do now. Clearness doesn't mean you must have your entire life figured out. But you still need to work and progress towards some goals, and God will iron them out along the way. "Many plans are in a man's mind, But it is the Lord's purpose for him that will stand (be carried out)" **Proverbs 19:21 AMP**. So what did your hands find to do? **Ecclesiastes 9:10 NIV** states, "Whatever your hand finds to do, do it with all your might." What comes easy for you while others find it challenging? What actions will you take in the next twelve months to make the world better than when you arrived?

PILLAR 2: UNSHACKLE TO GET UNSTUCK

We all feel shackled and stuck at one phase or another, and we'll uncover it here in the **U** pillar. As we advance in life and business, stuckness happens at different stages of our growth journey. As you grow, you notice strongholds, habits, behaviors, and mindsets that have held you back in certain areas of life and relationships. But Christ has set us free for freedom, so we must live in our Christian liberty. **2 Corinthians 3:17 NIV** says, "Now the Lord is the Spirit, and where the Spirit of the Lord is, there is freedom."

Sometimes, you can do the right things but feel something isn't clicking. Regardless of where you're stagnating, it would be best to have support. Building momentum requires understanding and soul work. I'm not referring to working out a deal with God or laboring for your salvation. **Soul work** is submission and co-laboring with the Holy Spirit's sanctification to remove unaligned habits and strongholds plaguing the soul for transformation. Soul work gets to the root of misaligned mindsets that hijack your spiritual progress and identity in Christ. Like a release in a backed-up pipe, God's transformational power must bust through those repetitions to demolish the iron fences you're hiding underneath to unleash and release the new you!

Remember, you're as free as you want to be. Don't let excuses, blame, and a lack of doing the work keep you identity blind. Your life will transform when your mind, will, and emotions renew, but God won't change them for you. You'll get unshackled when you synchronize your mind with Christ's. When you move past this gap, you'll be unstoppable.

PILLAR 3: REIGNITE AND REWRITE

You've gotten robbed! Many years of your life have been stolen. Therefore, the **R** pillar is about reclaiming what the enemy stole and what you surrendered through inaction or missing the mark and praying to the Father to reignite and rewrite your future. Only God can recover the losses. He will readjust and restore your remaining days if you're faithful. After a seven-year famine, the Shunammite woman, whose son the prophet Elisha restored to life, asked the King to give back her land and the request was granted. **1 Kings 2:8 NIV** says, "Then he assigned an official to her case and said to him, 'Give back everything that belonged to her, including all the income from her land from the day she left the country until now.'"

Sometimes, things get taken from us in disasters, losses, and hard times. On other occasions, most believers give up territory in their lives, dreams, business, and relationships due to sins or passivity. Although Christ has won the victory, that doesn't mean we're to be idle and abuse grace while the enemy destroys and plunders us and our brethren blind. He's ravaging our homes, marriages, and relationships, harming our children, and ruining our dreams, businesses, and nation—and we're allowing him to do it. He's infiltrated our food supply, causing us sleep loss, poor health, depression, anxiety, and many other unnatural symptoms. You can no longer sit idly by while the devil and his army wear you and your family down. Stop letting him steal your dreams and customers. Stop voting for people who want to destroy our children, freedoms, cities, and nation. It's time to turn off the television, gaming system, and social media and pray. As one pastor said, "It's time to get off Facebook and put your face in **this book**—the Bible."

Satan wasn't skillful enough to tempt Jesus while He fasted because he had nothing in the Living Word to tempt. In that exchange, Jesus refuted Satan and slayed Him with Scriptures specific to the temptation (Matthew 4:1-11). As believers, we must check our desires to see why we keep falling for manipulations and the same plays. **James 1:13-14 NIV** says, "When tempted, no one should say, 'God is tempting me.' For God cannot be tempted by evil, nor does he tempt anyone; [14] but each person is tempted when they are dragged away by their own evil desire and enticed." Being hauled away means we give in and become victims. As long as the enemy finds an opening to steal, kill, and destroy your life and business, he'll do it! Use the Word of God specific to the areas where you're prone to cave. God offers strength and deliverance for you now. "Surely God is my help; the Lord is the one who sustains me" **Psalm 54:4 NIV**.

Prayer works. I've heard of believers who pray for hours a day. Prayer warriors enter the presence of God in the prayer closet like a sniper. They have various tactics, tools, and resources, including multiple Bibles and translations, commentaries, books, maps, and educational materials, to deepen their understanding of God and strengthen their faith before entering. Warriors are committed to Team Jesus and stand in the gap through prayer for the sick, lost, believers, widows, orphans, children, imprisoned, the poor, exploited, and the silenced. In addition, they pray for the church, nation, leaders, government, first responders, military, business owners, etc.

You can create a warfare prayer hour focused on different needs and topics. Ask the Father to open more room to pray, study, meditate, and memorize Scripture. Ask Him what books and resources He recommends—partner with your church, a good friend, or start a prayer group. Once you've identified the stolen dreams with God, repent of any wrongs and ask Him to reignite them (or something better) according to His will. Rewrite a new vision, set new goals, and devise a God-led plan for spiritual, financial, health, life, and business success.

PILLAR 4: ENRICH AND ENDURE

The final pillar, **E**, comes into play with faith-driven action. Development and persistence are essential as they involve executing plans with accountability and support for acceleration. Enriching and enduring promote implementing priorities, disciplines, and habits for success into a tactical strategy and system that strengthens and raises fortitude to do God's will until the end. **Hebrews 10:36 NKJV** says, "For you have need of endurance, so that after you have done the will of God, you may receive the promise."

Although building your strategy can cause you to work alone for a long while, you can't climb to new levels solo. Eventually, we'll work with coaches, consultants, mentors, or someone else to assist us in accomplishing our vision. Having a trusted pastor or a seasoned believer discipling us at our local congregation is also helpful. We need other people in our corner to walk us through various stages of life and business. That's why building healthy relationships with fellow brothers and sisters in Christ and investing in the help you need to accelerate is wise. Since teachers, coaches, and mentors have already been where you are, they can help you find your way out quickly. Movement happens when you have assembled your dream team of prayer warriors, partners, friends, mentors, contractors, staff, suppliers, vendors, etc. The coaching I had at different stages of my life is priceless.

Leaders taught and walked me through blind spots I never knew I had and solutions I never knew I needed. If you can't find or afford a coach, buy books or go to your local library and extract the nuggets from them. The author puts years of experience and wisdom into a book. Go to free seminars, find an SBA office or the Chamber of Commerce for additional assistance. Don't let money and egotism keep you stuck going around the same mountain when help is only a prayer, person, sermon, book, course, seminar, program, blog, video, or call away. God will show you how to soar—He's the way, the how, and why you live and prosper. **Deuteronomy 8:18 NIV** says, "But remember the LORD your God, for it is he who gives you the ability to produce wealth, and so confirms his covenant, which he swore to your ancestors, as it is today."

EMPLOYMENT VS. DEPLOYMENT

You'll need to know where you belong to ditch the comfort zone. Purpose-driven leaders must identify whether God calls them to employment, deployment, or hybrid/bi-vocational. Know whether you're an employee, business owner, or hybrid. Separating the three will give you the patience to endure trials and temptations. You can better discern the enemy's schemes when he tries to drag you away through the distraction of people, places, things, and ideas.

1. **Employment**—The dictionary defines employment as an activity or service performed for another, especially for compensation or as an occupation.
2. **Deployment**—According to Merriam-Webster, deployment is placement or arrangement (as of military personnel or equipment) in a position for a particular use or purpose. [2]

Yes, The Lord can deploy us through employment, train us through a bi-vocational model, or instruct us to lead our organizations full-time. Suppose you're working a job with a career you love. In that case, that's beautiful because that's a purpose, such as a construction foreman, manager, skilled laborer, teacher, firefighter, police officer, detective, public defender, first responder, etc. Sometimes, our assignment links employment and deployment in a hybrid way, such as a pastor who also works full-time. You may be a non-profit leader by evening and a C-Suite executive by day. Abraham

Hamilton III says, "Many of you are transitioning from your part-time job where you make an *income* to your full-time job where you cultivate an *outcome*." Either way, we must align with Elohim's missional obligation to be His light, hands, and mouthpiece wherever we find ourselves.

PURPOSE-DRIVEN BUSINESS

Since the full-time entrepreneurial deployment is highly purpose-based, you'll have to unlearn some mainstream methodologies related to working as an employee and adopt servanthood to apply the acceleration principle successfully. First, know God sends us out for *specific* assignments and undertakings. Therefore, the Almighty's financial compensation, methods, standards, and pacing differ from what we learned as employees.

As saints, we are Christ's diplomatically deployed ambassadors. As His representatives in a foreign land, God deploys us to use our specific and unique gifts, talents, skills, roles, positions, ranks, education, and backgrounds for His kingdom. Think of the background of David. His training included caring for and tending the sheep, fighting for their welfare and protection, producing music, and writing poetry. His later deployment into his kingship involved everything from his prior training as he bumped up to the nation's overseer and military leader and added the roles of husband and father.

Who's dream and legacy are we building? If we're building a business, is it purpose-driven? I know the financial need is the main reason why we stay employed. But like a child growing up depending on their parents for provision, we must grow in our faith to trust God by knowing the money will come when we put God's will before our own.

If we spend every waking minute dedicated to building up someone else's dream and legacy through a misaligned job, when will we have time to work on God's assignments and expand the body of Christ? How can He deploy us into the marketplace as full-time leaders if we're employed somewhere else? How can we thrive if we're identity blind? When our faith is activated, God can deploy us for the greater good of His vision. Deployment allows us to operate to our fullest potential. Our energy and output move us at God's speed—His supernatural spiritual pacing.

GOD-SPEED

When we accomplish things by faith in the spiritual realm, it looks like lightning-speed in the physical because we align with the Holy Spirit's power. There's a supernatural acceleration that's taking place. Therefore, *The Acceleration Cure* involves living purposefully and trusting God to guide your steps toward succeeding in what truly matters and counts for eternity.

When people encounter those living accelerated lives, they think they're out of their minds. People even said these same things about Jesus and the Apostle Paul. **Mark 3:21 NIV** says of Jesus, "When his family heard about this, they went to take charge of him, for they said, 'He is out of his mind.'" **Acts 26:24 NIV** says of Paul, "At this point Festus interrupted Paul's defense. 'You are out of your mind, Paul!' he shouted. 'Your great learning is driving you insane.'" They wonder how we can choose to live so differently. I have two words—salvation and purpose! You have to ditch and remove your old mind and take on the mind of Christ. When you know why Jesus saved you and your purpose, it takes a lot to take alternative paths.

In school, intelligent kids focused and devoted to the right things are considered nerds, outcasts, and out of touch. They remind me of believers like us who dedicate themselves to Christ and His purposes. Many reject the thought of trusting the Bible and dealing with revealed sins. And they think we're out of our minds for obeying and praying for ideas and strategies for business and financial growth. Some individuals avoid pursuing a financially prosperous life because they believe Christians should merely scrape by. But the Bible I read tells me of Abraham's, Isaac's, and Jacob's wealth. Also, don't forget Joseph, King David, King Solomon, Job, and Boaz, to name a few. You and I are royal sons and daughters—our Father owns everything! We can approach Him and ask for things we need to provide for our families, missions, and businesses.

By embracing your identity, advocating for your family, and living your purpose, you can experience greater abundance in every aspect of your life and business. In the coming days, you will explore twenty-eight biblical principles for spiritual growth, overcoming setbacks, living by faith, and overall acceleration. I encourage you to read one principle daily to absorb its teachings entirely. Additionally, I highly recommend taking notes in the margins or in a new notebook to annotate your ideas, document your insights, and consider reading it with a friend or group for an expanded discussion.

Biblical
ACCELERATION PRINCIPLES

Part 3

EMOTIONAL ACCELERATION

Day 1

PUT OFF ANGER

Just recently, I watched the Los Angeles Orange County local news cover the story of a twenty-seven-year-old man who shot and killed a six-year-old boy strapped in his car seat due to a road rage incident.[1] I can't imagine how the child's family must feel. This avoidable, tragic, and heartbreaking incident demonstrates the dangerous depths of sin's bottomless dark hole for prideful and selfish angry outbursts. Flying into a rage is when one quickly reaches volcanic, uncontrollable, unsubmitted emotions. Endless evils, crimes, and tragedies occur at the other end of someone's momentary egocentric wrath. Irrational impulsiveness is like an unsecured city. **Proverbs 25:28 KJV** says, "He that hath no rule over his own spirit is like a city that is broken down, and without walls." People pull out their cell phones to record everything these days, and in an instant, one outburst of madness can go viral and suddenly destroy everything one has worked to achieve, and leave a trail of victims.

As a passionate person, I struggled with anger upsets in my youth and romantic adult relationships. I'd get outraged when people said something I disagreed with or if I wasn't heard. Their lies, poking, gaslighting, manipulation, crossing boundaries, lack of accountability, and blame-shifting from others caused me irritation, leading to internal outrage. I simply had some sinful, prideful, hotheaded ways. The guilt and shame associated with my angry outbursts always made me feel remorseful, ashamed, sad, and far away from God and those I got mad at. I struggled to control my emotions and fiery anger that suddenly consumed me. I wondered how the

0 to 100 quick angry reaction got there. I was irresponsible for behaving like a city with no walls.

As an adult, I tried to pray and fast it out of me, and I cried many nights as I continued falling for the same temptations. Due to the fast 0 to 100 response, I was afraid of myself and where my indignation could take me—prison or maybe even worse! The angry habit felt like a part of my identity as I couldn't release its hooks from me. To this day, it still attempts to have me; it's crouching at my door, but I'm better equipped to stand through it with the whole armor of God and self-control. It doesn't win anywhere near as it used to. I learned to rely on Scripture memory and submit to The Holy Spirit to overcome this stronghold. The truth is, I cannot react in my fleshly state. I must walk in the Spirit and be accountable for responding and reacting to things that trigger me. I know that my areas of weakness will always be an opportunity for the enemy to pounce on me through conflict, accusations, pride, disrespect, irritation, noise, and other perceived violations. So, I learned to study my habits, patterns, cycles, triggers, and the desires within. I replayed some past incidents and poured over them with the Lord to see what I could do differently the next time something similar occurred. I identified what fires me up and went to God to dig its roots. Ultimately, I'm responsible for my actions.

SYMPTOMS

In some cases, aggravation is a symptom of a medical issue. Such as in my case, I've dealt with anxiety since I was a teen. The anxiety means that when I'm anxious, my brain, body, gut, and nervous system are generally in defense mode—fight or flight. I didn't realize the extent of these challenges until I sought professional help around thirty. These imbalances with insomnia can cause irritation and quick exasperation due to the state of the brain.

Some people may not experience an outward expression of their feelings, but they're holding them inside covertly repressed, and it's only a matter of time before the lid explodes. Therefore, just because no one can see their fury doesn't mean God can't perceive it. To overcome this, I pray and fast to cause my flesh to stand down, refresh myself in the Lord with worship, and strengthen my inner being by meditating on His goodness. Fitness routines, sunlight, diet changes, herbs, sleep, reading motivational books, and supplements help immensely.

Although you'll overcome the guilt of an angry outburst like me, the person on the receiving end permanently imprints the sinful display. Most won't choose to deal with you again. They'll share their experience with others with screenshots and even publish a bad review online about your business. Depending on the severity of the incident, you can catch a case, go to prison, or pay legal fines. Refusing to tame and put off the beast of the monster within is d<u>anger</u>ous because hidden in d<u>anger</u> is anger. No matter how great the business, ministry, product, mission, or service is, once the word gets out that you go ballistic on your family, volunteers, clients, and employees—nobody will want to do business or serve with you. God isn't glorified if He platforms your gifts and talents in this condition. Likewise, contempt can soon turn to hatred, resentment, and envy. Because of fury, Cain murdered his brother Able. Haman plotted to kill Mordecai and the Jews. Amnon hated his sister Tamar after he raped her. Nothing good ever came from unrighteous indignation throughout history. Wrath and rage are indeed the devil's dream and purpose destroyers! There's no way to sugarcoat its effects, so we must put it off now as God commands and behave as children of the light.

Accelerated Power – Colossians 3:8 KJV But now ye also put off all these; anger, wrath, malice, blasphemy, filthy communication out of your mouth.

Fury is connected to insecurities, irritation, selfishness, control, fear, and self-righteousness and will open the door to many other sins. In his book *If You Bite and Devour One Another*, Alexander Strauch shared how anger and conflict destroy churches, ministries, and relationships. He's observed and has been privy to learning that many in leadership behave childishly, ungodly, and selfishly during disagreements, which causes churches to split. He teaches that conflict is unavoidable, but we decide whether to represent Christ or ourselves during disagreements. [2]

BREAK IT

If you have hatred in your heart, the Bible teaches that you're a murderer. "Anyone who hates a brother or sister is a murderer, and you know that no murderer has eternal life residing in him" **1 John 3:15 NIV**. Cain committed the first murder in rage and jealousy. "And Cain talked with Abel his brother: and it came to pass, when they were in the field, that Cain rose up against Abel his brother, and slew him" **Genesis 4:8 KJV**. Remember, the **C** in the **CURE** pillar stands for *clarify* and *commit*. We must clarify our identity and purpose in Christ and remember our conversion story and redemption journey. He's forgiven us and given us a new life and identity rooted in Him. Therefore, we must be faithful and commit to allowing God's purposes to prevail. Our abiding delivers power to us to submit by faith and obey His commands. God wants you to clear up and address what's hiding under the surface and crevices within your heart and soul. No boxer jumps in the ring to fight an opponent without first knowing what they're up against and training for months. The devil and culture have trained and refined patterns, traps, and snares for thousands of years to destroy you. The Almighty God is calling you to prepare as a warrior. You must stand firm in battle and train for months and years to overcome this!

God is righteous and holy, and He hates sin! God's hatred for the sickness of sin is why He came with a divine plan to save and redeem us from the penalty of it and gave us the Holy Bible (instructions for living righteous) and the hope of His second coming to keep us far away from sin and the tricks of Satan. The Bible commands us to put off vexation because it quickly manifests pride, wrath, malice, blasphemy, and filthy communication. **Ephesians 4:26-27 KJV** says, "Be ye angry, and sin not: let not the sun go down upon your wrath: Neither give place to the devil." God gives us emotions to gauge wrong actions from ourselves and others and to navigate situations. However, how we handle the information signaled by our feelings is vital. We can be upset without sinning and going to bed hanging on to it. That's why we must be clear-headed and alert. "Be sober, be vigilant; because your adversary the devil, as a roaring lion, walketh about, seeking whom he may devour" **1 Peter 5:8 KJV**.

How we manage unsettled feelings can transport us into sin if we're not resolving problems with love and reacting instead of responding. Our priority is to behave like God is in the room—because He is. Sadly, many hold onto the right to harbor offense and wrath instead of surrendering it to God. But the Most High commands us to adjourn indignation right away. Take it off speedily—hurriedly. Forcefully remove fury from you before it catches like fire to set your soul ablaze and scorch your life, business, relationships, and reputation. Remove it before it settles into the cracks and crevices of your heart and mind. We're responsible for our actions and reactions. Acknowledge the injustice, wait for God's intervention, and continue to do good. "Wherefore let them that suffer according to the will of God commit the keeping of their souls to him in well doing, as unto a faithful Creator" **1 Peter 4:19 KJV**. Retribution belongs to God, "Dearly beloved, avenge not yourselves, but rather give place unto wrath: for it's written, 'Vengeance is mine; I will repay,' saith the Lord" **Romans 12:19 KJV**. When you carry hostility, you sin and give place to the devil's influence and power. Name *one* good thing that can come about from an angry outburst—I'll wait. Outbursts block intimacy with the Holy Spirit and others. How can we know how to parent our children and be there for our spouses and friends if we don't hear from God? We must have clarity!

DO UNTO OTHERS

"So in everything, do to others what you would have them do to you, for this sums up the Law and the Prophets" **Matthew 7:12 NIV**. We sometimes treat clients and customers better than our families and employees when we're seething about something. Those closest to us get it the worst and often feel the wrath of our contempt. It's one thing to have righteous indignation, but crossing that barrier is when it turns into a sin. As a leader, you'll be privileged to encounter many people from many backgrounds. Therefore, please handle the precious souls God puts in your path carefully. Being gentle with people doesn't dismiss sternness and passion or keeping silent about wrongs and injustices. However, we live in such an overly sensitive society where anything you say against what someone believes is considered aggressive and combative. So, take responsibility in advance by guarding your response and tone. Slow down your speech and delivery, and do your best to explain your position with God's love and truth.

 The Creator isn't holding you back from success. You're responsible for your choices and temper. God doesn't leave you alone when facing challenges. He wants you to gain clarity and understanding and prioritize your spiritual growth before granting you success. Do unto others—remember? How do you want others to treat you? First, do you treat and talk to yourself internally gently and kindly? Do you have self-respect? Anger will hinder, delay, block, and possibly forfeit your blessings and dreams. Sinful hostility is like trash; the stench will foul up the whole room if you don't throw it out before it settles in and lingers. A little garbage in the disposer can smell up the entire house. "A little leaven leavens the whole lump" (Galatians 5:9).

Jesus is concerned about you—the individual—and the lives of those you'll touch. He loves you too much to leave you where you are, just as He loves others and doesn't want them hurt by you. The consequences associated with contention are just too significant to be left unresolved. Bitterness, rage, pride, hate, murder, and abusive speech are joy killers; we can't afford their remnants and residue to linger. I never felt good about myself after losing my temper to anyone, but I always feel good when I handle things God's way. It can be challenging to put off infuriation, but God gives an escape. **1 Corinthians 10:13 KJV** says, "There hath no temptation taken you but such as is common to man: but God is faithful, who will not suffer you to be tempted above that ye are able; but will with the temptation also make a way to escape, that ye may be able to bear it."

People deserve your best, and so do you. You deserve a sound, calm mind. Kindness builds people up. Let God's love, peace, and kindness reflect in your life. Treat people as though you're in the presence of God and that they are valuable. Give grace to those who are furious and disrespectful. If your loved one is raising hell, refuse to fall for the bait or take it as a personal attack. "We wrestle not against flesh and blood but against spiritual forces in the heavens" (Ephesians 6:12). The enemy is always looking to break you down like a battering ram and penetrate your areas of weakness like a feeble dam. Please don't fall for his bait, plots, tactics, and traps to lure you into an angry exchange.

If you feel you go from 0 to 100 too soon, immediately submit to God when annoyance, frustration, and irritation are on the horizon, and pray and ask Him to unveil your blind spots. Say, "Father, can you give me time to check in with you when I feel anger rising?" Get up early to pray to set the day's tone and get ahead of turmoil. We must not be ignorant of the devil's schemes and devices. You can resist the devil by humbling yourself and submitting to God. **James 4:7-8 NIV** says, "Submit yourselves, then, to

God. Resist the devil, and he will flee from you. ⁸ Come near to God and he will come near to you. Wash your hands, you sinners, and purify your hearts, you double-minded." Be encouraged, my beloved.

Ask others to fast and pray for you, surround yourself with supportive fellow believers, and respond to complex situations rather than reacting to them. Map out a strategy with God using Scriptures in advance so He can help you anticipate attacks. Watch for physical or emotional triggers and care for your physical and mental well-being. If you desire joy and transformation, God will not let you fall. You've already overcome through the blood of the Lamb. Master your soul and live your victory through a self-controlled, fruitful spirit and disciplined life. Rid yourself of identity blindness and see yourself as happy, loving, patient, kind, and gentle.

Acceleration CURE Actions:

- **Clarify** your triggers. Identify and write a list of what words, behaviors, people, places, occasions, times, dates, and things cause you to get offended and irritated and easily fall prey to anger. Find relevant Scriptures regarding anger and love to meditate on and memorize. I recommend a deep study of the Book of James. Commit to a disciplined and regularly planned devotions and warfare strategy. In the morning and before bed, pray those Scriptures and ask the Holy Spirit to fill you with His fruit and strengthen you during triggers.

- **Repent** of any revealed sins of pride, bitterness, and contempt, and confess to God and the offended party to get unshackled and unstuck.

- **Journal** about your struggles by getting to the root cause. Write about how good you feel. Join a support group if you need practical skills to slow down your emotions. The more you release the pinned-up emotional baggage, the more God will reignite and rewrite your mission and transform your mind to His will. Refocus on the foundation of your faith and reclaim God's promise of peace.

- **Enrich** your mind by focusing on the things above and how we are to honor, respect, and love others. Read inspiring books and devotionals to help you be a better person. *If You Bite & Devour*

One Another by Alexander Strauch is a good read. Faithfully endure and persevere through the acceleration principle (pray + obey + faith + wisdom = accelerate).

Prayer

Dear Heavenly Father, you know my struggle with anger, and I'm asking you to please help me to overcome this. I no longer want to be used as a tool for evil. Soften any hardened parts in my heart and blockages that aren't allowing your Word to penetrate and heal effectively.

Please permit me to meditate on, and study related Scriptures to conquer this stronghold. I submit to walking in the Spirit, and ask if you can show me how to watch for attacks during the day and guard my blind spots. If you want me to seek professional godly biblical counseling or outside support, I'll obey and seek out the help.

I have let bitterness seep into my heart when friends, workers, clients, and contractors don't keep their commitments. Sometimes, I even deal with my loved ones harshly. I get defensive when not being seen, heard, or taken seriously. Forgive me for carrying these sins in my heart.

Open my heart to be more loving, gentle, kind, and joyful, and remove the cloud of anger from hovering over my mind, purpose, calling, and mission.

In Jesus' name, I pray, Amen.

Day 2
RELEASE ANGER TOWARD GOD

Over a decade ago, God revealed that I was carrying anger toward Him for a season. I believed He had forsaken me by denying me a successful marriage, a child, and a flourishing business. I didn't understand my complicated life journey. I didn't know how to process the feeling of being unseen by the Lord. Therefore, I unknowingly harbored anger, bitterness, and resentment toward the Most High in my ignorance for years. The Holy Spirit's conviction and revelation of my hardened heart and sin were brutal realities when I became aware. The Lord lovingly revealed the poison of hostility in my heart and led me to repentance. Our relationship instantly changed once I repented and dealt with the issue, and His love overflowed within. God knows the depths of our hearts, and our true colors will always appear given the right circumstances.

> **Accelerated Power – Psalm 22:1-2 KJV** My God, my God, why hast thou forsaken me? Why art thou so far from helping me, and from the words of my roaring? ² O my God, I cry in the day time, but thou hearest not; and in the night season, and am not silent.

Have you ever found yourself in a situation where you questioned God's presence in your life? Like King David, who expressed his feelings of desertion in some of the Psalms, you might have felt forsaken by God, too. Despite his feelings, David's faith in God's character and integrity, which he had learned since his youth, kept him from despair. He believed that God's silence was temporary, and this belief sustained him.

Jesus took on the wrath of God due to our trespasses and iniquities. He felt and bore all the raw, brutal stings of death, torture of the body, and guilt of our sins. He was stripped, flogged, beaten, bruised, shamed, and nailed to the cross like a criminal, yet was without sin. During the crucifixion of our Savior Jesus Christ, on Calvary, He even asked the Father about being forsaken, and He knew His Father's love. "And about the ninth hour Jesus cried with a loud voice, saying, 'Eli, Eli, lama sabachthani?' that's to say, 'My God, my God, why hast thou forsaken me?'" **Matthew 27:46 KJV**. God is holy, and He judges and punishes sin. The innocent Lamb took our place on the cross, death, and the grave to save us. Because of Christ's righteousness, we can enter into the presence of God through our High Priest and Savior by grace through faith, which means we're not forsaken.

HONOR THE LORD

When Christ bore our sins (past, present, and future) upon and within Himself, He took on Father God's full cup of wrath for us sinners. Sin severed the relationship and broke the fellowship between us and God. There was no other way to bring us into right standing except through the sacrifice of the sinless Lamb. But if we believe Jesus is Lord and came to reestablish our connection, we can't harbor anger against our God and make Him out to owe us anything.

Some people find themselves angry at God because they believe:

- He didn't answer their prayers.
- He's not blessing the business with new clients.
- He didn't move fast enough to an urgent situation like the death of his friend Lazarus.
- He was far away when something terrible happened during childhood or marriage.
- He allows an injury or diagnosis to snatch their dreams.
- A close loved one passed, and they have yet to heal since the loss

because they feel it wasn't their time to go.

Why people are mad at God goes beyond this shortlist. However, He's already paid the ultimate price for us, and our life must now honor His love sacrifice regardless of what we're internalizing. Yes, we can ask our Lord God questions about things we do not understand and grow in our relationship with Him, but we must show reverence and thanksgiving. Resentment towards our Creator is sin, and I encourage you to identify its root so He can cure and fix the brokenness.

I heard a blasphemous and heretical statement made by some professed Christian teachers. They teach that you must forgive God! Where is this in the Bible? God is holy, perfect—and without sin. If you find yourself making such a statement, please repent immediately for this wrong because it's not biblical and does not come from above. We must humble ourselves before the Lord.

I know that trusting God's plan is easier said than done when you're living with the battle scars of childhood molestation, lost both of your parents or one of your children, or discovered your spouse was unfaithful or decided to leave you after years of marriage. Anger will not solve the problems or improve the situation, but God can show you the next step in the process of healing. You can communicate with the Lord about it all. God gets it and can fix it! Our God is the problem solver.

GRATITUDE FOR SALVATION

If Jesus is your Redeemer and Lord, you must display gratitude, worship, and appreciation for His love, grace, mercy, and rescuing power. Sometimes, we forget all He has done and is doing for us continually. Anger toward the Almighty, who gives us His breath to breathe, is misplaced, as we shouldn't be upset with the holy and righteous King of kings. If so, we must rid ourselves of pride and false conviction and look within for the cause.

Nobody wants to feel deserted and abandoned—especially by God. Sadly, this feeling of the dark soul will be an eternal reality for those yet to set their faith and trust in Christ for their salvation. The writer of Hebrews says, "It is a fearful thing to fall into the hands of the living God" **10:31 KJV**. Eternity in hell without Christ is tragic and permanent. You can't have a do-over when you die. "No one is to trample the Son of God underfoot and insult the Spirit of grace" (Hebrews 10:29). "In our trials, we find grace through suffering to strengthen, establish, and settle us in Christ Jesus" (1 Peter 5:10).

GOD IS COMPASSIONATE

Remember, we serve a loving, compassionate, and merciful God (Hebrews 4:14-16). No matter how painful the experience was, you can address it today. Even if you're grieving a loss, He's the only answer to EVERY problem. Fellowship with God isn't possible when the barrier of unforgiveness blocks intimacy.

Resentment will deter blessings, stop prayers from being heard or answered, hinder personal and business progress, and disrupt your relationship with God and others. Any accomplishments you experience unaligned and not rooted in God aren't flourishing. However, there's an acceleration cure if we address the obvious.

The motive and attitude behind our actions matter. Whatever we do for the Lord counts for eternity. Obedience to God and what He says is what success is. Anything outside of glorifying the Lord in our work, thoughts, words, and deeds "will burn in the fire" (1 Corinthians 3:15). "Whatever you do [whatever your task may be], work from the soul [that's, put in your very best effort], as [something done] for the Lord and not for men, [24] knowing [with all certainty] that it's from the Lord [not from men] that you'll receive the inheritance which is your [greatest] reward. It's the Lord Christ whom you [actually] serve," **Colossians 3:23-24 AMP.**

We serve Christ, and our inheritance comes from Him. Therefore, when we trust Him, we'll expect that everything He does is for a good purpose. We won't need to get mad or upset because we know He has a plan designed just for us. Look at Job's life. Can you imagine what he endured spiritually, mentally, emotionally, and physically, yet he didn't sin against God?

TALK IT OUT

A godly character is the precursor of good business and relationships. If you're angry with God again, please talk it out, repent, and escape the self-imposed prison. Let it go, no matter the cause. Talk to the Lord about why you're hurt, and don't hold back anything—He can take it! Let it all out passionately but respectfully so you can start a new level of your fruit-bearing relationship. Maintaining the right standing and intimacy is vital for moving forward. **Ephesians 4:30-32 KJV** says, "And grieve not the holy Spirit of God, whereby ye are sealed unto the day of redemption. [31] Let all bitterness, and wrath, and anger, and clamour, and evil speaking, be put away from you, with all malice: [32] And be ye kind one to another, tenderhearted, forgiving one another, even as God for Christ's sake hath forgiven you."

God has forgiven you for past, present, and future offenses. Every breath you breathe now is courtesy of Him to preserve your life. He is always there for you even when you feel He isn't. The Scripture tells us to put away *all* bitterness, wrath, and anger. Get rid of the things that God disapproves of. Cease grieving the Holy Spirit. Think of how grief causes you to feel and imagine how the Spirit of God feels. The passage ends by reminding us how God has forgiven us for Christ's sake. Because of Christ, we have a chance at life again. We can encourage and love others because we're among the living. We're blessed with a fresh start and new beginnings to keep pushing toward our purpose. Don't give up on God due to what was lost when He has you here for a more significant reason. Our dreams will bear good fruit and multiply. The Lord will reward faithfulness.

Refuse to let another moment pass without freedom in your heart. God wants to bless you. He wants you to dream big goals and pass your tests. Please put this book down right now, talk to God about the pain you're harboring, and then return to this chapter's actions and prayer.

Acceleration CURE Actions:

- **Pray** and clarify what's causing your concerns, and commit to getting to know the Almighty's character by spending time with Him in the Word.
- **Repent** and remember all the good things God has, is, and will do in your life to get you unshackled and unstuck so that you will never again be at odds with the Lord—your Maker.
- **Trust** and believe that God will direct your path. When you align with His will, He will reignite your dreams and rewrite and edit the manuscript of your story.
- **Focus** on enriching and enduring your faith by meditating on God's

promises. Then, read helpful books about the things you're struggling with and watch your relationships accelerate in every other area of life.

Prayer

Dear Heavenly Father, I ask you to forgive me and cleanse my heart of all unrighteousness, bitterness, and anger towards you. Accepting that you still have a plan for me is tough because I've been hurting from my past. I struggle with believing you'll come through for me or the business because I often came to you in all sincerity, and my prayers seemed to go unanswered. I don't understand your plan, but I know that you love me and have already planned to finish the work you started in me. Please help me to rest in your faithfulness and timetable for my life and business success. God, please reveal to me whatever I did outside of being bitter towards you that's blocking intimacy.

Starting today, if I have concerns or questions about anything I don't understand, I will respectfully talk to you.

In Jesus' name, I pray, Amen.

Day 3
PRACTICE FORGIVENESS

Have you ever rewatched a movie several times and found something different you never noticed each time you viewed it? You see something in the background—such as production mistakes or a new person, and then hear an unfamiliar line from a character. What has changed? You! You've changed and now view the film from a new vantage point through newly collected experiences because your awareness and discernment are increasing.

In contrast, when we read the Bible, there is always something fresh to take away. But we often miss the Holy Spirit's attempt to show us new things from His vantage point because we don't approach God's sacred and living text with changing in mind. Therefore, we gloss over the *familiar* passages, failing to grasp the more profound meaning because we don't deem the *same* Scriptures as newfound or necessary. In turn, we dismiss the significance of learning what the Spirit is trying to teach. But each time we open the Bible, God talks to us, and it's not only in descriptive ways but also prescriptive and instructional. The holy Word isn't meant to find *you* or only *good feelings* in the text—it's written to continuously transform your mind into Christ's.

We reflect and study for it to cut and perform surgery as per **Hebrews 4:12 NIV**, "For the word of God is alive and active. Sharper than any double-edged sword, it penetrates even to dividing soul and spirit, joints and marrow; it judges the thoughts and attitudes of the heart."

Sadly, many professing Christians are holding unforgiveness, grudges, and resentment against others and are reading the Bible regularly, believing it's pointing the fingers at everyone else. This poison is ruining them, and they're grieving the Spirit due to their unwillingness to address it. Failure to clear the blockage leads to distance from God and others.

Accelerated Power – Matthew 6:14-15 KJV For if ye forgive men their trespasses, your heavenly Father will also forgive you: ¹⁵ But if ye forgive not men their trespasses, neither will your Father forgive your trespasses.

My friend, God makes it clear—He looks at forgiveness precisely as He stated, "But if you forgive not men their trespasses, neither will your Father forgive yours." Practicing unforgiveness is a massive, cancerous, unholy issue in the body of Christ. But how can that be when our eternal security is based on God reconciling our sins? We cannot choose whom to forgive, as God has set the conditions. We're to forgive anyone who has wronged us. Mercy is an acceleration cure that frees us from bondage and the impact the offense will have on our lives and purpose. Building upon Christ's foundation is expressing His virtuous behaviors and agreeing with what He deems righteous.

Additionally, compassion allows the power of the Holy Ghost to move through us with no spiritual blockage. We must trust God to avenge us and handle the offense to accelerate. Sometimes, we read Scripture passages like Matthew 6:14-15 and race past fundamental parts.

We bypass the simplicity and truths of Jesus' teachings and move on with life, believing they're for other people. But mercy demonstrates true conversion to Christ, love, obedience, and spiritual maturity. The prayer Jesus modeled in Matthew 6:12 for His disciples references forgiveness: "forgive us our debts, as we forgive our debtors." When Peter asked Jesus how many times he should forgive, "Then Peter came to Him and asked, 'Lord, how many times will my brother sin against me and I forgive him *and* let it go? Up to seven times?' ²² Jesus answered him, 'I say to you, not up to seven times, but seventy times seven'" **Matthew 18:21 NKJV**. We're sinning if we're harboring offenses against someone right now. We're loudly declaring disobedience towards God's command to forgive. We can't ask God to forgive our debt, but we are unwilling to forgive the offender's debt.

If someone needs to seek you for mercy, is your heart positioned for absolution? Forgive them anyway if they don't seek it because you may never get an apology. You're held accountable for choosing only to be a hearer but not a doer of the Word. **James** writes in **1:23-24 NIV**, "Anyone who listens to the word but does not do what it says is like someone who looks at his face in a mirror [24] and, after looking at himself, goes away and immediately forgets what he looks like."

Some people will die without seeking your exoneration, but because your heart can forgive, you can get unstuck from the offense and move on with your life. Choosing unforgiveness will hinder your growth, block your blessings, and affect your life and business acceleration.

YOUR SOUL CURE

No forgiveness, no soul cure! Forgiveness is to anyone you've encountered, connected with, or had or currently have a relationship with who has wronged, disrespected, or harmed you—professionally, in passing, or personally. Additionally, just because you've forgiven them does not mean you must restore the connection. Sorrowfully, I hear many stories of brutal, sinister, and nefarious abuse and violation toward children. I've cried many times over the violence and harm I've seen adults manage to live through since childhood damage. The tragedies nearly ruined them, and the pain runs deep, but if one desires, God can make them whole if they desire healing. Forgiving someone for the most horrendous acts committed against you is truly the power of God's love within. Forgiveness is proof you have a new nature and Christlike character. It's the devil who used those people to kill, steal, and destroy you—not God! No matter how terrible the deed or how deeply hurt you are by it—you're commanded to forgive. Jesus can and will cure your soul and soften your heart. Christ asked the Father to forgive those who brutally murdered Him on the cross of Calvary—"Then said Jesus, 'Father, forgive them; for they know not what they do'" **Luke 23:34 KJV**. Take the first step and forgive, then allow Christ's love to restore you. What better way to glorify God? Be grateful to God for freeing you from any further harm the person may have caused if He hadn't rescued you at the time He did.

You don't want the enemy to have a stranglehold over your life in this way. The cost of holding on to unforgiveness is too high, bankrupting you spiritually. I'm sure you've heard this often, but forgiving them is for God and you! Some say that's unbiblical, but you experience freedom when you're free from that bondage of shame, bitterness, and grudges. Clemency opens up intimacy in every relationship, darkened by sin remnants. Embrace your God-given dream and consider how to serve God and the people you desire to inspire as a free person.

The more we flourish, the more often we can perform a soul check-up to gauge unforgiveness. **Soul work** is submission and co-laboring with the Holy Spirit's sanctification to remove unaligned habits and strongholds plaguing the soul for transformation.

The **soul check-up** is also a way to check on a few other important areas of your spiritual life, similar to a financial budget or a blood pressure check with a clinician. Like a doctor asks questions and runs tests to check on your body, I've created a soul check-up to help you see and stay abreast of the condition of your heart, mind, will, and emotions. Its self-reflection questions are designed to help identify possible blockages that may prevent you from functioning optimally spiritually, mentally, emotionally, and physically. It isolates what's keeping you from accelerating by addressing the Holy Spirit's concerns and prevents us from becoming desensitized to unforgiveness and disconnecting from the Vine.

MAKING IT RIGHT

In your prayer time, confess any unforgiveness you harbored against others. The people you have an issue with have gone on living their lives. If your offender is a Christian, the Holy Spirit will impress upon their heart to deal with the wrong, but don't wait around for it because this can take years, if it happens at all. Also, their guilt and shame may be too heavy if they think about the offense, and they'll never come forward. Whatever the case, you must forgive them whether they decide to apologize or not. **Proverbs 19:11 KJV** says, "The discretion of a man deferreth his anger; and it's his glory to pass over a transgression." God will judge and vindicate. Please free that person from your prison and pass over the transgression by leaving it in Jehovah's hands. Forgiving someone who hurt you allows you to identify deeper with the sufferings of Christ. Pray for your enemies as Jesus commands, "But I say to you, love [that is, unselfishly seek the best or higher good for] your enemies and pray for those who persecute you," **Matthew 5:44 AMP**.

God wants us to keep our lives right with Him. It's one thing to harbor sourness toward others, but we must also ask the Lord God to forgive us for our trespasses when we violate His commands. Ask the Holy Spirit to search your heart for hidden faults, too. The psalmist writes, "But who can discern their own errors? Forgive my hidden faults" **Psalm 19:12 NIV**. No matter how good of a person you believe you are, you will indeed wrong others and have wronged someone. If there is any role you played in sinning against someone, don't hesitate to take accountability. Don't make excuses or justifications for your actions. We're not good. The rich young ruler called Jesus a Good Teacher. In this statement, Jesus proves His deity and authority to forgive. "Why do you call me good?" Jesus answered. "No one is good—except God alone" **Mark 10:18 NIV**. Someone may be pondering an offense you've done towards them because we can also be victimizers by treating people wrong. We must learn to quickly say, "I'm sorry," to keep peace. We don't usually think about ourselves as the offenders, but avoiding offense and conflict in relationships is impossible. And since Jesus loves us, and we're a part of the body of Christ, He gives us His spiritual bread for a reason. We're responsible for what He feeds us when we read.

Don't let anything or anyone hold you back. Make things right with God and others, and get on with your life. Please rectify if you championed, agreed, and stood for something the Most High God is against. God is always faithful in forgiving you no matter what you do and what you've done if you repent. The Word of God promises that "If we confess our sins, he is faithful and just and will forgive us our sins and purify us from all unrighteousness" **1 John 1:9 NIV**. If we confess, God extends His grace and mercy regardless of our sins when we ask for them. He bore your sin because He's concerned about your sanctification and eternal life. Live in the freedom and abundance that Jesus promised you, and maximize the rest of your life for God's glory. If you need help getting into a rhythm with checking in on your soul a printable, check-up is offered at https://cure4thesoul.com/soul-check-up/ and in the Dream Big Goals Planner.

Acceleration CURE Actions:

- **Forgive** others quickly, and make a list of anyone you are holding hostage with unforgiveness. Clear heart and soul clutter, clarify and commit to the things of God, and pray for your enemies.

- **Refuse** to mediate on past, present, and future offenses. Turning your attention to the things above, your purpose, and serving others will help you get unshackled and unstuck from unforgiveness.
- **Focus** and know that God will take care of any person or problems you face due to what you went through. Thus, through confession and restoration, God can bless you by reigniting the dreams He gave you and rewriting a clearer vision.
- **Patiently** endure, have compassion for others, give people grace, find joy in trials, and overcome hurts through forgiveness to unlock enriched mercy through abiding in the Holy Ghost.

Prayer

Dear Heavenly Father, forgive me for the sin of unforgiveness and reveal any hidden wrongs I committed against you. I am coming to you today asking for your help and forgiveness for (person's name who wronged you). Please help me to accept that many people are broken and need a real relationship with you, Father. Today, I pray for them to get in the right standing with you so the enemy will no longer claim victory over their soul. Let my heart bend to forgive them because I no longer want to live in an emotional prison. I have no idea why they did what they did to me, but you do. Satan wants to see me hurt, destroyed, devastated, broken, crushed, shattered, shamed, and guilted by others, but you won't let his plans succeed.

For the people I wronged, place them on my heart so I may seek reconciliation if possible. I ask that you touch their heart to forgive me as well. Set me free from the painful experiences I've encountered so I can do the work you called me to do. I want prosperous and blessed relationships. I desire to live the rest of my life with joy. Please remove the pain I experienced and the memories lodged deep in my heart and soul and work it out for my good.

In Jesus' Name, I pray, Amen.

Day 4
CONQUER DEPRESSION

Artists who aren't making a living creating feel like fish without water. Some lean toward pessimism when they hit a roadblock and struggle to share their ideas and creativity with the world because they feel disconnected and misunderstood. They often fight a dark side wrought with gloom to accomplish their goal. Unfortunately, social conditioning makes it hard to tell when someone struggles internally, especially among artistic types and founders.

In the Forum of Christian Leaders, research shows artists and creatives are more prone to depression and loneliness due to their hypersensitive brains and temperaments. In his lecture, *A Thorn in the Flesh: Is Depression Relevant to Artists?* Christian psychiatrist Pablo Martinez reflects on how King David's sensitivity mirrors an artist's soul.[1] The Bible shares that David was a loving shepherd and warrior—a talented, gifted, skilled musician, writer, poet, and devoted King. Martinez references a medical framework and Psalm 31:9-10 as a starting point for this biblical analogy.

Accelerated Power – Psalms 31:9-10 NIV Be merciful to me, LORD, for I am in distress; my eyes grow weak with sorrow, my soul and body with grief. My life is consumed by anguish and my years by groaning; my strength fails because of my affliction, and my bones grow weak.

King David experienced bouts of despair to the point where his soul and body were pained, his eyes overflowed with burden, and his body ripped with grief. But, he spoke kindly to the Lord. Also, the psalmist expresses, "Why, my soul, are you downcast? Why so disturbed within me? Put your hope in God, for I will yet praise him, my Savior and my God" **42:11 NIV**. Please note how he spoke to himself. He encouraged himself with calmness. He didn't try to force himself to get over and on with it. He took his thoughts captive and waited for God's help to pull him from that darkness.

2 Corinthians 10:5 NIV teaches, "We demolish arguments and every pretension that sets itself up against the knowledge of God, and we take captive every thought to make it obedient to Christ." Most creative and high-achievers face mountain-top highs and deep valley lows. Our situation changes when we lovingly and gently talk to and remind ourselves of God's Word. **Proverbs 16:24 NKJV** says, "Pleasant words *are like* a honeycomb, Sweetness to the soul and health to the bones."

THE DEPTHS OF MELANCHOLY

Depression's symptoms can include withdrawal, insomnia or sleeping more, agitation, self-criticizing, weight gain or loss, gain or loss of appetite, trouble focusing, and anger. Depression isn't only related to what you're thinking and feeling. Physiological issues can contribute to despair, such as brain injury, stress, and anxiety. Sadness can overwhelm us when we lack vital nutrients, vitamins, and minerals. Battling excess body weight, inflammation, high blood glucose, poor gut health, hormonal imbalances, insufficient physical movement, sleep loss, and an absence of sunlight decelerates our victory. Other underlying health disorders or traumatic events may often trigger these feelings of gloom. Yet, as visionaries, we rarely share or open up about these experiences, as entrepreneurship can be lonely. As believers, we must stay connected with our local church, build a consistent exercise routine, and maintain healthy relationships to minimize these blows.

Going against the grain is a huge responsibility. Within the first few years of starting a company, the losses often outweigh the wins. Without substantial financial savings, availability of business credit, investors, or start-up capital, one can quickly run into money issues that lead to depression. Psychology Professor Dr. Jordan B. Peterson's lecture, *The Curse of Creativity,* discusses how creative people often suffer financially due to their inability to monetize their creative talents.[2] He also clarifies that everyone isn't innovative in the same sense as gifted, creative people, which is why they struggle deeply. Blues can quickly set in when these losses happen back-to-back due to the avalanche of debt and the need for a quick solution. Many fully functioning business people can still be pressed down, pushing through without time to nurse the wound, but it shows up in other ways, like anger and withdrawal.

THE TRIUNE MAN

I believe the Creator formed us in a trichotomy—spirit, soul, and body. I accept the soul is the mind, will, and emotions that intersect our subconscious mind, personality, and intellect. It's thought that the heart is the seat of the soul that bridges our spirit with the conscience. **Hebrews 4:12 NIV** says, "For the word of God is alive and active. Sharper than any double-edged sword, it penetrates even to dividing soul and spirit, joints and marrow; it judges the thoughts and attitudes of the heart." The Godhead is the Holy Trinity—One God in Three Persons. God the Father, Son, and Holy Spirit—and we're created in God's image. The Holy Tabernacle and Temple (Moses' and Solomon's) were also made of three parts—the *outer* and *inner* court and the *Holy of Holies* (the most holy place). God also gives the gift of salvation in the past, present, and future.

1 Thessalonians 5:23 NIV says, "May God himself, the God of peace, sanctify you through and through. May your whole spirit, soul, and body be kept blameless at the coming of our Lord Jesus Christ." When God's Word speaks of sanctifying us wholly, He covers the entirety of our makeup—spirit, soul, and body. Likewise, **Proverbs 20:27 NKJV** says, "The spirit of a man *is* the lamp of the LORD, Searching all the inner depths of his heart."

You get to partner with the Holy Ghost in your restoration when you better understand your human makeup, just like a doctor needs knowledge of anatomy to treat the body. Take, for instance, the ear. It's composed of the outer ear, middle ear, and inner ear. This analogy is just one example.

Dr. Donald Grey Barhhouse was a notable faith warrior recognized for his expository teaching of the Book of Romans. During his pastorate, he parked his Sunday sermons in the book for three and a half years, teaching exegetically verse by verse. He was faithful to sound doctrine and research, spending countless hours studying, and a pioneer in spreading the gospel through media with radio broadcasts and his magazine.

As a Presbyterian pastor and businessman for thirty-three years, he authored *Romans Expositions of Bible Doctrines*. In it, he says, "The image of God which was placed upon man, and which man lost in the fall, is a spiritual image. Man, like God, is a trinity." He explains that although a tree's body is visible, it doesn't possess a soul or spirit. Likewise, animals have a body and soul but not a spirit. God created man as a living soul along with a spirit and body fashioning us in God's image.

His artfully painted analogy of a bombed building's *third floor* (spirit) collapsing into the *second floor* (soul) expresses how the fall in Eden affected the new makeup of unregenerate man. The visible cracks from the bomb's aftermath show on the exterior and *first floor* (body). The original foundation was destroyed along with the divine spirit, leaving the man to live out life soulish and spiritually dead.[3]

Christ's redemption and regeneration gave us a new spirit imparted by the Holy Spirit to reset us back to God's original design. We won't always agree on the trichotomy and secondary doctrinal beliefs, but I hope we agree about the correct view of God, the gospel of Jesus Christ, and the core tenets of the Christian faith.

As new creations in Christ, we were used to living soulish, and often, we find ourselves reverting to that familiarity. Soulish living is how we once operated as spiritually unresponsive non-believers. Without consulting God, you can still decide with your mind, will, and emotions. You can still explore fresh learnings with intellect and charm with your personality and heart.

When wrestling internally, it takes the Spirit of Holiness to untangle the intricacies. Sometimes, you can sink so far down. But there is hope! "We wait in hope for the Lord; he is our help and our shield. [21] In him our hearts rejoice, for we trust in his holy name. [22] May your unfailing love be with us, Lord, even as we put our hope in you" **Psalm 33:20-22 NIV**. We must pray, sing aloud, and worship God with our inner man. Also, talk to the Counselor about what's causing your heavy soul. Adoration and dependency on God for assistance will drown out adverse mindsets because He inhabits our worship space. Ask someone else to pray for you, too.

THE INNER WAR

I've publicly discussed my struggles with depression through my ministries, which led me to research this connection with creative people and founders. I battled with soul-sickness in my twenties and thirties. The heaviness of my emotional climate occasionally dragged me into an internal storm. Consequently, my weariness came from relational and business disappointments, financial setbacks, rejection, and seasonal blues. I'm also an overcomer from an unhealthy relationship that the enemy used to try to devour me and execute my joy and purpose.

I've experienced tremendous victory over depression for the more significant part of now thirteen years, but it still tries to rear its ugly head sporadically. We're always prone to falling back into the things we've overcome. Two months before the final edit of this book, I got hit with a brick of despair that lasted for three weeks. When an avalanche of deleterious thoughts and fiery arrows closes in, there's only so much one person can take. When people are pressed down, their habits break, and everyday tasks are complicated. The soul isn't well, and it needs nursing back into recovery mode. Revival and working back into restarting consistent habits are equally taxing as the prior crushing and require time to readapt. Nonetheless, your functions will be back once you overcome the soul afflictions.

CHECK YOUR THOUGHTS

Founders and creatives turn thoughts into things for a living! Most of what they think about becomes a reality, whether massively accepted or not. You may be overwhelmed by thoughts of mounting debt, an unbearable marriage, and providing for your children and employees. Your goals may not work as expected, and you may feel tired, grieved, ashamed, and embarrassed. You don't want to cut jobs, close down the company, or get a divorce, but it's a lot to manage.

The wrong spiritual and mental outlook on life and a dreadful loop of invasive thoughts have severe consequences. We all get overwhelmed and stuck occasionally. It's not a weakness, but we must seek biblically sound help. Suicide and hopelessness are no laughing matter, but when you turn it over to God, He solves every problem, no matter how big and bad things appear. You're not alone, and I dislike that you're feeling this way, but ending your life is not the answer. If you need intervention, please seek spiritual, medical, or professional help today.

Dr. Sherry Walling, PhD, discussed in an article on entrepreneur.com how entrepreneurs are at a higher risk for suicide and mental thrashes. She explained that even though founders may have a team around them, they often work in solitude and isolation, making them vulnerable. Their networks are more prominent than their social circles. She also emphasized the grave nature of her findings, citing instances of successful entrepreneurs who tragically ended their lives and how dangerous business ownership can be psychologically speaking. [4]

Christians—we must deal with our inner man to address the darkness of the soul. We can intentionally meditate on good things habitually. Those who have pursued creative passions or managed a full-time business can truly grasp the profound sense of heartache that can accompany these endeavors. It's the difference between someone who's been married to a narcissist as opposed to just being in a bad relationship. They won't understand the mind traps and conditioning that a person puts you through to increase your tolerance to manipulation and pain. They say things like, "Why did they stay." "Why don't they just leave." Likewise, a person facing the complexities of despair can't just turn it off like a light switch. However, there's good news!

2 Corinthians 1:3-4 NIV *says,* "Praise be to the God and Father of our Lord Jesus Christ, the Father of compassion and the God of all comfort, ⁴ who comforts us in all our troubles, so that we can comfort those in any trouble with the comfort we ourselves receive from God." Thank the Father for His comfort and compassion. The Father promises to comfort you in ALL your afflictions and sanctify you wholly; therefore, you don't have to stay pressed down. Life doesn't always work how we want, but it gets better. The Word of the Lord can instantly change your heart and soul because it's alive and active. Ask the Holy Spirit to override your sadness and inabilities. The Creator will free you from abuse, low self-worth, melancholy, and constantly toiling to do things alone. You can choose what you want to focus on each day. If needed, take off for a few days or a week and do something you enjoy. God will care for your financial needs because you need spiritual and soul rest and nourishment.

There are churches and online ministries where you can call for prayer if you don't have anyone to pray with. Cure 4 the Soul answers prayer requests on its website. The purpose the Creator kept you alive for is vital to the lives of those He wants to use your testimony to impact. And in these dark times, we need all hands on deck to spread the good news. The business and skill set you have to offer the world are needed, and that's why the enemy is trying to keep you low. Choose your level of hard Soulful. It's hard to lose, and it's just as hard to conquer the win.

Growing in the knowledge of Jesus Christ, studying and reading specific Scriptures that are key to my related concerns, and drawing near to God changed my life. In addition, I enjoy reading, researching, and using herbs and plants, which offer natural remedies to balance my moods. The Lord God won't let the righteous fall. "Cast your burden on the LORD [release it] and He will sustain *and* uphold you; He will never allow the righteous to be shaken (slip, fall, fail)" **Psalm 55:22 AMP**. Use your spiritual weapons to accelerate past destructive thinking. Your weapons are in **Ephesians 6:10-20**—"the helmet of salvation, the breastplate of righteousness, a belt of truth, the sword of the spirit, the shield of faith, the gospel of peace, and prayer."

MORE THAN A CONQUEROR

Above anyone or anything, the Holy Spirit is my recommended Counselor. No clinician can penetrate the deepest, darkest wounds of your hurts, pain, and past. I recommend getting some good, godly Christian counseling to help you sort out your thoughts and offer practical tips for working through your pain if you need to talk to someone. Don't neglect, but care for yourself so you can care for others. Look into changing your diet, juicing, nourishing your gut, brain, and internal systems with natural herbs and nutrients, getting some sun, moving your body for at least thirty minutes four times a week, and resting. When you focus on the Lord and hide and abide in the Vine, you'll find less room to think about what you don't have.

Acceleration CURE Actions:

- **Clarify** the enemy's ploys he's using to keep your soul anguished and anything you're meditating on that's causing you to dread. Then, commit to replacing them with new ones focused on the goodness of the Lord and your blessings. Identify one person you can contact to help you find ways to monetize your creative endeavors.

- **Remember** how God already unshackled and unstuck you from the soul's depression. Address loneliness and despair by memorizing and praying Scripture, connecting with understanding people, exercising, and eating nutritiously.

- **Mediate** on the Lord's goodness in the Psalms. Ask Him to reignite your suppressed happy emotions. Rewrite your goals, journal your thoughts, research natural supplements, and seek biblical counseling to reclaim your sound mind, balanced emotions, and healthy hormones.
- **Pray** for other business owners to be lifted from the blues and experience an enduring and enriching joy in the Lord.

Prayer

Dear Heavenly Father, I thank you for speaking to my heart about depression. Thank you for showing me that I'm not the only one who feels this way. Today, I seek your help because my heart is heavy with depression, discouragement, and hopelessness about _____. Please restore my joy, peace of mind, and sleep. Please help me understand that things work on my behalf even when I don't see them. God, allow me to challenge and change my defeating thoughts and replace them with your life-changing Word and singing your praises. I pray for every business owner who may be experiencing depression or suicidal thoughts. Please deliver those trapped in seemingly helpless situations. Vindicate your righteous children facing hard days ahead in the legal system because of standing for righteousness. I know you have an excellent plan for my life, so help me keep my eyes on you and the people I'm to serve and lead. I'm praying for the wisdom to return to my business with a sound mind. Assist me to see that you're more significant than any problem I encounter.

In Jesus' Name, I pray, Amen.

Day 5
DESTROY JEALOUSY AND COMPETITION

Within two years of God revealing my purpose, I launched my coaching program, "Dream Big Goals Accelerator," rebranded, separated, and created a new business and website for Cure 4 the Soul and C4tS Ministries. I published projects, including "Dream Big Goals" and its two printed companions, which I deliver to your front door in beautifully branded boxes. I also released my first non-fiction book, "The Acceleration Cure." Although I initially completed the chapter weeks ago, the Spirit urged me to include this introduction story.

During these project releases, I've sought understanding from God Almighty about the evident spirit of envy plaguing the body of Christ. On my birthday, October 14, as I announced the book's pre-order on multiple social platforms, I spoke to the Lord about the jarring dismissal from people in the car before me celebrating at Pappadeaux Seafood Kitchen.

When I went into the restaurant's restroom to wash my hands, the song—*Smiling Faces*, released in 1971 by The Undisputed Truth, blasted piercingly as speaking directly to me—yet warmly in the speakers. I know it was the Holy Spirit responding to our talk. The tune's lyrics paint a picture of a friend or someone close who smiles in your face but is envious of you under the surface. As I unpacked this feeling further on that day, He confirmed my suspicions that many people who say they love and respect you don't even like you. Some will go as far as expressing support but still show signs that it's out of compulsion instead of pure desire and generosity. Some just aren't interested in what you offer, and that's okay.

In contrast, others are preoccupied with their cares and aren't purposefully ignoring you—but many aren't delighted about your progress, success, or level up. They prefer you struggling, down and out, busted and disgusted, because they're okay with you winning a little as long as you aren't winning more than them. So, in their heart, they secretly dislike, ignore, belittle, compete with, and sabotage your success.

However, as an avid observer of people, I've been fortunate to discern and understand things I might not have noticed if I hadn't released these projects, been in solitude, taken months away from social platforms, and backed away from close contact with people for a season. If I were the pre-Dallas unhealed version of Tanya or relied on others' endorsement, I'd feel heartbroken and resentful; thankfully, I don't, primarily since I've grown and gone through much hurt, recovery, and soul work and found solace in expressing the thoughts behind these twenty-eight biblical principles.

THREADS AND STITCHES

Throughout the Holy Bible, we see threads, stitches, and traces of jealousy, competition, and selfish ambition rearing their ugly heads. This dangerous emotion fused with pride, resentment, criticism, arrogance, anger, and discontent can quickly turn poisonous if not immediately stopped. When it takes root, its vicious venom will destroy the lives of those it plagues and others.

Satan is jealous of the Most High God, and he hates everyone made in His image. He is exceedingly envious of God's children, who dare to believe Jesus Christ is God and Lord, and his green-eyed ways are infectious. King Saul was once favored by God and admired by the people. However, Saul's initial admiration for David eventually turned into jealousy and a desire to kill him. **1 Samuel 18:7-9 NIV** teaches "As they danced, they sang: 'Saul has slain his thousands, and David his tens of thousands.' Saul was very angry; this refrain displeased him greatly. 'They have credited David with tens of thousands,' he thought, 'but me with only thousands. What more can he get but the kingdom?'" [9] And from that time on Saul kept a close eye on David." And in **1 Samuel 19:1-2 NIV**, "Saul told his son Jonathan and all the attendants to kill David. But Jonathan had taken a great liking to David [2] and warned him, 'My father Saul is looking for a chance to kill you.'"

Accelerated Power – James 3:14-16 NIV But if you harbor bitter envy and selfish ambition in your hearts, don't boast about it or deny the truth. [15] Such "wisdom" doesn't come down from heaven but is earthly, unspiritual, demonic. [16] For where you have envy and selfish ambition, there you find disorder and every evil practice.

RID THE POISON

Demonic ways in our hearts and actions toward others are sins; when they're present, all other ungodly disorders appear. Joseph's brothers envied him and sold him into slavery. And shall we forget about Esau and Jacob, Haman and Mordecai? Hagar and Sarah—Rachel and Leah. This poisonous human soul-sucking selfish emotion is too dangerous to let linger, and guess what? No matter how holy we appear, none of us are immune to it catching us off guard. As soon as jealousy rises, we must pray immediately for the Holy Spirit to take it away. We must tell the Lord God the genuine reasons for our impression and ask Him to help us focus on our security, blessings, and identity in Christ. The Creator made us all unique with individual abilities, talents, and treasures to glorify Him. Whatever we want and need, we can ask our Father for it.

NO EXPECTATIONS

Throughout the years, I've faced a lot of rejection. Through it, I learned that the people God wants to do business with you aren't necessarily those closest to you. Sometimes, your family and friends may support you, but your core supporters are usually strangers. It can be deeply hurtful when those we love and count on seem to overlook our need for support and encouragement. It's disheartening to feel a lack of acknowledgment or appreciation, especially from those who profess to care. A simple word of encouragement, a kind comment, or a heartfelt congratulations can make a difference and lift our spirits during happy or challenging times. Feeling down, hurt, unwell, or injured can be discouraging when others don't check in or offer support. A little godly kindness can make a big difference. Additionally, pay close attention to people's words and actions surrounding special occasions, significant accomplishments, and before a new year. I've heard and noticed the strangest behavior from people. God will always reveal the heart behind said words, silence, actions, and inaction. People will go around you to compliment you on your nails, shoes, hat, shirt, curtains, floors, rugs, pets, sofa, and photo background to avoid giving *you* a compliment, congratulations, or encouraging words.

Although I've learned to overcome these soul-aching incidences of people's insecurities and inferiority complexes, many of God's children haven't reached that point yet. They're trying to sort these digs of passive-aggressive occurrences out. Therefore, I want to share some truths of reassurance. Jesus didn't rely on men's support, words, or praises because He knows their hearts. "But Jesus, for His part, did not entrust Himself to them, because He knew all *people* [and understood the superficiality and fickleness of human nature]" **John 2:24 AMP**.

Soulful, the sooner you recognize that only God can supply all your needs and you must be solid and non-reliant on anyone's opinions of you, the better you can navigate your life and business without spiritual, emotional, and mental blockage and co-dependency. People are dealing with different things, and their minds can change, like the Texas weather. My dear brother and sister, as a servant of Christ, please vow today to release 100% of your expectations for people. Commit to serving God anyway, and expect the best of yourself as salt and light, as well as how you handle rejection in leadership. Realize it's a *them* and not a *you* problem. Pray for people and remove yourself from taking rejection personally. Don't desire or require anyone to see, notice, or do anything for you. Never await a compliment, a helping hand, a phone call, a sympathy card, or a congratulations. Do those things for yourself. Learn how to put all your dependency on God alone. Love people without hesitation through your transformation, as any inspiration you get above your low expectations is *a motivation* that leads to godly appreciation. Vow to rise above their intentional belittling.

COMPETITION AMONG ONE ANOTHER

Some spouses compete with each other and even turn their children to compete against their brothers and sisters. Some parents are even jealous of their children. Additionally, the business world is highly competitive, and getting caught up in what others do is easy. No believer has to take orders from the flesh anymore because we're hidden in Christ's life. **Romans**

13:12-14 NIV says, "The night is nearly over; the day is almost here. So let us put aside the deeds of darkness and put on the armor of light. [13] Let us behave decently, as in the daytime, not in carousing and drunkenness, not in sexual immorality and debauchery, not in dissension and jealousy. [14] Rather, clothe yourselves with the Lord Jesus Christ, and do not think about how to gratify the desires of the flesh."

Brothers and sisters, let us put aside dark actions and thoughts and live spiritually as God's light-bright children by clothing ourselves in peace and a Team Jesus mentality. As Christians, Jesus Christ isn't calling us to compete with our family, friends, other business leaders, or the world. We're known for our love, light, salt, and sweet aroma that radiates from Christ. We're all victorious if we focus on what God calls us to do. Everyone brings something unique and valuable to everything. God gave us each a lane to run in and a heart to work so we can bloom and flourish.

LEADERS IN THE RACE

The Apostle Paul told us to finish our race. As leaders, it's okay to want to overachieve, be the best in our fields, hone our skills, and surpass an industry record, but realize that whatever we do has to please God. The all-powerful Lord empowers us to run because He provides the race in the first place. Woefully, many believers and leaders in Christendom and in the business world become so competitive that they become obsessive. After the ascension of Jesus Christ, the Apostles boldly preached the good news and expanded the church. The high priest and Sadducees, envious of their Holy Spirit-empowered ability to perform miracles and heal, opposed them. "Then the high priest and all his associates, who were members of the party of the Sadducees, were filled with jealousy. [18] They arrested the apostles and put them in the public jail" **Acts 5:17 NIV**. They also were jealous of Stephen's Holy Spirit-empowered wisdom, and they killed him by stoning. **Acts 7:54, 57-58 NIV** teaches, "When the members of the Sanhedrin heard this, they were furious and gnashed their teeth at him. At this they covered their ears and, yelling at the top of their voices, they all rushed at him, [58] dragged him out of the city and began to stone him." Leaders are coaches, trainers, and servants. Christ sanctifies us to behave maturely, unlike Sadducees and Pharisees. When we think like some of the ancient Jewish leaders, we've reached beyond the point of doing our best to achieve. So, we can't afford to let the traits of our pre-converted lives linger.

EVERYONE ELSE

Worrying about the what, when, why, and how of others is causing you to be distracted from the glorious vision God has for you. This perspective sheds light on the growing issue of identity blindness we're experiencing today. God can do something extraordinary in your life and business when you're detached, unbothered, and unconcerned about someone else's efforts. Unless you're contributing to their growth and mission, God wants you to care for your business and fulfill the assignments He has for you. Remember, everything you have comes from the Lord—all of it. If you have 100 or 100k followers or 10 or 100 sales—God blesses you with them. "For who makes you different from anyone else? What do you have that you did not receive? And if you did receive it, why do you boast as though you did not?" **1 Corinthians 4:7 NIV**. We don't have to be jealous of anyone's life, looks, wealth, success, product, service, likeability, or social influence because it's a trap set up for failure. In Christ, you're already flourishing if you're living by His will. Galatians 5:19 lists jealousy as one of several deeds of the flesh. Instead of rolling over thoughts about others, let's pray for God to bless us and learn how to please Him. Asking God for what we desire eliminates fights and quarrels.

James 4:1-3 NIV confirms that we should check our motives and ask for what we want. "What causes fights and quarrels among you? Don't they come from your desires that battle within you? ² You desire but do not have, so you kill. You covet but you cannot get what you want, so you quarrel and fight. You do not have because you do not ask God. ³ When you ask, you do not receive, because you ask with wrong motives, that you may spend what you get on your pleasures." Ask yourself, what's causing me to feel like this, and what motivates my desire for things? Is it love, greed, fear of lack, ego, competition, or something else? In **3:13**, James expresses, "Who is wise and understanding among you? Let them show it by their good life, by deeds done in the humility that comes from wisdom." If your motives are pure, in humility, you'll see God do fresh things and answer your prayers.

When God is your CEO, there's no such thing as wrestling with insecurities, competition, envy of other's success, the industry being too small, someone taking all the market share, or financial lack. If you feel there's no room for your gifts right now, or you're in a season of lack, there's something else God is working on and preparing you for. It's God's nature to make something out of nothing and provide exceedingly abundantly above all you ask or think (Ephesians 3:20). He is the Creator—the Author! He is the owner of everything. You can have all worldly success, but without love and the genuine desire to love and see others win, why would it matter? **1 Corinthians 13:4-7 NIV** highlights, "Love is patient, love is kind. It does not envy, it does not boast, it is not proud. [5] It does not dishonor others, it is not self-seeking, it is not easily angered, it keeps no record of wrongs. [6] Love does not delight in evil but rejoices with the truth. [7] It always protects, always trusts, always hopes, always perseveres." Because your business and dreams are rooted in Christ, you can express love while championing and respecting other's gifts, talents, and successes.

FOCUS ON SUCCESS

Every artist offers something unique to the creative craft, and God isn't expecting me to be like them or produce an identical experience or work of art. The good Lord blessed you with your own big canvas. Therefore, you never have to compete with anyone else. The creative key is to find your unique treasure and talents and authentically produce your masterpiece. God has a personal plan for your success and territory. He maps out your journey with detours, tests, trials, and challenges so that He can extract the power of the potential He placed in you. When you observe the sheep with the shepherd, you don't see them pushing another out of the way to graze in the pasture land—why? Because there's *abundance* in God's infinite storehouse. The Good Shepherd will lead you to overflowing rivers, green pastures, and a place to rest. As a Christian business owner, your joyful job is to bring glory to God. Since His Spirit lives in you, your work will reflect His influence. If you abide in Jesus Christ and continue building your life and business on the Rock, you'll be the success story He already knows you are. God has abundant money and patrons for you to grow a profitable, purpose-driven business in the marketplace. You'll accelerate far beyond anything you dream in your heart. Nothing is too complicated for God Almighty. If He puts something in your heart, He wants to see *you* be all you can be in Him. You can and should genuinely compliment, praise, and encourage others from a pure heart.

Acceleration CURE Actions:

- **Thank** God for clarifying that there's room for your uniqueness and removing possessiveness. Commit to your purpose and praise Jehovah for the gifts, skills, talents, plans, and business He gave you while remaining focused and grateful.

- **Eliminate** envious and unnecessary criticisms from your thoughts to get unshackled and unstuck from the works of the flesh. Think of kind reflections about someone before reverting to denigration.

- **Reignite** and rewrite a new narrative when green thoughts and competition appear out of the blue. Instead, be happy, pray for people, and wish them the best. Then, turn your focus on worshiping the King.

- **Endure** the turbulent bitterness and refuse to let it control you. Enrich and immerse yourself in meditating on the Scriptures, reflecting on loving your brothers and sisters.

Prayer

Dear Heavenly Father, Please forgive me for giving in to a jealous heart towards others. I realize you gave me my life to glorify you, and I don't want to waste any more time concentrating on anyone or anything else bitterly. I'm to focus on cultivating my gifts. I want to love and encourage everyone who positively impacts the body of Christ. Please guard my heart against competition and envy with my friends and family in church, in my workplace, on social media, in business meetings, and at industry-related events. Teach me to pay attention to what I think about to ensure I'm not getting caught up in selfish ambition. Please help me to lean on your Word and Spirit to overcome my insecurities. Thank you for providing all I need as my Good Shepherd.

In Jesus' name, I pray, Amen.

Part 4

SPIRITUAL AND PHYSICAL ACCELERATION

Day 6

UNLOCK THE VISION

After having a farewell Detroit dinner with my youngest sister, Denise Gooden, at Olive Garden on Sunday, I had trouble using my bank card. So I went to check into it after our meal. At the ATM, the balance on the screen didn't match my monthly statement or account register. My stomach sank, and tears welled when I realized my account was negative $1600. That's the number I saw when I learned I had no funds to access the week of my move to Atlanta in December of 2000. This issue had to be some big mistake. How was my money gone after saving up for my move? Where is it? I wanted to know. Who has my money? Indeed, I thought a phone call to the bank in the morning could resolve the misfortune. They'd clear it up, and things would return to normal—but that didn't happen.

Sadly, I learned there was nothing to settle or clarify. That's when I had to accept my ignorance of how credit worked. I owed a credit card money from a judgment. I stopped paying the minimum agreed settlement to save for my move to Atlanta a few months prior. They took the entire balance I owed on the judgment instead of taking the few back payments. So, I cried and tried to get the money other ways. Finally, I let down my pride by Wednesday and went to my father for help. And he secured the funds of over $1200 for my move. Praise Mighty God! Thankfully, I also had a few paychecks in the clutch that I hadn't cashed, which helped tremendously. Dad knew the power of a dream because his parents, my grandparents George and Lucy Quinn, owned a successful store on Rosa Parks (12th Street) in Detroit when he was a child. He and my mom also started a few ventures, such as a successful landscaping business. Although I'm sure my parents and sister preferred me to stay in Detroit as a family, they knew I had dreams and blessed and supported me in moving forward.

THE BON VOYAGE

Like Khadijah on Living Single, I dreamed of publishing about six months prior, which sparked my move. What first started as a newsletter idea morphed into a full-color version of a magazine I could see a vision of. My daddy told me, "Okay, Tanya, media publishing is a huge call because you're standing in as a mediator and sharing crucial information with people." That power-packed statement sticks with me to this day. I also set my heart on songwriting. I had done as much as possible with my music in Detroit, and Atlanta would be the right place to explore that dream due to its thriving and evolving music and film influence.

By late Friday evening (almost a week later), my dad, my brother LaFrance Quinn, and I packed my U-Haul truck for the early Saturday morning trip. The weather in Michigan was warm and mild when we left, possibly in the low 50s, but Ohio, Kentucky, Tennessee, and then Georgia were dealing with inclement weather and ice storms.

Daddy drove the truck, and I drove my 1998 Chevy Malibu. We went through the worst ice storm in the Midwest and South to get me there on December 16th. I had that date written as a goal. I wanted to get there before Christmas and the New Year.

Those freezing conditions were scary, but God's hands guided us. When we arrived at my apartment in College Park, the complex was locked, and barely any snow was on the ground. I burst into tears. I had minimal skills in overcoming complex trials yet. My daddy said, "You can't cry over everything, Tanya. You gotta learn to be patient and find solutions through prayer and the Word." I calmed down, and I felt the Spirit's power. I had to survive, and tears weren't the way to make it through.

The apartment complex manager knew I was to arrive, so when I called, she rushed over to give me the keys and let us in. We moved everything in right away. My dad and brother left the following day. Here I was with a vision but no job or income source. I looked for work all of Monday and got a job for a mail sorting company I started that night. I had no idea how to survive my new life, but I knew God was uprooting and providing for me.

Last Sunday, I had a drained bank account and no extra financial means to move to Atlanta, and by that Saturday, I was living in my apartment in College Park.

In my first few months, I attended an industry event and met Christa E. Jackson, a seasoned event marketer and writer. She became my Editor-in-Chief and helped build a team of talented writers and other help. I found an independent artist, Crystal Cunningham—Pure Element, to write songs for. She introduced me to businessman and marketing talent Sean M. Rush, who joined my team as the Operations Director. He mentored and taught me business strategies and how to lead a team.

I was ten times more ambitious in my twenties than I've ever been moving forward, partly because I've learned to readjust my pacing within God's wisdom, which is the reason for this book. I assembled a squad of go-getters within a year for my magazine. Although my dream wasn't aligned with my life like it is now, a vision from God will use our past to move us into purpose in His timing. A God-vision provides hope, direction, protection, provision, and eternal life.

Accelerated Power – Proverbs 29:18 KJV Where there's no vision, the people perish: but he that keepeth the law, happy is he.

Do you feel delighted and blessed? If not, what does your vision and outlook on life look like? Living by God's standards, embracing His direction, and adopting your Christian identity is essential for gaining a clear vision and joy in life. Although my magazine wasn't faith-based, God gave me my irrevocable gifts and talents, taught me how to depend on Him and run a publishing business, led me to overcome my childhood battles with fear, and how to identify the quality of a good team player. I did the best I could with what I had and knew at the time over twenty-five years ago. If I had stayed in Detroit that day, I'd never have known the possibilities of potential God placed within me.

TEAR-BASED STRATEGY

Instead of doubling down on biblical principles, I sometimes defaulted to sobbing. A tear-based strategy involves crying and waiting for God to rescue you. However, this can work in some circumstances, such as when Hagar cries out when she runs out of hope and water for Ishmael and other disasters or losses.

However, after the Israelites marched out boldly from Egypt, God hardened Pharaoh's heart, and they came after them. **Exodus 14:10-12, 15 NIV** reads that "As Pharaoh approached, the Israelites looked up, and there were the Egyptians marching after them. They were terrified and cried out to the LORD."

They resorted to a tear-based strategy followed by complaints and fear-based statements. "They said to Moses, 'Was it because there were no graves in Egypt that you brought us to the desert to die? What have you done to us by bringing us out of Egypt? [12] Didn't we say to you in Egypt, 'Leave us alone; let us serve the Egyptians'? It would have been better for us to serve the Egyptians than to die in the desert!'" Moses motivated the people, told them not to fear, and assured them the Lord would fight for them (verses 13-14). [15] "Then the LORD said to Moses, '**Why are you crying out to me**? Tell the Israelites to move on.'"

God required them to move on and stop weeping. In many cases, this is what He's saying to us! My tears didn't bypass God's will or move His hand to grant me long-term success in my magazine or art business at the time because I had to deal with my spiritual and soul work. I had to learn to fit into His plan, not to continue doing my own thing. I had to move on. Whatever moving on looks like will gust you into where He wants you to end up. The Lord's vision will push beyond your cries and limitations—otherwise, your vision dies. The bride of Christ is the light that illuminates and makes vision possible to the world. When God gives sight, he unlocks the dream, and the benefits continually expand visibility beyond ourselves.

WHAT'S THE PLAN

Failure to write a plan is like a builder building without a blueprint or a surgeon operating without a strategy. There's no such thing as working from a marriage, parenting, life, or business vision floating in your mind. A purposeful business is one of significant servanthood—it's the mission God created you for. Focused intentionality produces intentional results. Nothing is confirmed until you imagine it, map it out, and organize a written plan. What you don't write now can often get lost and never recovered. Writing and praying over ideas causes acceleration because God has a seed of faith with which to work. It shows God you believe it will bear fruit and multiply. Yes, God will intervene and adjust your plan through His sovereign will. However, faith is about trusting He knows the correct route to take us.

Even the God of all planning works from a plan called His divine will, and the entire Bible is His mind. *God wrote His thorough plan* and gave it to us for life, godliness, wisdom, encouragement, correction, salvation, instructions, rebuking, answers, and teaching. "All Scripture is God-breathed and is useful for teaching, rebuking, correcting and training in righteousness, so that the servant of God may be thoroughly equipped for every good work" **2 Timothy 3:16-17 NIV**.

- The Lord reveals Himself and His plan through the alive and active written Word.
- God stays on course with His plan regardless of who's on board.

The strategy has a beginning, middle, and end from Genesis to Revelation. If God Almighty—the Creator of everything has a plan *in writing* and follows it, shouldn't we have a life, ministry, and business plan, too? He took the time to write the program and share it with us because He loves us. We're living out His vision now.

WRITTEN VISION UNLOCKED

While the book was in the last to the final stage, I got a new title from the Holy Spirit. *The Acceleration Cure* is the fourth title. God used my friend coach Tamika R. Dunner to mention how she believed God was giving me book titles that included the word *cure*. I understood what she was saying, but I couldn't see how that could even fit this book because coming up with the phrase acceleration took some research. A month later, the Lord illuminated that truth from Tamika. He presented and confirmed her words in a way that amazed me, solidifying the words *cure* and *soul* He gave me years prior and *acceleration* from my coaching program. As a creative visionary, the title expansion unraveled my imaginative storehouse and expanded my passion for writing and publishing. If we stick with the Lord and let Him usher us into fulfilling our ultimate purpose, we'll experience an unlocked written vision. He gives us acceleration greater than anything we envision. Our life is fruit-bearing, so it's not only about us—it's about pleasing the Father and serving others! We're overcome by our testimony and the blood of the Lamb (Revelation 12:11). God wants to use your experiences and deploy you to go and find your other brothers and sisters who belong in the sheepfold to build His family.

The bride of Christ will share in Christ's victory over death and the Lamb's supper. "Let us be glad and rejoice, and give honour to him: for the marriage of the Lamb is come, and his wife hath made herself ready." "And he saith unto me, 'Write, Blessed are they which are called unto the marriage supper of the Lamb'" **Revelation 19:7, 9 KJV**.

Now, do you see why you need to write down everything? Write down what God gives you because it's important to where you're going and where you'll end up. Writing whatever God lays on your spirit is a blessing. I encourage journaling to track your experiences or creative brainstorming sessions to generate fresh thoughts. Also, if you're going to write a book, ask God's help in recalling details of specific events for inclusion.

A PLAN FOR EVERYTHING

Before you proposed to your spouse or fiancé, did you have a vision, goals, and a plan? Jehovah God has a vision for your life, marriage, family, work, career, and business. Write down what God is illuminating through Scriptures and while fasting and praying. Before you started your business or ministry, did you take the time to write out a business and marketing plan? Before you quit your job, will you have a documented guide? At the least, you must have a vision statement. Without a clear vision, your marriage, family, mission, and business may not be as successful as they can be.

You're already in trouble if you're unsure where you're going, who you're targeting, what your company or mission stands for, how or where you'll market your product or services, and your revenue goals. You can't hire contractors or staff without a company vision. A vision helps you to say how this *can* happen as opposed to how this *can't* happen.

When life and business felt overwhelming, I'd ask God to rescue me instead of staying focused on His promises by faith. I lost my way in the past. I often got off track from inconsistency and not following my written plan because I took my eyes off vision and lost focus. Follow a strategy diligently and consistently. When you pray for wisdom, the Spirit gives you a blueprint.

VISION AND TECHNOLOGY

We live in the day of technological advances. Writing, typing, texting, voice notes, recordings, digital note apps, and instant printing are convenient privileges. How can the Almighty bless something of yours that He can't see? He's not even sure you see it because you didn't spend time documenting it. Look at all God went through to bring us the Holy Scriptures in writing. Can you imagine how the Bible came to be with all the persecution experienced in the early church? The sixty-six books by forty authors over 1500 years had to be God-breathed. Gotquestions.org shares how the sixty-six books aren't unrelated or disconnected but present God's interconnected plan. [1]

Look at all the prophets of old endured. Think about all the research from the early church, founding council, and our Bible translations today. Think about the stones and parchment they wrote on. The time and technique to learn to scribe. The hand-drawn letters and calligraphy. The distribution networks and first printing presses. They manually cross-referenced Scriptures, analyzed, researched, confirmed, and vetted multiple books to see if the Holy Spirit breathed them. They translated and transliterated the Hebrew, Greek, and Aramaic texts into English and numerous languages. The history of God getting His written Word to us has much blood, death, and heartbreak. Now, we all have multiple digital and printed Bibles.

Soulful, it's time to get serious about your life and pen it on paper. Yes, you can have faith in and love the Lord immensely, but God needs to see you put a plan in His hand to bless your life and business goals. It's not okay to go from the top of your head and go with the flow—we can no longer wing it and waste precious time this year.

Consider these questions:

1. If money wasn't a problem, what would you want to do with your life to serve God?
2. How does this vision serve and strengthen others?
3. Why do you want to do this kind of work?

4. What vision is God pressing on your spirit?
5. What's holding you back from doing these things?
6. How can you spend two hours a week working towards this idea?

Once you ponder these questions, try compiling them into goals with a start and end date.

COMMIT THEM TO GOD

Proverbs 16:3 KJV says, "Commit thy works unto the Lord, and thy thoughts shall be established." The NIV version says, "Commit to the Lord whatever you do, and he will establish your plans." The AMP says, "Commit your works to the LORD [submit and trust them to Him], And your plans will succeed [if you respond to His will and guidance]."

Commit your thoughts to God. Planning is profound in business because it involves clarity, organized thoughts, commitment, and formation. Faith is on full display. If God calls you to do something, He will teach you what to document and how to do it. God is intentional, and as His child, you're to be this way, too. After all, where will you be flowing if you go with the flow? Who are you following, and where are *they* going?

Getting off track in a bind can be easy, but that's where a strategy comes in. Within the CURE pillars, the vision starts with the C for clarity and commitment and R for reigniting and rewriting. **Proverbs 21:5 NIV** teaches that "the plans of the diligent lead to profit as surely as haste leads to poverty." Faith leads us to create a proposal and carry it out with fruit-producing prayer and persistence. Throwing anything into the marketplace quickly leads to poverty. Belief drives you when you can't see clearly. And thoroughness in operating in that plan allows God to order our steps. "In their hearts humans plan their course, but the Lord establishes their steps" **Proverbs 16:9 NIV**. As long as our plans are within the Lord's will, things will work out, and what's not meant, He can and will realign them. When you follow the direction God has for you, I promise whatever He has in store is a million times better than anything you could come up with, especially when you get off track. Obedience and spiritual insight wake up the accelerated mustard seed faith that can move mountains.

God is faithful in finishing what He started. Think of how an author writes a book or a screenwriter writes a script. They know the end before you do. You see the film and read the finished book the creators already wrote. So once the producer produces scenes and talent acts the movie out, they perform the script from beginning to end.

Although a screenwriter's play can bend, the Bible can't fit what we want. However, we can undoubtedly pivot by adjusting as detours occur. When we get off track from our goals, we can consult with the Bible, pray specific prayers for realignment, and tweak the written script as God establishes our steps. Please don't give up. What you create can accelerate! Your successful business is already in your soul. Your purpose and mission are prosperous and necessary for the marketplace. Your life and business is God's life and business because He's the Originator and Creator of life and business! Don't let the devil steal your dream, and don't give up. Your company is another vehicle to share Christ with others. It's a selfless plan, not a self-plan. Therefore, God wants to see your venture grow and profit. Capture the vision, dream the dream, set big goals, make grand plans, and watch the outcome unfold in God's hands.

Acceleration CURE Actions:

- **Clarify** your assignment by refining your purpose. Ask: Why am I here, and what should I do now, Lord? Then, commit to drawing near to God to learn how He wants you to navigate your mission.

- **Find** the beauty in chasing purpose and after the things God loves. Dedicate time daily to think about your vision to get unshackled and unstuck from going with the flow and inconsistency. How do you want your mission to impact others?

- **Ask** God to show you how He wants to reignite your dreams and mission, and enjoy the process of rewriting the vision. What do you want me to document, Lord?

- **Move** forward in faith by sharing the gospel and dedicating time to unlocking your vision. Endure hard things to improve every area of your life, enrich your experience, and maximize your time, talents, and relationships.

Prayer

Dear Heavenly Father, I pray you can clarify my mission and assignment. If it's slightly different from last year, please let me know. Thank you for entrusting me with a vision that's bigger than me. I ask that you bless the vision for life and business. I need help starting or updating my plan. Please show me the areas that need tweaking. I look forward to laying the revised plan for instructions at your feet. Thank you for entrusting me with managing and growing a business to help and bless others. I pray that this mission reaches the lost and that my light will shine bright for your glory. Please protect the vision from any harm or evil plots and plans of the enemy. Please teach me to keep moving by faith when I don't see clearly. If there are flaws in my character or any sin in my life that I have not confessed, please reveal them to me so as not to hurt the vision. I pray you show me how to run a successful business. Starting today, teach me your wisdom, knowledge, and understanding.

In Jesus' name, I pray, Amen.

Day 7
USE WISDOM AND DISCERNMENT

In April 2023, I was overwhelmed and anxious when I launched my first live webinar, Dream Big Goals Challenge. A week before the event, I still had countless tasks, insufficient time, and lacked the technical expertise to reach the destination. After running a test ad, brute-forces attacked the landing page I had built. Brute force attacks are cyber wars hackers employ to break into and breach websites and online platforms. It reminds me of battering rams in ancient times—huge wooden and iron bars, military siege engines enemies used to break down the walls of their opponent to capture a city. They attack it until the wall becomes weak, vulnerable, and collapses, and the troops move in to obstruct the city.

The site hacker's attack left me with security and technical issues with some website code. After spending time trying to resolve the assaults with the hosting company's tech support, I was left with many other matters that weren't connecting the dots to launch in time. It wasn't a hosting issue; it was a security issue. The attacks were coming so fast that it slowed the site down. Another big problem was whenever I tried to update the site, which could be tweaked by resetting some parameters. I still had to learn new webinar software to present the teachings and work on my presentation and biblical content. The tests to successfully launch my product got so intense that I couldn't even run a search online to try to ask for what I was looking for. It felt like the devil was deploying a brute force attack on my mind. I had no idea how to articulate what I needed. So, I took my hands off of the project for a day. That decision was critical because I was on a tight deadline.

I prayed to God for more profound wisdom than I'd been praying daily. He promptly answered and told me exactly what to do. The insight God gave me is simple yet weighty. He also presented me with the word *STOP*! Obeying The Lord God's wisdom to *stop* gave me the answer and a way to solve future problems as a leader. The insight He provided in my tight time frame was mind-blowing. Whenever I run into a roadblock that can potentially take me endless hours of mental looping while trying to learn and figure out anything, I must—*STOP*! Then, immediately seek the Father in prayer, asking for specific wisdom for unequivocal difficulties of the present concern.

MAKE A HABIT OF ASKING

Likewise, every believer is encouraged to make a habit of asking God for wisdom and discernment daily. Wisdom is God's way of sharing how to classify and distinguish what's good, while discernment is to judge through His lens. However, wisdom isn't just about knowledge and getting answers; it's about applying instructions. God is the only One who can show you how to live as a wise person.

The wisdom and discernment we discuss are from above—from Yahweh's mind. In the first chapter of James, the Bible tells us to count trials as joy because enduring them produces perseverance, leading to a complete and perfected life that lacks nothing. Not that trials and suffering make us happy, but what they produce is joyfulness. When needing help, we must ask for the Lord's guidance and wisdom to guide us through storms and trials. Through God's foreknowledge and all-knowing nature, He spiritually nudges us before employing, doing business with, or marrying someone. He guides us into making competent decisions and upholding godly character. Our choices are better based on righteous judgment, not feelings or others' thoughts. Our security and confidence must rest in God, not our or someone else's beliefs.

When you dedicate your life work to God, consult with Him throughout your day to keep the line of communication open. The continuous conversation is an example of prayer without ceasing. We can properly assess an individual or project, but our first refuge is talking it over with God by seeking Him. Some*thing* that you invested in previously or *someone* who worked for you last year may not be what God has for you now. Discernment comes from above and gives spiritual understanding to clarify any unanswered questions. **Proverbs 1:7 KJV** says, "The fear of the LORD is the beginning of knowledge: but fools despise wisdom and instruction." When we reverence and respect God's purposes and leadership, He gives us insight and understanding. But we foolishly behave when we despise His direction and step outside of abiding in the Vine.

> **Accelerated Power – James 1:5 NIV** If any of you lacks wisdom, let him ask God, who gives generously to all without reproach, and it will be given him.

Jesus Christ is wisdom incarnate, and His knowledge exceeds anything the world can offer. Paul writes in **1 Corinthians 1:20 KJV**, "Where is the wise? where is the scribe? where is the disputer of this world? hath not God made foolish the wisdom of this world?" Our wisdom to live right and discern God's will for our lives is paramount and supernatural. The Spirit dispenses everything we need because it's hidden secrets from above. Paul's prayer in **Colossians 1:9-10 NIV** said, "We continually ask God to fill you with the knowledge of his will through all the wisdom and understanding that the Spirit gives, [10] so that you may live a life worthy of the Lord and please him in every way: bearing fruit in every good work, growing in the knowledge of God." Living as a wise person leads to joy, peace, freedom, and blessings from the Lord. **Proverbs 1:5 NIV** says, "Let the wise listen, add to their learning, and let the discerning get guidance." Let's continue adding training and judgment to keep in step with the God of heaven and earth.

SOUL WORK IT OUT

We touched upon soul work earlier in *Chapter 3, Identity Blindness*. James expresses throughout his letter how faith without works is an oxymoron—it's dead, as saving faith produces good works that model Christ's nature. James gives examples of godly sense in contrast with demonic intelligence. He addresses social sins such as partiality, taming the tongue, disobedience, pride, oppression, envy, selfishness, boasting, and wrong desires. Our foundational saving faith produces righteousness. Therefore, working through the revelation of our social sins with the Holy Spirit will always give insight into our hearts. I call it soul work. **Soul work** is submission and co-laboring with the Holy Spirit's sanctification to remove unaligned habits and strongholds plaguing the soul for transformation. Sanctification is God's work in separating us from the effects of sins and conforming us to the image of Christ. Since we learn through repetitive behaviors, adjustments are essential for living in the Spirit to reprogram habits and paradigms that keep us stuck and unable to move ahead into God's sanctifying transforming power.

Unfruitful habits hinder us from the next level, and identity blindness will not progress us beyond where we are today. I'm reminding you of the acceleration principle here: **pray + obey + faith + wisdom = accelerate.** Active participation in sanctification is how to live as an insightful, fruit-producing person of loyalty and understanding.

Like renewing the mind to know the will of God, soul work is our responsibility because it involves *doing work* to match our convictions. **Matthew 7:21 NIV** says, "Not everyone who says to me, 'Lord, Lord,' will enter the kingdom of heaven, but only the one who does the will of my Father who is in heaven." Do not be misled. Participation-based spiritual growth is vital to accelerate. What we do to develop spiritually will spill out and overflow into the soul and the body. True wisdom is our profession of faith in Christ lining up with our thoughts, words, and deeds. Strengthening a robust, overflowing, and saturated internally mature life will address the faulty areas of our lives and help us become better, more developed teachers, leaders, and students of sound doctrine. Picture Niagra Falls showering a local South Texas river experiencing a drought with months of 110-degree heat. The abundance and stream of the Falls shower the parched river with the drenching and quenching it needs to replenish. That's how the Holy Spirit fills us when we walk by the Spirit and meditate on the Scriptures. The benefits of our joy-filled spirit being satisfied will overflow into our souls. We're then living by faith—refreshed and restored.

James 1:25 NIV says, "But whoever looks intently into the perfect law that gives freedom, and continues in it—not forgetting what they have heard, but doing it—they will be blessed in what they do." **James 4:6 NIV** declares, "But he gives us more grace." That is why Scripture says: "God opposes the proud but shows favor to the humble." God gives grace to the meek. When people are too proud and know everything, they don't need the Spirit's recharging. The Holy Ghost goes where He can work without resistance through submission. Wisdom is gifted when we humbly ask for it, submit to it, and act on it. The Heavenly Father can and is willing to help when we *need* Him to lead us.

EXPERT ADVICE

The world offers advice on marriage, parenting, relationships, careers, success, wealth, and investing. They also provide *insight* into new-thought philosophies, the universe, the law of attraction, manifesting, the soul, mind, healing, psychology, and religion. These resources dismiss Jesus Christ as the One True Living God, the Way, Truth, and Life. So, they combine and extract practices and principles like an all-you-can-eat restaurant buffet and form beliefs that make them *feel* good, enlightened, and philosophical. Most of these teachings steal from and excerpt parts of the Holy Bible's principles without paying homage to the Author—the original Creator—Jesus Christ. But Satan isn't original in anything he does. Everything about him involves deception, counterfeiting, thievery, plundering, masquerading, and manipulation.

The All-Wise God gave me firsthand insight into how crafty the devil is in the marketplace. Last year, I sat in group business coaching sessions with others from different walks of life. Some were Christian or corporate women. Others happened to be psychics, energy healers, and yoga instructors. This picture of those in business leadership demonstrates why God calls us to the marketplace as light and salt. To win the day and show others the way, Christians must show up with excellence in God's presence. It's necessary to stay rooted to represent The Lord Almighty daily with the filling of the Spirit overflowing from us to push back the darkness with our prayers and influence.

Social platforms are also full of people claiming to be experts at all sorts of things. However, no matter how much you learn from these individuals, even those who profess to know Christ, please ensure the Lord approves their instructions. Obtain counsel from the Lord and run it by another wise brother or sister in the faith. The lessons may be great, but He may give you the wisdom to use a unique strategy or a hybrid type for your mission.

Use discernment when you choose to partner your business with someone. Involving your organization in a project with the wrong people can be harmful. People and specific developments may seem promising initially, but God will reveal the truth about them if you ask Him. The devil often sends people to distract and trip you up at what seems to be the right time, so be watchful. They'll use Jesus' name and a redemptive testimony to bond with you. Posers want to access your business acumen and assets without intending to compensate you. Pretenders sit under you to glean insights and take your ideas as theirs. If you let them in, they'll learn your system and take your customers. These grifting wolves are not who they appear to be.

Hold firm to your procedures in business and relationships because when you do, they're guardrails to repel wrong things from occurring. If you usually take deposits before starting a project, continue. If your rates are standard across the board for every client, continue to charge those rates. After establishing an ongoing relationship with the person or company, God will lead you to adjust rates or offer a custom option, and that's fine. God will impress upon your heart to help someone.

DISCERNMENT IN THE CHURCH

It's imperative to vigilantly discern wolves in the church, causing division, conflict, and spiritual warfare. **Matthew 7:15 KJV** says, "Beware of false prophets, which come to you in sheep's clothing, but inwardly they're ravening wolves." God wants you to watch out for seemingly discreet people looking to fleece the sheep and claim to be of the faith. For instance, many black preachers teach their congregants the woke social gospel, critical race theory, and to vote Democrat. They highlight racism, black lives matter, reproductive healthcare, justice, and threats to democracy as reasons. But a further look behind the curtain reveals how their policies are anti-God and catastrophic to our Christian liberty, nuclear family, children's future, constitutional rights, national and border security, economy, and black communities.

My question is, what biblical values are these so-called pastors voting for? Christians conserve a biblical worldview. Therefore, before joining a church, see how they preach the gospel and learn their doctrinal beliefs about the faith and theological stance about the Godhead. Are they Oneness or Trinitarian? Are they in a denomination? How do they teach the Bible? Is it topical only, or is it expository and exegetical? Do they subscribe to the core tenets of the Christian faith? Does the pastor have leadership and accountability? Are they more interested in the gospel of wealth and self, growing members and programs, or seeing people transformed? Do they teach about hell, sin, end times, current events, and Israel? Do they disciple new believers? Are the churches led by the Holy Spirit or by the traditions of men? Find out if they are more conservative or liberal in their biblical and political views.

When do they believe life starts? Although they can try to justify their feelings and give things a fluffy name, abortion isn't reproductive healthcare—it's pre-meditated murder and genocide amongst the most innocent living souls—God's precious image bearers. God says to **Jeremiah 1:5 NIV**, "Before I formed you in the womb I knew you, before you were born I set you apart; I appointed you as a prophet to the nations." Sadly, blacks lead the statistics of this barbaric procedure. Margaret Sanger of the eugenics movement started Planned Parenthood to spearhead this mission and garnered support from the black church leaders. Pastor Clenard Howard Childress said, "The most dangerous place for an African American is in the womb."[1] God asks us to seek wisdom by learning about laws and policies because many so-called pastors are wolves.

DISCERN HISTORY

Carefully studying the Democrat's history and policies will highlight their radical and deadly origins since 1800, such as the party of slavery, Jim Crow, and the Ku Klux Klan. Consistently, they try to rebrand and disconnect themselves from who they are—enemies of God and you! They've propagandized mainstream media to gaslight Americans with untruths. Their demonic agenda promotes the ungodly *isms*— Femin*ism*, Global*ism*, Social*ism*, Marx*ism*, and Commun*ism*.

There have been three assassination attempts, lawfare, media ambushes, and harassment on 2024 President-elect Donald J. Trump due to dishonest, defamatory, and inflamed narratives backed by fraudulent news reporting. Not only did they barely cover the assassination attempts, but they blamed him for them. Every claim and charge they threw at him backfired and garnered him the popular and electoral vote. It's clear that the hand of God preserved and saved his life, and he won the election *again* because God and the people chose him to lead America.

Now ask yourself, why do they hate DJT so much when he's been the most pro-life, pro-American, pro-economy, and pro-Israel president? What about the Abraham Accords? Did they hate him before he entered politics for the Republican platform? Please look into his past footage, which goes back over thirty years to his stance on political issues. He always wanted to fight to protect America. I'm not asking you to like or agree with him on everything; I'd like you to look beyond mainstream media for answers. Follow the trail and those pulling the strings behind the scenes. We must ask why those who once loved him turned and what they're trying to protect. Their maliciousness even ties in with Bible prophecy and historical and current events we must discern. While they call DJT the new Hitler, please check into who influenced and fueled the Nazis' ideas.[2] When discussing the Jews and the hatred that led to the Holocaust, it's essential to discern and remember the tragic, heartbreaking events that occurred.

Vince Everette Ellison wrote in his book *25 Lies: Exposing Democrats Most Dangerous, Seductive, Damnable, Destructive Lies and How to Refute Them*, he gives an entire chapter to the Democrat—Jim Crow—Nazi connection. He also shares how the primary goal of the Democrat party is to intensify hatred amongst blacks, whites, and Christians. This black man of God backs up his claims in the book with factual historical research. He went on to express how when our politics don't match our religion, our religion is just a hobby. [3] In other words, we can't claim to be God's discerning children and hold a fist against God at the same time. So, if a preacher or Christian influencer rejects God in their voting decisions and leads their members and supporters to do the same, what other areas in their lives lack godly truth and wisdom? An undershepherd wouldn't lead his beloved sheep to support the same things that God hates and made Him exile Israel into Babylonian captivity and disperse them from their land for nearly 2000 years.

While false prophets lie by declaring and decreeing about your breakthrough coming every year and seek selfish ambition to keep their attendance, merch sales, speaking fees, and donations coming—a whole spiritual battle is swelling under the surface. Every believer is encouraged to be well-informed and have a biblical understanding of government and policies. Unfortunately, many of us aren't accelerating because we're knowingly or unknowingly holding hands with the devil at the voting booth, idolizing our race, and attending false churches—but God holds us accountable. "Wherefore come out from among them, and be ye separate, saith the Lord, and touch not the unclean thing; and I will receive you" **2 Corinthians 6:17 KJV. Isaiah 5:20 KJV** shares, "Woe unto them that call evil good, and good evil; that put darkness for light, and light for darkness; that put bitter for sweet, and sweet for bitter!" Selfish, depraved people seek a victim to devour, just like their father, the devil. Continue to pray for people, even your enemies. Jesus says, "Behold, I send you forth as sheep in the midst of wolves: be ye therefore wise as serpents, and harmless as doves" **Matthew 10:16 KJV.** If you disagree with my political understanding and want to confirm what I shared, I encourage you to research and ask God if it's true. Start with Isaiah, Jeremiah, and Ezekiel. To gather historical facts about how Planned Parenthood's founder Margaret Sanger infiltrated the black church, I'll also share, *The Negro Project, Margaret Sanger's Diabolical, Duplicitous, Dangerous, Disastrous and Deadly Plan for Black America* by Bruce Fleury.

HOW BAD DO YOU WANT IT

The Holy Spirit—the Teacher—leads believers into God's wisdom through doctrinally sound study and prayer. All good and perfect gifts come from the Lord. He'll show you the ins and outs of things you can't see with your eyes because you'll observe them spiritually. **Jeremiah 33:3 AMP** says, "Call to Me and I will answer you, and tell you [and even show you] great and mighty things, [things which have been confined and hidden], which you do not know *and* understand *and* cannot distinguish." If you want to know something, ask. God will uncover the blind spots that you can't see. He can save you from exploitation, manipulation, and misuse in business and relationships. He will show us things we've yet to know.

Acceleration CURE Actions:
- **Make** it a routine to seek God first for wisdom, clarity, and discernment before committing to something or making plans. Father God, can you help me with…? Can you tell me the truth

about this or that? God, how should I vote locally and federally?

- **Discover** God's perfect will by growing in His knowledge and praying without ceasing to get unstuck and unshackled. Father, what will you have me to do and learn today?

- **Thank** God for sharing His life-abundant wisdom and discernment in His Word, leading to reignite, refocus, rewrite, and reclaim the fullness of God in your choices and actions. I encourage you to add a book on hermeneutics to help you study the Bible correctly. *Basic Bible Interpretation* by Roy B. Zuck is a good start.

- **Practice** stopping when you can't figure out something. Halting turns your face to God, who helps you find enrichment and endurance in your work and relationships and solve unanswered complex problems.

Prayer

Dear Heavenly Father, thank you for waking me up this morning and blessing me to see another day. I humbly come to your throne of grace to seek your face. But before I go too far into my prayer, I ask that you forgive me of my sins and any unrighteous choices. Forgive me for looking elsewhere for answers before seeking you. Lord, please impart your wisdom, instructions, and discernment today. Without you, I cannot navigate relationships, flow in my purpose, and operate this venture. Please rest on the throne of my heart. Please show me great and mighty things I don't know. I trust that you know what's best for me. Order my steps and teach me your ways so that I can make righteous decisions. Highlight the traps, plans, strategies, and tactics of the enemy. Show me people I should and shouldn't do life and business with. Show me churches, groups, political parties, and affiliations I should disconnect from.

In Jesus' Name, I pray, Amen.

Day 8

DON'T TRUST THE FLESH

One day, my siblings Shenetta, LaFrance, Denise, and I went to run errands with my mommy. When we arrived back home, Denise, being five years old, convinced my mom to give her the keys to the car. She didn't manipulate her. In fact, Neicy told her exactly what her intentions were. She said, "Mama, can I have your keys so we can drive to the store?" but my mom didn't take her seriously because she knew Neicy was a child who loved to play and express herself. However, moments later, my mom discovered the power of a child's vision, will, and mind. Me being older than my sissy by sixteen months, I, too, got in the Gremlin with her on the passenger side (I thought she was playing too).

After putting the key in the ignition, we pulled out the driveway. My mom, who happened to look up from the kitchen window, was terrified and in shock at the site of us operating and moving her motor vehicle. She ran outside to stop us because we lived on a residential block off a busy street—8 Mile Road near John R. By God's grace, the car sat stuck in the street at the driveway as my little sissy and I didn't have any wisdom, knowledge, skills, understanding, or visibility to take us anywhere or get us out of this mess. We could've been injured or destroyed someone's property.

Denise mimicked what she saw our parents doing when they drove and thought trying herself was fun. Without my mother Lynette's help, we'd be stuck with no hope of getting the car back in the driveway or covering up the disastrous situation. In this case, Denise depicts *the heart and soul* as willing to do their own thing. I represent the flesh, which went along and complied with the program without resistance. Although we can laugh about this incident now, the reality is that as adults, we enter into tragic situations when the wrong influence gets lodged in our hearts and souls and ignites collaboration with the flesh. Thank God for my mother's instinct and authority to rescue us from our decision-making disaster, which is what the Holy Spirit always does. Me and Denise's soulish fleshy ways could have turned out worse, void of intervention.

Soulful, we cannot succeed without God! Therefore, we need continuous filling of the Holy Spirit, who teaches, rescues, and keeps us from self-destruction. Sadly, Christ's followers face three daily challenges: the world, the flesh, and the devil. The world's culture and system of influence want to distract you from God and a biblical worldview. The devil and his demons look to scatter, confuse, sift you like wheat, and devour you like a roaring lion. And the fleshly body, your old man laden with sin remnants, wants to dominate, so you detach from the Spirit's power. However, nothing will test you more than your worst enemy—your flesh!

"The acts of the flesh are obvious: sexual immorality, impurity and debauchery; [20] idolatry and witchcraft; hatred, discord, jealousy, fits of rage, selfish ambition, dissensions, factions [21] and envy; drunkenness, orgies, and the like. I warn you, as I did before, that those who live like this will not inherit the kingdom of God" **Galatians 5:19-21 NIV**. The old self craves supremacy and needs constant feeding for intensity and strength. The more it feeds, the stronger the lusts, aggression, and destructive behaviors become. Unawareness of its anti-God ways means you're playing a role in your demise through passive cooperation.

Believers who choose to serve and resolve issues in their old, untamed, and unsaved disposition instead of submitting to the Holy Spirit will find it difficult to flourish in every area of life and business. That's because the flesh cannot be reformed, consoled, or coddled—wherever you are, there it is. It's your antagonistic narcissistic enemy and doesn't cooperate with the higher spiritual calling. Its language is *me, me, me!* Once that version of you teams up with the devil, you're warring against God for your best interest. Due to our unique Christian makeup, we can't just pick up a worldly motivational, self-help, or book a psychology counseling session and expect to see lasting change. God is the only One who can save us from ourselves. Everything we do must first filter through the Holy Spirit's truths and overflow in our spirit. When we allow our Teacher to teach and instruct us through the Holy Bible (Biblical Instructions Before Leaving Earth), we soar above falling into the world, flesh, and devil's schemes. The sinful nature is laden with longings, appeals, and customs for dealing with desires, conflict, and irritation. It loves the things of the world and the pride of life. The former yearns and pleas to come out of the closet and war with the Spirit.

> **Accelerated Power – Galatians 5:17 NIV** For the flesh desires what is contrary to the Spirit, and the Spirit what is contrary to the flesh. They are in conflict with each other, so that you are not to do whatever you want.

IDENTIFYING THE ENEMY WITHIN

Although we're born from above—the corrupt, unredeemed nature is easily identifiable because it's wasting away. There is no cure for it! That's why God gave us new lives and living hope; no salvation is possible in the law, which is why Christ came to fulfill it. Any good works done in the flesh to obtain righteousness are unacceptable, pointless, futile, and worthless (Matthew 5:17-20). To determine if you're obeying the flesh, ask yourself: "Do I easily give in to what I desire whenever I feel like it, or is there a battle within to fight against sin?" As Paul teaches in **Romans 8:5-8 NIV,** "Those who live according to the flesh have their minds set on what the flesh desires; but those who live in accordance with the Spirit have their minds set on what the Spirit desires. ⁶ The mind governed by the flesh is death, but the mind governed by the Spirit is life and peace. ⁷ The mind governed by the flesh is hostile to God; it does not submit to God's law, nor can it do so. ⁸ Those who are in the realm of the flesh cannot please God."

    The rescuing blood of the Lamb saved you, and Jesus has already overcome the world, the flesh, and the devil. The King has equipped His heirs to display power-filled grace in their conduct. Transformation flows by *taking off* the comforting and familiar dysfunctions and *putting on* life and peace. Intentionality in putting on the whole armor of God to navigate the flesh's pull into its shameless requests means you're walking in the Spirit.

    Verse 9 teaches "You, however, are not in the realm of the flesh but are in the realm of the Spirit, if indeed the Spirit of God lives in you. And if anyone does not have the Spirit of Christ, they do not belong to Christ." Indeed, it's wise to ask, "Does the Spirit of God live in me?" Do my daily actions reflect and allow the Spirit to live through me? The Precious Lord is Holy, and the Bible teaches in **1 Corinthians 1:29 KJV**, That "no flesh should glory in his presence." Fleshly behaviors are associated with non-conversion, and God grieves when believers choose the deathly mind over the Spirit's power.

Imagine if Denise always found new ways to *get the keys*. What impact would that have on the family? It strains and drains the relationship. The bond remains awkward and injured until she shows genuine repentance, respect, and a willingness to change the behavior. Likewise, as God's children, we're responsible for keeping the relationship free-flowing and healthy through obedience and removing self-imposed barriers and self-impaired bonds. The Bible highlights in **2 Corinthians 5:17 KJV**, "Therefore if any man be in Christ, he is a new creature: old things are passed away; behold, all things are become new." We must value our gift of eternal life. Just as a new baby is precious, so is our new life in Christ. We show appreciation by cherishing it, turning away from old desires, and embracing a deeper relationship with our Sovereign Lord God.

First, we can repent from repeating sins by seeking God's forgiveness and agreeing that we've missed the mark and are going the wrong way. Then, turn from the erroneous direction and get on track with following the way of truth. Genuine repentance is like Denise when rescued by our mommy—she was sorrowful for what she did, acknowledged going the wrong way, sought forgiveness, and never retook the car keys after restoration. Often, after repentance, we can struggle with the same sins, but a brawl is still evidence of a fight against the Spirit and our flesh. The problem arises when we give ourselves over to the things that destroy us. Finally, ask the Father to fill you with the Spirit. Whenever you humbly approach the throne of God, you remember to count the flesh as dead.

THE SOUL AND FLESH

The soul is you! Your mind, will, emotions, intellect, and personality! You were interwoven with the lust of the flesh before the Holy Spirit healed and filled your dead spirit. The soul's influence led the way when the flesh threw tantrums, burst out in anger, and wanted to indulge in illicit behaviors, perversion, gossip, slander, stealing, lying, gluttony, drugs, and other wickedness. *You* were a willing partner in the flesh's pleasures. The mind can only see change by adopting Christ's mind to understand and prove His will and living by the Spirit. I'm not speaking of works-based salvation. I'm speaking of sanctification we partake in for the mind's holy transformation. **James 2:14 NIV** says, "What good is it, my brothers and sisters, if someone claims to have faith but has no deeds? Can such faith save them?" Understanding God's will, living by faith, and growing in righteousness won't happen on its own or through osmosis. There must be intentional actions and a will to renew the mind and submit to the Spirit.

When God rescued you from the slave auction block, He rescued you from hell and the eternal penalty of original sin. During conversion, God gave you a new heart and set you apart. Why? Salvation is threefold—**phase one** is justification (past)—**saved** and born from above and rescued from the penalty of original sin, legally declared not guilty, and regeneration occurs; **phase two** is sanctification (present)—**being saved** from the power and effects of sins; and **phase three** is glorification (future)—when we die, we receive a new resurrected glorified body and eternal rescuing from the presence of sin. This entire process of salvation is a work of the Holy Trinity.

Let me try expressing these phases practically. One summer day, while we visited my grandma, Lucy, my brother LaFrance got hit by a car when he was ten years old. A man drove his car recklessly down the street, endangering several of us kids playing outside, but my brother couldn't escape. The vehicle ravished his leg, and he needed rescuing. **Phase one**—the ambulance rushed and took him to the hospital emergency. The doctors saved, pinned, and patched the leg up to prevent loss or further injury. **Phase two**—LaFrance was still involved with medical care and needed to participate in follow-up visits, rehabilitation, and recovery as recommended by the medical team. After spending weeks in a wheelchair, he transitioned to using a walker and then crutches, all while in a cast. During this time, my parents took care of him. In **phase three,** after full collaboration with the medical and rehab plan recovery, the cast came off, and his leg felt like new after a few weeks of strengthening the muscles. He then moved on and resumed the way of walking with his leg that God intended for him.

God is doing the work in us, but we must cooperate like healing from a broken leg. It also took medical professionals, caregivers, and equipment. When walking in this sanctification phase of Holy Spirit-infused supernatural power, we work out our salvation daily with fear and trembling, allowing the new Master to flow through us for a soul-transforming soul cure.

SUCH WERE SOME OF YOU

As believers, we will have incidences of daily sins in thought, word, and deed. Some are sins of omission and commission due to the depravities remnants that reside in our flesh's members because the flesh is not born-again. Omission is when you choose not to do what's right, although you know it's wrong, and commission is when you premeditate to sin in thought, word, or deed. **1 Corinthians 6:9-11 NIV** teaches, "Or do you not know that wrongdoers will not inherit the kingdom of God? Do not be deceived: Neither the sexually immoral nor idolaters nor adulterers nor men who have sex with men [10] nor thieves nor the greedy nor drunkards nor slanderers nor swindlers will inherit the kingdom of God. [11] And that is what some of you were. But you were washed, you were sanctified, you were justified in the name of the Lord Jesus Christ and by the Spirit of our God."

Such *were* some of you! We *were* once living as idolaters, fornicators, adulterers, homosexuals, gossips, crooks, and covetous people, but God rescued us from profane living into a righteous holy life. Although Christians will and do sin, *living in* sin isn't to be a *lifestyle*. A *lifestyle* is ordinary, usual behavior—an everyday way of life. If there's an overwhelming tendency to live a *lifestyle* in the flesh's pleasures, please take it to the Lord and confirm your calling and election. Please make sure you're one of God's own.

I had to do the same thing because some of my past actions didn't always reflect my new nature. Since all looked well outward to others, I wasn't asked by a loving believer to confirm my salvation and living patterns with God because I wasn't accountable to anyone. Again, the passage of Scripture in Corinthians ends by saying such *were* some of you, but you *were* washed, sanctified, and justified.

If someone can live the same way they did before they knew Christ—do they know the Jesus in the Scriptures or another Jesus? Sadly, many people think they're saved because they believe in facts about Jesus' life, death, and resurrection. However, one doesn't *know* a thing until what one professes to *know* and *believe* is expressed. Today, the Most High God asks you to come out of deception. It's impossible to live as a double-minded, double-life, double-agent believer who displays different versions of character depending on who's around or what environment they're in and still lives as a Christ follower.

NEW FRUITY HABITS

We can't ignore the issues of the flesh. If we focus solely on managing our business or relationships in our strength, we'll tire ourselves out and miss the blessings of moving in the Spirit. Believing there's good in the flesh will only lead to undisciplined outcomes. Attempts to improve will often fail, resulting in a cycle of constant frustration. Additionally, operating through willpower alone is unproductive.

Galatians 5:24-25 NIV says, "Those who belong to Christ Jesus have crucified the flesh with its passions and desires. ²⁵ Since we live by the Spirit, let us keep in step with the Spirit." God already crucified your flesh on the cross, but it's up to you to walk in the new life. Putting off the flesh and putting on the Holy Spirit isn't always easy, but it's a choice. Surrendering allows His fruit to overtake you. **Galatians 5:22-23 NIV** says, "But the fruit of the Spirit is love, joy, peace, forbearance, kindness, goodness, faithfulness, ²³ gentleness and self-control. Against such things there is no law."

God's Spirit is a superfruit. It's not *fruits* of the Spirit, it's *fruit* of the Spirit. It's His characteristic *fruit*! It starts with love and ends with self-control. Your new life is bursting with possibility, and the joy discovered while walking in the Spirit is incredible. It's where God dwells because He is Spirit. Therefore, you can live in freedom by worshiping Him in spirit and truth (John 4:24). While walking by faith, you'll find that the old nature stands down. Everything accelerates in your life and business when you abide in the Spirit as a fruity believer. Living in righteousness allows you to persevere through obstacles, see relationships flourish, accomplish new goals, finish projects, meet aspirations, navigate seasonal changes, and be long-suffering and kind to others. Fruitiness is your purpose and identity in Christ. Rejoice and be cheerful; lift your hands and shout for the King of Glory. Let His fruit flow from your spirit and touch your soul.

Acceleration CURE Actions:
- **Add** Galatians 5:22-24 to your memory scriptures and try meditating

on them throughout this week to clarify if you're operating in love and ending with self-control. Commit to living fruitfully.

- **Ensure** the world, the flesh, and the devil aren't your influence. Strengthening your spirit (through prayer, fasting, and studying) will get you unshackled and unstuck from the old you.

- **Reignite** your strength and dependency on the Lord, and rewrite your narrative by expressing how you want to start showing up for God and others.

- **Choose** to enrich, stand above, and earnestly endure the spiritual war and attacks the world, the flesh, and the devil are waging against you daily by developing new fruit-bearing habits.

Prayer

Dear Heavenly Father, I enter your presence with thanksgiving and praise. Today, I want to make my calling and election sure and confirm that I live a lifestyle rooted in righteousness. Also, I ask you to search my heart for any sin. Thank you for being my strength through the supernatural power of the Holy Spirit to accomplish your proposed assignment. I don't have to rely on my strength to walk in the Spirit and do the work you called me to do. Building fruitful relationships and running a business in my power is exhausting. Your Word tells me I can walk in the Spirit and not gratify my flesh. Please show me my vulnerabilities where I give into the world, flesh, and devil. Please help me to always call on you before I give in to my desires.

In Jesus' name, I pray, Amen.

Day 9
VALUE YOUR HEALTH

I gained 30 pounds during the 2020 pandemic primarily because I wasn't getting enough daily movement. I ate foods that comforted and fed my emotions instead of nourishing my body. Although I progressed several times to get the weight off by restricting processed foods, I couldn't get past removing 10 pounds. The stubbornness meant that my body weight had a new set point, and I needed to do something drastic to nudge it. I struggled with weight due to reduced sleep and hormonal imbalance. Though I didn't eat poorly overall, junk food affected my progress and increased insulin resistance. Sitting for hours working, having a bad diet, and lacking movement are the worst. I felt defeated because my mindset, body, and disfavored habits were in a cycle. So, I kept restarting to lose weight at the same starting point.

Before I moved in 2023, I prayed for specific things to support my spiritual life, work, and well-being. I established new goals for the environment I wanted to live in, created a detailed plan, and prayed. From there, I made a goals system and tracked my habits, meal plans, and fitness using my Dream Big Goals system.

I planned twice-weekly meal prep, tracked daily water intake, watched, listened to, or read one hour of health-related content daily, and did four 45-minute workouts weekly. One of my petitions was to live in an environment where I could walk outdoors. So God blessed me to live anchored by a park and beautiful residential areas where I can walk for miles.

By June, I had lost 10 pounds and another 21 during a twenty-one-day spiritual fast in August. I shed pounds by first asking for God's intervention.

During my spiritual fast, I ate one apple and a cup of pistachios around 2:00 pm and drank two cups of coconut water and apple juice in 50 ounces of distilled water daily. The process let my digestive system rest and repair, and my cells stopped insulating the fat and moved my body into ketosis. The Lord Jesus showed me that the bulk of my weight was emotional, and I needed to get in His presence to remove it spiritually. I also needed to bring down my body's weight set point so I wouldn't hit my highest weight again when I regained some of it. Good health is a gift, and we want to prioritize it, as the lack of consistency in moving and caring for our temple cannot be ignored.

> **Accelerated Power – Ephesians 5:29-30 NIV** After all, no one ever hated their own body, but they feed and care for their body, just as Christ does the church— [30] for we are members of his body.

The Apostle Paul wrote to the church in Ephesus about how a husband is to love his wife. In the letter, he expresses how one cares for his wife just as much as his body. "In this same way, husbands ought to love their wives as their own bodies. He who loves his wife loves himself" **Ephesians 5:28 NIV**. Since husbands love their wives like Christ loves the Church, we can still apply the wisdom and instructions of this passage to caring for our temples as an act of worship because, in them, the Spirit dwells. Christ cares, feeds, and nourishes His body—the Church and wants us to follow His leading. The sooner we can get into the habit of caring for our bodies with nourishing foods, herbs, hydration, and exercise—the better!

Jesus prioritized His spiritual and physical health in His natural body during His earthly life. His body had to be durable to bear our sins. He strengthened it by keeping it pure and prepared it to drink the cup of God's wrath and bear all sin and disease. As children sealed by the Spirit, He wants us to follow His example and do the same. We're to guard and protect our temple from the flesh's desire for gluttony. "And you also were included in Christ when you heard the message of truth, the gospel of your salvation. When you believed, you were marked in him with a seal, the promised Holy Spirit, [14] who is a deposit guaranteeing our inheritance until the redemption of those who are God's possession—to the praise of his glory" **Ephesians 1:13-14 NIV**. Since the Holy Ghost rules within, we can seek His help for things that are good for the body.

RESPECT FOR PROFESSIONALS

I respect and appreciate the doctors, practitioners, and advances in modern medicine and surgeries. They've saved many lives. A good physician is a blessing from the Lord and for the community they serve. Dr. Ben Carson is an excellent example of a purpose-driven specialist. However, I must address the elephant in the room. Most modern doctors *practice* medicine. Practice refers to acting out or exercising a system or method within pre-defined boundaries.

Therefore, when most doctors recognize symptoms, their default practice is to write a prescription, which usually places you on a monthly subscription. Your subscriptions help fund the Doctor's lifestyle and the pharmaceutical industry and lead to a lifetime of symptom management, visits, and submission to their practices. People take whatever the doctors say as truth-proof without consulting God's divine wisdom or a second opinion because it's easier to take the pill or get the surgery. Those adverse medicinal and post-operative side effects pour into other body regions, causing problems. God wants us to remember that food is medicine. Some people benefit from medications, but others must change their eating and lifestyle habits. The Creator designed the body to repair itself. Submitting to a lifetime subscription to pharmaceuticals leaves people unwilling to do the extra work to let the body heal itself by switching to a healthy existence and eliminating the deprived behaviors that caused the problems.

Most Christians never think outside the box when caring for their precious health. Looking into old-school alternatives to heal the temple can do wonders. Consistent juicing, smoothies, and herbal infusions can often reverse some conditions. Feeding your spirit with daily manna is also imperative to strengthen your inner man and cultivate physical health. Moving your body will help you have a happy, productive day and stay alert to the world, the flesh, and the devil's tricks and pitfalls. The food manufacturers work tirelessly to create bliss points in their ingredients to keep us craving and thinking of ways to get them.

FEASTING

Jesus knew His submission to the Father was vital to defeating death and temptations. "For we do not have a High Priest who is unable to sympathize *and* understand our weaknesses *and* temptations, but One who has been tempted [knowing exactly how it feels to be human] in every respect as *we are, yet* without [committing any] sin" **Hebrews 4:15 AMP**. The enemy attempted to entice Jesus like he does us, but the Messiah emphasized the spiritual aspect of winning battles by not giving the enemy a foothold in His life. He didn't allow his hungry stomach (during His forty day fast) to distract Him from His purpose.

I don't think any of us hate our bodies. But let's paint a picture. For breakfast, you have coffee with sugar and cream, along with pancakes, syrup, and bacon. A bacon double cheeseburger, large fries, cookies, and a pop for lunch. Twelve honey BBQ wings and dipping sauce with a side of celery for dinner. Three scoops of ice cream and more cookies for a snack. How will you feel at bedtime and the next day? How many days does it take for all this food to digest and leave your body? Overeating these ultra-processed, sugary, acidic foods can quickly turn us into addicted gluttons and promote laziness, obesity, and severe health issues.

"Do not join those who drink too much wine or gorge themselves on meat, [21] for drunkards and gluttons become poor, and drowsiness clothes them in rags" **Proverbs 23:20-21 NIV**. The devil uses choice foods to move us away from God's optimal health. Recall how God's anger burned and destroyed some of the Israelites in the desert for their cravings for fish, garlic, and leeks in **Numbers 11:4 NIV**. "The rabble with them began to crave other food, and again the Israelites started wailing and said, "If only we had meat to eat! [5] We remember the fish we ate in Egypt at no cost—also the cucumbers, melons, leeks, onions and garlic. [6] But now we have lost our appetite; we never see anything but this manna!" **Psalms 78:18 NIV** says, "They willfully put God to the test by demanding the food they craved." Our US manufacturers use ingredients in our foods that other countries label toxic. Their cravings were for foods we classify as healthy because now our thirsts are for lab-made ultra-processed foods.

But what if I eat all that junk and add *celery*? When we fill our temples daily as opposed to occasionally with mock, processed, and fast foods, we feel the effect of fake and dead ingredients rather than fresh, living, and whole-nutritional ones. The counterfeit components and harsh seed oils such as cottonseed, vegetable, canola, and soybean aren't suitable for the body. Therefore, the few celery stalks demonstrate the sprinkle of spiritual food we throw into our routines for the illusion of goodliness. Some only get nourished for an hour on Sundays and starve spiritually for the rest of the week, while others sprinkle it in twice weekly.

ATTRACTION AND STRENGTH

Many of us take better care of our hair, skin, clothes, shoes, vehicles, homes, gardens, offices, and pets than we do of our bodies. When we neglect proper rest, hydration, minerals, and nutrition, the effects show up in every aspect of our lives. This lack of care for our physical health primarily impacts our spiritual well-being, leaving us feeling unwell, tired, and defeated.

While prioritizing spiritual disciplines and well-being are essential for nourishing our spirit and soul, self-care also reflects love, self-discipline, self-respect, and a connection to godliness. Regardless of our preferences, people often judge us based on our appearance. Why? Because it forms their first impression. They see us before truly knowing us, and there's a natural attraction to beauty and well-groomed aesthetics.

A fit physique, hydrated skin, good grooming and hygiene, stylish clothing, and a warm, friendly smile can draw others to the light of God within us. The better we feel inside, the more confidence radiates outward. Remember that our good or bad habits with health and grooming will heavily mirror how we function in our lives and businesses. As the saying goes, "You are what you eat." Working long hours with minimal sleep isn't healthy either, but I guarantee that God wants your spiritual, soul, and body health to take priority over the company. Unless you've established the business structure with operations, officers, and a trust, if your health fails, there goes your business.

Friend, good nourishment, and a healthy lifestyle are vital to your life and business's survival. Food intake is essential to your calling as a husband or wife and parent. Good physical condition helps us to serve Christ and others. What you eat affects everything. Therefore, we must do what we can to make no provisions for the flesh and its indulgent temper tantrums. **Romans 13:14 NIV** says it plainly: "Rather, clothe yourselves with the Lord Jesus Christ, and do not think about how to gratify the desires of the flesh." When we exercise, eat, and rest properly, we can do the Lord's work and will while crucifying our flesh. It's crucial to exercise for a minimum of thirty minutes four times weekly and elevate the heart rate to over 120 if medically possible. Interval training is ideal for strengthening and pushing the body out of its comfort zone. Our efforts will support our well-being while pushing blood to the brain, gut, organs, cells, nerves, muscles, joints, vessels, hair, skin, and nails.

The body God gave you in your mommy's womb has been fighting for you since He formed it. Elohim made your body for acceleration and movement. When I refuse care and attention to my physical body, it shows me that my spiritual health isn't aligned. How do you show appreciation to God for the beautiful machine of a body He gave you? By God's design, your body is fighting internally harder than you ever could imagine. We're supposed to help and assist our bodies to do their best work, not work against them as enemies. So, we suffer when we neglect to treat the body in ways that promote optimal performance. We wouldn't want a spouse, friend, employee, or business partner who worked against us, so why do we work against our bodies?

If not maintained, ponder how much more complex our vehicles have to work in Canada's cold or Mexican desert-hot weather. They'll likely hold up in all conditions when we regularly preserve them if appropriately maintained. The manufacturer made them to withstand wear and tear. If product manufacturers stand behind and guarantee their creations, imagine how God backs up those He calls His children—made in His image. The Creator designed our physical inner workings to weather way more than a vehicle manufacturer could ever fathom. The body design is to push and accelerate through sickness, gashings, bruisings, attacks, and challenges at a high threshold. We must maintain our assets by restoring the proper fuel and nutrients.

HEALTHY HEALING HABITS

The devil uses food and sorcery in his temptation weaponry. Spiritual warfare started in the Garden of Eden when the serpent incited Eve to eat the forbidden fruit. The rabble in the wilderness began a war against God by complaining about the daily manna when they wanted tastier foods. Daniel and his friends opted out of the king's choice of delicacies and looked better than the other men when they consumed only fruits and veggies. Must I remind you that your calling is first a personal mission? The wrong food choices can and will alter and cloud your thinking and shift your mood, leading to deceleration. Purpose-driven leaders don't let their gut rule their lives because they have self-control and self-discipline. They choose what they want to consume instead of allowing their cravings to control them. This health message is stern to hear, but this book is about the acceleration cure.

When setting up new health systems, I also want you to be on the lookout and prepare to maintain your habits before and after vacation and in the grueling, cold winter months. So, what healthy healing habits can you adopt to meet your obligations when you don't feel like doing what's right? Jesus arose early in the morning to spend time with God, fasted to deny himself any physical food, and consumed sustenance that sustained His body, like figs and fish. Jesus also walked a lot (one of our body's most natural forms of exercise) and slept well, as we read about on the boat during the storm.

The demands placed on us in this fast-paced technological age can wear us out if we're not spiritually and physically fit. Our eyes, hands, legs, and brains can suffer sitting in front of the computer or standing on our feet all day. It's been said that sitting is the new smoking. Sitting all day at work messes with the body's system and brain like that of a smoker. Sitting in a car all day commuting in traffic or running a transportation company without exercise is not what God desires for our temples. Those unhealthy behaviors only wear the body down. Our immune system, gut health, brain neurons, cells, organs, muscles, bones, and blood vessels need our assistance to fuel them. That energy from the foods and the oxygen we get into the body from movement helps boost the body and brain and take care of the internal working systems.

Suppose we're unhealthy for no reason of our own. Indeed, God still wants you to live from your inner man and treat your body as best as possible. He still wants you to use your measure of faith to feel your best. "O LORD my God, I cried unto thee, and thou hast healed me" **Psalm 30:2 KJV**. God is our healer—Jehovah Rapha. He can pull you up if you want it.

Here is a sample of healthy healing habits:

- Pray to God to deliver you from poor habits around health, wisdom to remove excess weight, and how to care for your

temple.
- Prepare all meal prep ingredients for delicious, fresh meals over the weekend and mid-week.
- Drink warm lemon water and honey, with a dash of cayenne pepper and apple cider vinegar, daily upon waking up to flush the digestive tract, liver, and kidneys.
- Eat within a six to eight-hour window.
- Do a juice-only diet for three days a week/month.
- Go on a spiritual fast one to three days monthly, or take on one whenever you need supernatural strength to overcome food temptations and addictions from three to twenty-one days.
- Do a quarterly detox to support colon, liver, blood, kidney health, gut, etc.
- Schedule all weekly workouts on a calendar.
- Incorporate exercises like interval walking, rowing, elliptical, bike riding, jumping rope, kickboxing, swimming, or HIIT exercises for at least thirty minutes four times per week. Aim to raise your heart rate to over 120.
- Eat a loaded veggie salad with herbs and olive oil for lunch.
- Take a probiotic, supplements, or medication with meals as recommended.
- Stretch for ten minutes in the evenings.
- Read/watch a video about health for thirty minutes twice weekly.
- Replace an hour of TV and social media with reading or research.
- Use a habit tracker to track daily habits and goals.
- Get an accountability partner to share progress with.
- Move around at home by cleaning up or walking in place.
- Explore one new healthy recipe or meal per month.
- Find a few restaurants in your area that make healthy entrees and eat there when you don't feel like cooking.
- Drink 64 ounces of water daily.

- Consume your last meal no later than four hours before bedtime.
- Go to bed on time and get proper rest.

Your calling in life is far too significant to neglect your body and treat it poorly. When you allow yourself to look and feel unhealthy, it affects your well-being. It reveals itself in your energy levels and overall physical demeanor—others will undoubtedly notice the difference. By taking the time to care for your body, you send a powerful message about how much you value the incredible gift of life and the unique vessel you have been given. Prioritizing your health is an act of thanksgiving and appreciation; it enhances your physical strength, mental clarity, and emotional resilience, empowering you to fulfill your purpose with vigor and enthusiasm. Embracing a lifestyle that promotes well-being signifies your commitment to living fully, purposefully, and authentically honoring God. I hope you can implement some of these practical ideas to maintain a lifestyle that reflects your dedication to growth. It's possible to shed excess weight and develop healthier habits now. Remember, your life, body, relationships, work, and business should bring glory to God.

Acceleration CURE Actions:

- **Research** and clarify if your eating is emotionally based. Try not to eat past your fullness. Locate and try new, healthier food options and commit to eliminating the ones that don't serve you as a purpose-driven leader.
- **Investigate** the food, chemicals, supplements, and ingredients you put in your body to break free from food enslavement and control what's going into your system.
- **Rewrite** your goals and devote yourself to refocusing by working out four days weekly for a minimum of fifteen minutes (until you can reach thirty minutes or more) to reclaim your health and reignite your well-being. Then, slowly add another day or two to your routine for a four—or five-day fitness plan, even in winter.
- **Join** groups, read health books, connect with others, and watch videos with like-minded people to effectively achieve, endure, and

execute your health, body goals, and plans and stay on course to enrich your journey.

Prayer

Dear Heavenly Father, please help me to prioritize my health and take better care of my body. I know that if I'm in better shape spiritually, it will allow me to be more disciplined physically. I know I'm to be sober, vigilant, and self-controlled in every area of my life so as not to give the enemy a foothold. Sometimes, I don't want to work out or eat healthy foods, so I need your help, Lord. People say food strongholds are difficult to break, and if I'm addicted to foods in any way, please break down the stronghold of pleasure and gluttony from me. I want to be motivated to nourish and take care of my temple. At this time, I'd like to pray about _____. I'm praying for healing and restoration from these things.

In Jesus' name, I pray, Amen.

Part 5

FINANCIAL ACCELERATION

Day 10
MASTER YOUR FINANCES

In November 2023, Cassandra Ventura filed an injurious $30M civil lawsuit alleging many heinous and nefarious acts against her ex-boyfriend, Sean "P Diddy" Combs, business mogul and founder of Bad Boy Entertainment. Combs denied the allegations but later issued an apology when leaked footage of him attacking Cassie in a Beverly Hills hotel surfaced. Since then, many suits have been filed. Months following a Homeland Security raid, Combs was arrested and indicted for racketeering and sex trafficking. Additionally, Puff has a thirty-year reputation of allegedly being notorious for withholding payment to his artists and stripping them from publishing and royalties. Yet, allegedly, he spent multi-millions on unthinkable debaucherous parties and pleasures to gratify his insatiable appetite for lust.

Although Combs is not a believer, we know from a spiritual perspective how Satan fuels the works of the flesh and sets up shop in an unbeliever's vessel through sacrifices, rituals, dark arts, occult practices, and witchcraft. Power, control, and money are satanic tools to hide perverse, deviant, depraved, illicit, and illegal activities, such as child molestation, rape, sex trafficking, murder, and drug distribution. When professing Christians or non-believers team up with satanic agendas, he will give them everything they lust for to bring about his demonic program—but it's a quid pro quo, not a gift. After all, he doesn't give gifts because he neither owns nor originates anything. However, he's returning to collect the payment he's owed, and money can't buy a way out when God's longsuffering and mercy are exhausted and wrath and judgment come.

Some people hide deception behind their walls of money and authority. They have the capability, connections, and sophisticated operations to shut people up and blacklist them if they don't cooperate with their wicked proposals and advances. There's also no shortage of people willing to sue, slander, lie, manipulate, blackmail, extort, or do anything to get a piece of someone's money bag. Through various means, we've witnessed people longing for nothing more than to be music, entertainment, or movie stars. In their desperation, they're easy targets for spiritual and financial manipulation. The starry-eyed big dreamers consciously bypass their moral compass and turn a blind eye to criminal acts to go into what they *think* is the upper echelon of society. Soon, they realize their talent has a high price tag tied to selling their soul to moguls to ravage their God-given abilities for fame and money. Once they enter these industries, they must continue overlooking bad things and doing what they never envisioned to get to the A list and keep the money rolling in thereafter.

In my twenties, I respected the moguls in these industries. So much so that my magazine *Industry Status* focused on the behind-the-scenes moguls, tastemakers, and creative talent who made everything we see and hear in these industries come to life. I wanted to write songs for their artists, too. I was also very close to partnering my magazine with someone who worked for Bad Boy Entertainment for many years. We spent a few months going back and forth about collaboration. I was up close and side-by-side in rooms, exclusive invite-only events, and VIP sections from Detroit and Atlanta to Miami with well-known big shots, producers, DJs, and artists. My experiences were way before the popularity of social media and celebrities opening up their lives online. So, I witnessed firsthand why people are attracted to getting into these industries and being around celebrities. There's a pleasurable excitement in the atmosphere.

As I look back over my life, I see the hand of God spare, block, and protect me from wicked, greedy men and a debaucherous industry in my ignorance. The music, film, entertainment, and fashion industries function in a hierarchy and doors are opened and closed by high-power people and forces of wickedness through gatekeepers. Their chiefs operate in a mob-like manner fueled by evil, pride, greed, selfish ambition, manipulation, lust, and power. Behind these industries are the promise of influence, wealth, and riches, but most of their powers are witchcraft-fueled and demonic.

Accelerated Power – Matthew 6:24 KJV "No man can serve two masters: for either he will hate the one, and love the other; or else he will hold to the one, and despise the other. Ye can't serve God and mammon."

Hate and despise are strong words. Love and hatred are extreme contrasts. Matthew's writing provides a framework Jesus taught for deciding between serving God and money. Many professing Christians are being misled to serve a false Jesus. They think they prosper from the Lord when their heart is far from Him. They haven't avoided the temptation of filthy lucre. But God's children aren't greedy or serving the master and god of worldly wealth because they chose loyalty to the Maker of heaven and earth. Greedy business owners who cheat their workers will pay the penalty. Leaders professing the name of Christ and using money to bait people into bondage will answer to God. Attraction to fast money over integrity puts our hearts and motives on display.

- What good is money if it's an idol?
- What good is having funds that God didn't bless or approve?

1 Timothy 6:9-10 KJV says, "But they that will be rich fall into temptation and a snare, and into many foolish and hurtful lusts, which drown men in destruction and perdition.[10] For the love of money is the root of all evil: which while some coveted after, they have erred from the faith, and pierced themselves through with many sorrows." Unauthentic and disingenuous men of the cloth face ruin because their true desires led them to serve money. Their love for it is the foundation on which they build everything. Therefore, how can a person be upright who's led to chase money by any means necessary? If money is their motivation, nothing is off limits—they'll cheat on their spouse, steal, delude people, and do all sorts of ungodly things to meet their goals and obsession. Some will wander from the faith for the notoriety it offers.

If our sole motivation for starting a business is financial gain, then it's not a purpose-driven venture. Because we're hidden in Christ, God-honoring businesses and assignments come from Him. Remember: Our primary reason for living is to serve God. In obedience, the Most High

God will bless the enterprise with patrons and financial rewards. The temptation to pursue money presents a snare, leading to hurt, destruction, and punishment for you, your employees, and your family. People who serve Satan don't care whose lives they destroy to get what they're pursuing. The Scripture clarifies that money isn't evil, but the love of money is *the root of ALL evil*—not some—but **all evil**. Once someone becomes too consumed with chasing after it, they'll find that sorrows and loss follow.

GREEDY AND HOOKED

So many people got caught up in PPP (Paycheck Protection Program) loan scams during the COVID-19 pandemic. Since then, many people have been arrested. Though highly necessary, the finances are secondary when you start your mission on Christ's Cornerstone. Remember, as believers, we can't use God's principles for money without genuinely connecting with Him. He saved us because of love, not to be used as an angel or seed investor for our desires.

Our wealth is meaningless if we become multi-millionaires without an intimate relationship with our Lord Jesus Christ. Greed isn't godly. "He that loveth silver shall not be satisfied with silver; nor he that loveth abundance with increase: this is also vanity" **Ecclesiastes 5:10 KJV**. The affluent have their rewards now, "But woe to you who are rich, for you have already received your comfort" **Luke 6:24 NIV**. Riches obtained by the world's success system profit nothing eternally. The prosperity of the wicked belongs to the just, "A good man leaveth an inheritance to his children's children: and the wealth of the sinner is laid up for the just" **Proverbs 13:22 KJV**. And if you haven't created a financial plan to leave with your children's children, it's not too late to ask God for wisdom. See, God wants to bless whatever you put your hands to and give you the desires of your heart when you *sincerely* seek Him first (Matthew 6:33).

When you're on the outside looking in, it may appear that all wealthy people are living the big American dream, but this isn't necessarily the case. God knows the heart of all men, and everything in them lays bare (1 Samuel 16:7, Hebrews 4:13). Many rich people are spiritually bankrupt. Riches are all an illusion if God isn't the affluent person's Master. It's not the money that's evil because currency is a tool, but the greed others have for it exposes corruption in their hearts. Money is a resource from our God to help us accomplish the work of The Lord and bless others. Money answereth all things, *"The officials* make a feast for enjoyment [instead of repairing what is broken], and serve wine to make life merry, and money is the answer to everything" **Ecclesiastes 10:19 AMP.**

WHEN YOU NEED MONEY

I focused on the money in my business because of my bills, overhead, and contractors I wanted to hire. So, I got up each morning to pray and read the Word. I spent the rest of the day on other work and revenue-driven activities (RDA). Throughout the day, I talked to God about the business. You may not see anything wrong with my actions, but God did. I was preoccupied with doing my part to be profitable due to fear and worry of not paying my bills. I trusted my efforts and wasn't resting in the Lord in my heart. I needed to seek Jehovah Jireh—my Provider, for peace and wisdom.

I also learned that everything God asks us to do isn't what He wants to use for our ultimate purpose or financial advancement. He uses them to bundle into our treasure box of skills and business acumen to lead us further into purpose. Patience in the economic area is challenging. God gave me gifts that don't monetize quickly. I'm mainly in the creative, knowledge, and publishing business, with an arm of coaching and consulting. Although revenue is needed, we mustn't work for it from a position of lack, fear, deprivation, and desperation. He knows how to send customers and clients our way. When we trust the Lord, He will finance whatever He calls us to do. He will set up our financial function so we can serve Him without worrying about how to bring in money.

The Father has infinite, far more excellent resources and strategies than you can contain in your finite mind. The world's strategies don't have the final answer to your financial dilemma. Their understanding of life and business is secondary to what God can show you because Christ is the wisdom of God. He gave King Solomon wisdom and wealth; there has never been and never will be anyone as rich as King Solomon (1 Kings 10:23-29). Note that Solomon didn't petition God for wealth, possessions, honor, or the death of his enemies—Solomon asked for wisdom to govern God's people. Since his heart first inclined to God's leadership, God happily blessed Solomon with things He didn't ask for (2 Chronicles 1:11-12). If He gave Solomon the abundance and astuteness for financial prosperity beyond anything anyone will ever witness, surely He can provide the money to pay your monthly expenses and lead donors, clients, customers, sponsors, investors, and partners to join in on your vision. Is there anything too hard for God (Jeremiah 32:27)?

SOW AND REAP

Remember the law of sowing and reaping. You reap what you sow (Galatians 6:7). We can't sow to our flesh and trespass against the Lord God and think everything (including our relationships, children, businesses, and money) won't be affected. When we give into the work of God through church and ministries, paying our debts, and taking care of our families, employees, contractors, vendors, or suppliers, we reap a harvest. I'm not saying that you give to get. Giving is a heart and soul matter and a display of spiritual growth in righteousness. Unfortunately, we cannot bypass God's financial principles, refuse to study and apply them, and look for a harvest. If we're not sowing by working for the Lord and serving others, there won't be any fruit to enjoy.

If you disregard time and discipline for consistent business success, you cannot expect positive results. Sowing inconsistency will only yield inconsistency. Should we look for apples during harvest if we don't plant the seed in the ground for our apple tree? Generosity is an act of worship for the New Testament church, and we aren't taught to tithe but to give a genuinely purposed offering from the heart. We do not seek returns with a motive. Still, when we serve God wholeheartedly and rest in Jireh's promises, He will supply our needs by making grace abound for our sufficiency. **2 Corinthians 9:6-8 KJV** says, "But this I say, He which soweth sparingly shall reap also sparingly; and he which soweth bountifully shall reap also bountifully. [7] Every man according as he purposeth in his heart, so let him give; not grudgingly, or of necessity: for God loveth a cheerful giver. [8] And God is able to make all grace abound toward you; that ye, always having all sufficiency in all things, may abound to every good work:"

WHO'S YOUR MASTER

Please don't fall for the *finance-first* baited hook that makes you depend on yourself to figure it out and make things happen financially. Pride in financial matters causes us to serve money and fall into temptations. You don't own anything here on this earth, but God is gracious enough to let you borrow and care for the things you have in your possession. Your purpose and vision belong to Him. God wants you to experience joy and peace with His blessings because they come with no sorrow. Remember: He cares for you and wants to protect you from the evils stemming from the love of money. Seek Him for financial wisdom and growth opportunities. His arms are open for you to discover and gather clarity on where He's leading you so that He can care for you financially while you work on accelerating your purpose and building your dreams for His glory. Since your business idea belongs to God, steward your financial resources well. Give the best portion to God because you can never out-give the Lord. Serve the Lord and others from a pure heart with the right motives. Freely give and bless people the same way God freely gives.

Acceleration CURE Actions:

- **Consult** the Lord for clarification on and self-discipline in applying the wisdom of the Word to your financial acumen, then commit to trusting His guidance.
- **Focus** on reproducing fruit in line with godly standards. When you plant seeds in good soil, you'll get unstuck and unshackled by reaping the harvest of progression and honorable character.
- **Consider** providing financial support or volunteering to help others further their mission however possible. Rewrite, reignite, and reclaim your financial outcome.
- **Plan** a one and five-year monetary plan to help you grow through enriching endurance in financial management.

Prayer

Dear Heavenly Father, At times, I've been guilty of chasing the money at times more than I pursue after you, and I ask you for forgiveness.

I've had a hard time trusting you with my finances. I've misused the resources you blessed me with a few times because I didn't seek wisdom.

I'm asking that you forgive me. I lacked insight and understanding of finances, and I'm praying that you grant me a fresh start. I submit to your leading because you're the All-Wise God, and your will is perfect. Please grant me wisdom, knowledge, and instructions on managing my income and investments. Please lead me to the applicable Scriptures, instructors, books, and courses to expand my understanding. Please lead me to the proper CPA, bookkeepers, and financial and legal services. Please show me where to give and spend and how to clean up debt. Teach me to lend and not have to borrow. Father, please prosper me in my finances so I have the resources to do your will.

In Jesus' name, I pray, Amen.

Day 11

LOOK AT YOUR FINANCES

My siblings and I had chores and allowances as kids. When I was around thirteen, my youngest sister Denise and I earned additional money by proposing to do extra household tasks. My mom learned housekeeping at a major hotel group sometime back and quickly got promoted to the front desk, so naturally, we wanted to model and mimic her expertise. So we proposed cleaning our parents' bedroom. Neicy cleaned it one week, and I'd do it another. We also got paid to pass out flyers for the family's lawn care business.

My high school, Pershing, offered work co-op programs for honor students in eleventh and twelfth grades. My first job was at fifteen, and I worked as a moving company administrative assistant at Janush Bros. Moving & Storage. Though it was a good position, after a few months, I sensed that God had something else in mind. The school's program had a dream opening. For my last two high school years, I landed the best role ever as an Office Assistant at Courville Elementary School, just minutes from our house. I loved the beautiful ladies in the office, the principal, the teachers, the support staff, and the many loving children who always sang, "Hi, Miss *LaTanyaaaaa*," whenever I walked into their classroom to hand out announcements and notes.

When we got licensed to drive, some of our responsibilities included making it to work, getting our nephew Emmanuel Quinn from school and ensuring he got his homework done, cheerleading practice, dance, and games for Neicy, and attending events and leisure activities. Mom pretty much gave us her 1986 Ford Cougar when I got my driver's license, while Dad handled all the maintenance and repairs. Driving our gray coupe taught me about vehicle accountability and helped me diagnose car issues later. I'm forever grateful to my parents for blessing us with our first car and showing us responsibility.

SAVINGS

Saving chunks of cash was a pattern I developed since my allowance days. My daddy always referred to me as a tightwad (a conservative spender—a cheapskate). I didn't find it necessary to spend money on things that I didn't have to have. That nickname became a part of my finance and money management skill set. I was also taught about spiritual giving at church early on. So, I often saved two to four paychecks at a time and was a consistent giver of 10% or more for decades. I didn't just hoard all of my funds. I spent money on things I liked and wanted but still managed to save. I remember as a little one how my parents taught us to take a portion of our funds and put them in church for the offering. I loved being a giver, and I still do to this day. I know managing money in that way and sacrificing to delay gratification is the gift of wisdom from God.

Even when I struggled financially during some of my years, I remained a giver. And I never have been down to my last dollar, even when I say things like, "I don't have money." That same wisdom from above is how I later paid off nearly $25k in debt in eighteen months (when I moved to Dallas). The Bible says, "Honour the LORD with thy substance, and with the firstfruits of all thine increase: [10] So shall thy barns be filled with plenty, and thy presses shall burst out with new wine" **Proverbs 3:9-10 KJV**. He spoke of literal fruit here, but the principle still applies to all we do and have. Giving is simply a principle and an act of obedience, discipline, and sacrifice that demonstrates good stewardship, generosity, and gratefulness. Jehovah Jireh doesn't need your money because "The earth is the LORD's, and the fulness thereof; the world, and they that dwell therein" **Psalm 24:1 KJV**. I constantly thank Jireh for letting me live in His home and use His resources.

Examples of giving include but are not limited to allocating funds to your local church regularly, supporting businesses/ministries, and supplying help and essentials for others. You'll want to consult God to ask where He'd like you to give, as all of your earned income shouldn't remain with *you*. You're blessed to be a blessing. Write down your budget expenses, and have your savings automatically deducted and placed into another account.

MANAGE THE LITTLE

When I was twenty, I financed my first brand-new car from the Pontiac dealership with my father's co-sign and automotive discount. I saved my money like I was paying my monthly payments first before asking for his help. Like that, my dream car—the 1997 teal Pontiac Grand Am coupe, was mine. It got totaled six months later when me, Neicy, my baby niece Danasia, and nephew Deontae Quinn drove from church one Sunday. A lady having a seizure hit us in a collision nearly head-on. I thank God we all didn't have significant injuries. After the insurance payout, I got a new car, a 1998 green Chevy Malibu, with my dad's signature again.

> **Accelerated Power – Luke 16:10-12 NIV** "Whoever can be trusted with very little can also be trusted with much, and whoever is dishonest with very little will also be dishonest with much. [11] So if you have not been trustworthy in handling worldly wealth, who will trust you with true riches? [12] And if you have not been trustworthy with someone else's property, who will give you property of your own?"

Still, so many believers miss the point. How you handle little is a test of how much more—if any—you can handle. How we steward tiny things matters to our future responsibilities because they are rewards, gifts, and blessings from God. The passage says, "So, who will trust you with true riches if you have not been trustworthy in handling worldly wealth?" True riches are our eternal life, blessings, and relationships with our believing brothers and sisters. And if you have not been trustworthy with someone else's property, who will give you your property?

How are you treating your bus ride, bedroom, vehicle, rental living space, job, and other belongings you're to steward? How are you keeping and accounting for your time, resources, and ideas? How are you treating your relationships with the saved and unsaved people in your life? Consistency in building our spiritual, personal, and financial lives on Jesus Christ so the foundation won't crumble is stewardship.

BUILD A FOUNDATION

In every place I've ever rented, I kept it neat and clean as if I owned it. I learned this instinctively because my parents were homeowners. Living in apartments, I notice how many parents who raise their children in multi-family dwellings aren't considerate or respectful to their neighbors. They allow the children to be loud and unruly. Even some Christian parents overlook consistently teaching their children how to clean or pick up after themselves. But kids must learn and be taught how to assist with whatever age-appropriate tasks they can for their own good. Some parents dismiss this wisdom with statements such as, "I want my kids to be kids." However, their learning responsibility isn't disallowing them to be kids, as parenting is about teaching them about building life skills and good habits.

I've watched my nephews Emmanuel, Deontae, and niece Ashley Williams as toddlers. They loved lending a helping hand and getting rewarded. Watching them move with such energy to accomplish the mission was fun for me as their aunt. Toddlers enjoy helping around the house and hearing "Thank you" and "Good job." They enjoy assisting, serving, and giving when it's taught as long as the guidance is in the proper context. We must also instruct our little ones to share things with other children and to give financially from their allowance or gifts from their aunts, uncles, grandparents, or peers. If you're raising kids, please don't miss out on sharing financial and work principles with them early.

UNSOUND PERSONAL FINANCIAL DECISIONS

I made a poor financial decision when I married from a place of brokenness and sinful living. My rebellion towards God through fornication carried into my finances, and there were long-term consequences for my actions. Sin instantly separates us from God's presence, will, and hidden wisdom. Likewise, other sins are present in multiple areas of our lives when we grieve the Holy Ghost. Don't be deceived. If one lives in open rebellion while confessing salvation in Christ, this book is a call to address it before it's too late. God is longsuffering, but we can't play with His grace and mercy long without suffering consequences.

I say this with love because I want to see more believers set free. Please don't let consistent church attendance and financial giving deceive you into thinking you live a holy life. We can't expect to live how we wish without reaping the wages of sin. Trust me, if there's fornication—there is lying; if lying—there's stealing and cheating in some form. If thievery is present—so is jealousy, pride, and gossip. If prideful gossip—then idolatry. I repented for that sinful season of my life, and it drained my spiritual, relational, and financial blessings and resources superfast.

I was making good money but lost it all. At thirty-one, I had a mortgage with a new construction townhome, a brand new Cadillac CTS, excellent savings, good credit, and profit sharing. But because I yearned for a husband and children. I got impatient and thought I could prosper living like the world. My unequally yoked marriage drained me spiritually and financially because I paid *all* of the bills and stayed stressed out from gaslighting and other forms of hurt. In other words, I had already been paying all the bills as a single woman, but instead of finding relief and rest in my femininity and womanhood, I took on a life of unrest and more bills. I was in bondage in my spirit, soul, body, and home to the consequences of my sins, and I had no peace.

We cannot live in sin and think we will prosper from God's hand. Many of us are financially pierced because of our sins in other areas. I'm responsible for my choices and actions. My behaviors caused me to go through much painful discipline from God. I later surrendered my home in bankruptcy and let it foreclosure. I struggled with those poor choices for ten years and had to go back to low-paying jobs and live in noisy apartments with disrespectful neighbors who didn't value peace or property. I always say God used my art business to sanctify me. It wasn't meant to succeed then because I had to repaint a new reality, learn some hard lessons, and have my faith tested by God to be trusted again.

UNSOUND BUSINESS FINANCIAL DECISIONS

In business, I didn't always manage my finances as I wanted. When I hit some financial pinches, the times in my life were usually because I always used my funds to invest in my dreams. But it's gotten better over the years, and I'm improving because I know how my financial journey started, both the good and the bad. However, God can work miracles to override a financial trial for you when He's testing your faith in that area. Nonetheless, He usually gives us financial principles to incorporate into our life and business. He won't entrust us with monetary wins if we don't manage or choose to squander what we have because if we get it, we won't keep it.

People typically don't start a corporation to lose money, break even, and not turn a profit! They start profit organizations to help customers solve problems and make a living from their expertise. Of course, you plan for losses initially and give the endeavor time to ramp up, typically three to five years. However, the business will struggle to grow until the product or service demand is there. Supply and demand lead to financial profitability. Therefore, financial sacrifice starts at home and bleeds over into our creative and missional endeavors. We can still learn and apply the correct principles but can't skip steps, so go back to the foundation—to the root.

Many owners use their credit, 401K, savings, business loans, or investor's capital to float until growth. Suppose you don't have the funding options due to your creditability score. Consider OPM (Other People's Money) in other ways, like pre-orders, GoFundMe, personal lending from someone you know, peer lending, grants, sponsors, or partners for specific projects. You can also look into bartering your skills, services, or products in exchange for something you need from another business. It's also wise to work full-time and save money to invest in the company if possible.

Never despise small beginnings and financial pivots and shifts. I worked a job many times off and on over the years to pay business expenses and cover my household overhead because all of my endeavors cost quite a bit. If you must work for a while to support your family, home, and business, it's okay to be bi-vocational for now. You can grow the enterprise part-time until it grows with sweat equity. Work diligently at that job as if it's your own company and accurately manage the finances God entrusts to you. Regardless of how you work the financial plan, ask God to give you wisdom and show you how He wants you to finance it and use the funds.

Don't fret if your finances are out of balance and you have more liabilities than assets. God can turn this around because properly stewarding the finances starts now in your secret place of prayer. Like the widow who gave all she had into the treasury by faith, simply start with where you are. Return to your financial plan and update it frequently if the needle isn't moving. Faith in God's economic management is mandatory for acceleration. If we're broke or managing resources poorly, we can't:

- Give to the purposes of the gospel
- Extend financial help to those in need
- Pay professionals, experts, employees, and contractors to help with business growth
- Acquire assets, intellectual and commercial property
- Invest in other business opportunities or sponsor other's vision
- Pay taxes, retainers, expenses, fees, insurance, and debts
- Expand into new territories and markets
- Launch, test, and develop new products
- Provide for our families and their interests
- Take time off to care for ourselves and our loved ones
- Think clearly and creatively
- Take breaks from work to travel or vacation
- Buy ourselves or others something nice

WHERE TO GO FROM HERE

So what do you do when money isn't up and up, and God tells you to start a business requiring lots of capital and resources? Although it may be tempting to grab a book or watch a YouTube video quickly, seek God's wisdom first. Ask God to give you the insight, knowledge, and understanding to do what He wants you to do. Then, you can venture into the financial resources available from books, experts, coaches, podcasts, and advisors. The Almighty will lead you to the right people, places, things, and ideas.

Also, make sure your credit is intact with a 700 or higher score so that it aligns you for business credit opportunities for its legal structure. I also recommend opening accounts (savings/checking) with different banks to organize your finances and savings. Those relationships help you when you apply for business credit for their institutions. The acceleration cure occurs when you're generous and not trapped in debt. Financial riches can be deceptive outside God's will, so you must be careful. The Father wants you to be rich in abundance and become Christ-like by the Spirit instead of the flesh.

If you file a claim with your insurer for something outside the policy coverage, you won't receive reimbursement for your damages. The insurer can't compensate you because the loss occurred external from the contract. Although God can snatch you from wrong financial deals or funds mismanagement, you don't want to make unaligned methods the norm. Therefore, stay within God's ethics and boundary markers so that He can work things out according to His success standards. Apply the acceleration principle: pray + obey + faith + wisdom = accelerate.

Here are a handful of 2350 money Scriptures to hold on to:

- Deuteronomy 8:18, 15:10, 16:17
- 1 Chronicles 29:11-17
- Ecclesiastes 5:8-20, 7:12, 10:19
- Proverbs 3:27, 10:4, 22, 11:24-25, 13:11, 21:21, 22:9
- Galatians 6:6
- 2 Corinthians 9:6-11
- Acts 20:35
- Hebrews 13:16

God loves you and wants to give you good things. Him blessing you with finances is of His good pleasure. Money is a blessing that helps you accelerate. And you can overcome any financial challenge when you understand how money works and adopt good habits. When you apply yourself to become a student of studying biblical money principles, laws, economics, and consumer and business credit, you'll know how to use the knowledge as a means. Also, give freely to support the things God presses on your heart.

Acceleration CURE Actions:

- Evaluate, clarify, and audit your current finances monthly by adding up your assets, liabilities, unpaid/unfiled taxes, funding needs, etc. Pull your credit report as your name and score is your credibility in business, so keep track of your score. Document your due dates and put reminders on a digital calendar for important ones. Steward your resources, work with a budget, and stay disciplined with your spending. Here is a budget and debt repayment tracker I used to manage my finances and pay off debt. Cure 4 the Soul https://cure4thesoul.com/finance/
- Study financial principles about money and stewardship to break free from unhealthy patterns and limiting beliefs about money. Get the kids involved with serving and giving early.
- Reignite and rewrite new economic growth targets and plans. Hire a professional to help you get on course with your funds, bookkeeping, and taxes to reclaim your financial position. Buy some good books about money management, watch videos, take classes, and attend seminars.
- Enrich and endure any consequences of poor money choices and team up with your spouse or an accountability partner to stick to your new game plan for the next twelve months.

Prayer

Dear Heavenly Father, I welcome you into my personal and business finances because my life and company are yours. Forgive me for my sins that have caused me to enslavement to unfit money habits. Please lead me to your financially sound wisdom so I can handle my finances according to your principles. Reveal the areas in my life in which I'm mishandling funds. Please forgive me for the times I held back, mismanaged, and recklessly spent the money and resources you provided. I pray you show me how to settle the matter for those I owe money to. I pray for the complete restoration of my finances and the wisdom to manage, allocate, grow, and budget funds correctly. Teach what projects and ideas to invest in.

Father, please show me where to hire the right accountant, bookkeeper, and tax advisor. Father, show me what vendors and suppliers I will do business with so I won't sow into infertile soil. Tell me where to give an offering. Teach me what product and service offerings are not profitable so I can eliminate them, and show me which ones are worth the investment. Bless the work of my hands and direct the motives of my heart so I can work diligently to generate a profit. Please download the correct prices and financial wisdom for business growth. Please help me to apply the knowledge and information for transformation. Lord, bless me financially so that I can bless others.

Also, if you want me to leverage credit as a tool, I pray that you make me wise in using it and staying away from long-term debt. But Father, if I must utilize debt in the form of credit cards, loans, and lines of credit, let me use it wisely by paying it off each month and only extending its resources through prayer and wisdom.

In Jesus' name, I pray, Amen.

Day 12

OVERCOME FINANCIAL EMERGENCIES

I remember when members of my church, Bible Community Baptist, on Detroit's West Side, pastored by George Gooden, occasionally had various emergency financial needs. Whether for a car repair, roof leak, or unexpected expenses, the church members came through. It still amazes me how they instantly pulled together to meet the needs. This quick gathering of resources reminded me of the early New Testament Church in Acts. I rarely see this *pulling together* with larger churches, possibly because they have sophisticated systems behind the scenes.

However, I know churches still help in benevolence. Some houses of worship give *loans* for financial assistance, and I learned this the hard way. During my first year in Atlanta, I visited churches and looked for one to call my own. As a non-member, I attended for months and gave weekly financial support to New Birth Missionary Baptist Church during Bishop Eddie Long's pastorate.

So, back to the loan story, here's why I needed help. I moved from my College Park apartment two weeks prior and lived with my friend Crystal in Doraville due to me losing contract work. I was also getting back into doing nails but was only breaking even after booth rent at the Sandy Springs salon suites and working on my magazine. I was battling with the temp agency about unemployment after the assignment ended. They gave me unemployment insurance but denied my claim weeks later and took me to a hearing, and I could no longer afford my rent. Then, she lost her job and couldn't afford to pay hers. I needed the finances to help her, or we both were going to be homeless. I asked New Birth for benevolence assistance, and they offered me a $300 loan to pay back in thirty days. That loan would cause me additional hardship, so I opted out. Fortunately, she went to non-profit charities, including a church, and got the help. She also met a security guard for Dillard's, and he told us they were hiring. We interviewed, and both got jobs there a week later. Praise God! I got a new apartment six weeks later in Roswell and and found a new contract job offering unlimited overtime after learning the role.

Accelerated Power – Philippians 4:19 KJV, And my God shall supply all your need according to his riches and glory by Christ Jesus.

Nonetheless, where there's a need, God promises to supply them all. His riches and glory are glorious and reach beyond financial provision. When, where, why, who, and how He provides is up to Him. The goal is to keep moving and trust in His promises. The Lord Jesus intersects all your necessities abundantly in His perfect timing. "Now to him who is able to do immeasurably more than all we ask or imagine, according to his power that is at work within us" **Ephesians 3:20 NIV**. So we don't just get the blessing of answered prayers. The gift comes with God's lavish, unspeakable glory.

RISKS AND REWARDS

Have you heard the saying, "The rewards outweigh the risks?" I keep that statement top of mind when I *feel* I'm not making any headway. We can go months without making money and eventually see an avalanche of funds in one week. I'm sure you have experienced a great need for God to come through financially at least once in your personal life and business, and perhaps it didn't end the way you wanted it. But operating and accelerating your purpose-driven business is all about living by faith no matter what you see. Your faithful actions involve risks and sacrifice. And you're more than a conquerer if you live a righteous life. **According to Webster, an entrepreneur** organizes, manages, and assumes the risks of a business or enterprise. [1]

An entrepreneur takes on greater than normal *financial risks*. When you take *monetary chances*, not to be confused with *penitentiary chances*, you know there's no guarantee they'll pay off. The very word *risks* tell us that what we invest in is uncertain. That's why the rewards are more significant than the hazards when they pay off. As Christ's followers, we take on threats in life —it's called living by FAITH! We trust God for the outcome because we don't know how things will turn out. But we're in business because we believe in the best conclusion and continue pivoting until we see the fruit of our labor. And sometimes, you'll need to fast along with your prayers and mustard seed faith to see God's power blast through financial barriers.

BELIEVE

When believing God for a financial breakthrough, you must have unwavering and unworried confidence to accelerate through the gap because the things you're standing for—those hard things—often look like they will *not* happen. Jesus said, **Matthew 6:33-34 NIV** "But seek first his kingdom and his righteousness, and all these things will be given to you as well. [34] Therefore do not worry about tomorrow, for tomorrow will worry about itself. Each day has enough trouble of its own."

Life is a daily walk, and gratitude starts by thanking God for today's provision. Sadly, most believers will never risk ego, pride, and rejection by sharing even the gospel with a stranger or someone they know because of fear, let alone attempt financial and social risks. Most people who say they want a financial blessing or business growth are unwilling to invest $300-$5k into a life-changing program unless they can guarantee a return. But that's not an entrepreneur's or leader's reality. A mindset that lacks faith and sees scarcity struggles daily. The seeds you plant grow; if you plant doubt and worry—it shall be. It's impossible to please God without faith, and those who diligently seek Him get rewards (Hebrews 11:6). Learning from errors is also a way to profit from first-hand experience. To conquer financial giants and emergencies, we can't be passive and terrified to take on opportunities.

I put my money where my faith is by investing thousands of dollars into my businesses and ministries. I've poured cash into growing my spiritual and personal development, skillset, knowledge, and mission. I believe in what God gives me and invest in whatever it takes to accelerate the vision.

Sometimes, I can be conservative with my funds, but I see fruit when I release it to buy what I need. Whether I purchase a $25 book to add to my library or a $10k program, I'll go for it if God leads me to buy it. And the more you make, the heftier the risk and investment. For instance, if you're already bringing in $100K from your business, your coach or consultant to get you to $200K may be $25k or more to get you the desired results. Believe in your purpose-driven business because no one else will support you if you don't. When you don't have money, God blesses you with the time to dedicate to learning how to acquire new skills to level up.

God owns everything! His economy is abundant and overflowing with riches, creativity, resources, divine connections, appointments, and provision. He owns the cattle on 1000 hills, "For every animal of the forest is mine, and the cattle on a thousand hills" **Psalm 50:10 NIV**. So, God needs to come to us for nothing, but we must seek first the Kingdom. Refuse to think about things going wrong or failing when you're struggling. Do this instead:

- Consider what you'll do with the money when God answers your prayers for a financial blessing.
- What good will occur if you dedicate the first two hours of your day to reading, praying, and strategizing with God about applying biblical principles to your mission?
- Focus on the results you'll get from mastering the coursework you pay for and showing up for the coaching sessions that whip you into shape.
- Imagine the good that will happen if you let down your pride and ask for help from a mentor or someone who's already been where we're going.
- What will change if you invest one hour daily in reading and studying in the areas where you need the most help?

As Christians, we're supposed to excel in the things we do. However, we often lack confidence, belief, discipline, patience, habits, wisdom, insight, implementation, and execution—not money! As noted previously, I lost and squandered my material possessions, so I didn't have a money problem—

I had a spiritual maturity problem. Don't underestimate the importance of spiritual growth and obeying God. Reliance on the Godhead is the only way to accelerate in all you touch. God is your strength and the way to conquer anything.

At times, we're disinclined to eliminate the destructive, seemingly small things from our lives. Therefore, we suffer the consequences in our wallets. Reflecting on some lessons that hit my pocketbook makes me shake my head. The problem you're facing today with your funds *might* be present because of your unwillingness to forego something that is keeping you bound. Going the wrong way is not always why we struggle in this financial arena, but God uses these hardships to get us right in other areas. Other times, God wants to pull you out of your comfort zone and help you exercise your potential. Regardless of your battling and emergency financial need, don't give up. It takes an obedient individual to start a business and trust God for the economic outcome. You're reading this book today because you're one of the faithful leaders, and God wants to restore your finances if you believe and recommit this area of desire to Him.

15 IDEAS

Navigating monetary hardship is not easy. Financial losses can be enormous, and they affect everyone differently. If your operation is small, the inability to overcome it can quickly put you out of business, thus putting more stress on you, your family, employees, and contractors. However, assessing what's working and what's not is vital. Then, cut your losses. If your business is in deprivation and the monetary need is significant, consider the following ideas to find an acceleration cure:

1. List everything you intend to do with the finances you're praying for down to the penny.
2. Categorize expenses into critical and non-critical.
3. Reduce underperforming activities, products, and services, no matter how well-liked they are.
4. Negotiate payment extension and grace options with creditors and lenders.

5. Grab your financial documents, bookkeeping program, notebook, or spreadsheet, write down the business's economic weaknesses, and document your assets and liabilities.
6. Determine how to multiply and flip the cash, credit, and assets on hand.
7. See if you have any clients you can collect early payments from at a discount.
8. Schedule 3-6 hours of weekly planning sessions with God in solitude and repeat them as often as needed. Go over Bible verses and the information from #1 and #5. Talk to God as if you both are in a boardroom strategizing the next move.
9. Email, DM (Direct Message), cold call, text, or contact past customers to offer or re-offer your services or request referrals.
10. Go on a seven-day fast with extended prayer time to seek God for wisdom, knowledge, and understanding to help you through this trying time.
11. Grab ten Scriptures on money and faith, and study and meditate on them.
12. Set a 1-hour timer and brainstorm with the Holy Spirit and your team to find fifty creative ways to turn a profit quickly.
13. Ask the Lord to identify and multiply what's in your hands (ideas, gifts, skills, money, products, services, connections, etc.).
14. Ramp up your social media posts and build your community by providing valuable answers to frequently asked questions (FAQs).
15. Send emails to your community focused on a new idea or angle to add value and keep them engaged for your upcoming sales and launches.

THE NEXT 30-DAYS

Stay focused on your emergency execution plan and put in longer than regular hours to work through the turnaround. Challenge yourself to keep your eyes concentrating on the promises of God for the next 30 days. Don't turn from them to the right or the left. Turn off any unrelated content that gets you off-focus and makes you unproductive. "Lazy hands make for poverty, but diligent hands bring wealth." "The blessing of the LORD brings wealth, without painful toil for it" **Proverbs 10:4,22 NIV**.

God knows how to get you out of a situation where you're strapped for cash to pay for your basic needs. Finding yourself in a dire financial situation doesn't mean you didn't consult or follow God's investment guidance. I've yet to experience a financial failure God didn't later use as a lesson to advance me beyond that loss. I realized that it's not the money or wins that ultimately shape and define us. How we handle and come out of storms is what matters. It's understandable to emphasize that God is a provider when you feel secure financially and haven't had the opportunity to invest in a vision. It's a different experience when navigating uncertainty and striving to bring your dreams to life.

Psalm 50:15 KJV says, "And call upon me in the day of trouble: I will deliver thee, and thou shalt glorify me." Will you call upon the Lord in the day of trouble? You can't go around, over, or under the financial hardship gap. If you get angry and shut down, it will not change that you still have to go through this situation to get out of it. **Hebrews 13:5 KJV** says, "Let your conversation be without covetousness; and be content with such things as ye have: for he hath said, I will never leave thee, nor forsake thee." Although you may feel alone in this—God promises never to leave or forsake you, so stand on His Word. It never feels good when you're going through the eye of a storm, but you can make it if you look up. God is taking you this route because of the places He wants you to go after that.

When I was in survival mode with my art business, God knew I didn't want to use my credit cards to pay my expenses and buy food for those months. However, He gave me the wisdom to leverage credit, which changed my life. That principle of leverage reminds me of the widow whose creditor wanted to enslave her two boys. When Elisha asked her what she had, she replied, "Your servant has nothing there at all," she said, "except a small jar of olive oil" **2 Kings 4:2 NIV**. Elisha told her to "*borrow* oil jars." The jar overflowed with oil, beginning with just a tiny jar. That abundance allowed her to pay off all debts and live off the rest. Without Elisa's help and obedience, she'd be hopeless and stuck. But when we least expect it, God sends us a ram in the bush. Borrowing when you have nothing to pay back seems out of sync with God. But your journey is faith-driven, not selfish-driven, so this borrowing isn't something you'd do otherwise. However, removing pride and asking for resources helps us build credibility with others and the banking systems we may need to grow our businesses later.

ENDURE THE TRIAL

Your strength to endure comes only from God. Sometimes, you must suffer experiences like this to get to your Promised Land. Like Joshua and Caleb, you must now see the land and vision. Don't be afraid to ask friends, family, and your church for help and prayer if you need it for your household. Feeling panicked, discouraged, and humiliated is common when your finances are in disarray, but someone is willing to assist you.

I've regularly witnessed God come through financially when I prayed, and my belief didn't waver. I have multiple testimonies of how He's come through in the fourth inning. For instance, as a manicurist, I usually went to college Monday through Thursday and worked in the salon (Thurs-Sat) around my schedule. One Sunday, I looked at my books for the week and found that I had only a few regular clients scheduled, which was odd. When I went to work that Wednesday at three, I had a few walk-ins, and I had to turn away clients. My books filled up for the rest of the week, and I continued to turn business away until Saturday evening. I didn't leave the shop until late at night those four days. When I calculated my earnings, I had the most significant week I ever had doing nails (outside of prom season), which was close to $800 when I'd typically average around $400ish on a regular week after paying booth rent and expenses (this was in Detroit, 1996/1997 working mostly three days). God sent a surplus of customers to get their nails done so I could pay my bills.

Friend, you will make it because God deployed you to this. All the potential and acceleration you need to make the money is already in your hands. Your success is in your faith rooted in the Rock. Buckle down, remove distractions, and let God accelerate you. Believe in Him. You will survive this test. You'll be firm when you come out of this examination of perseverance, faith, and endurance. Your business, book, program, training, membership, speaking engagement, invention, idea, and ministry are already successes. The Great I AM never promised that it would be easy, but He did promise that He would be with you through it. We've never seen the blameless abandoned. "I have been young, and now am old; yet have I not seen the righteous forsaken, nor his seed begging bread" **Psalm 37:25 KJV**.

Acceleration CURE Actions:

- **Take** action to clarify your priorities by choosing three items on the list of 15 ideas to navigate your hardships and committing to a financial emergency strategy.
- **Open** your heart to hear what the Holy Spirit has to say. Resolve to pivot wherever necessary while remaining steadfast in your mission to get unshackled and unstuck.
- **Resist** the temptation to worry about the taxes, rent, payroll, and other mandatory expenses due this week. Instead, stand firm on God's Word and rest in His promised peace to reignite your vision and rewrite your future.
- **Consider** and pray for others in similar circumstances to enrich and endure financial trials.

Prayer

Dear Heavenly Father, Thank you for this day you've blessed me to see. Your Word instructed me not to worry about tomorrow because it has its own problems. Lord God, I desperately need a financial breakthrough. Some bills need payment immediately for the business to stay afloat. The household expenses are also overdue. I've tried everything I know how to do, from prayer, keeping you first, adding new services and products, updating the marketing campaign, hiring a sales team, taking advanced classes in business, and giving financially to help others. At this point, the puzzle pieces are not coming together, and I'm drowning financially. Nothing is working so far to turn the business around. Lord, you said that I have not because I ask not; you said not to be anxious about anything but in everything through prayer and supplication with thanksgiving to present my request to you, and your peace would guide my heart and mind. Lord, I have been doing that, and I'm doing it again today.

Please hear my cry and come through for your child and your mission on this day. Please make a way as you did for Israel with the Red Sea and the Jordan. Slay this financial giant like you slew Goliath through David. Please give us wisdom to joyfully endure. Be my shield so I won't sin against you with angry thoughts. Quiet my anxieties and racing mind. Help me recover from this hardship and these financial setbacks so you can bless and trust me with more to do your will. May you move the hearts of those who need our products and services this week and send them to us.

I pray for everyone affected by the financial decisions—my family, employees, vendors, suppliers, creditors, and landlords. Please give them peace during this process so they won't hold this against me. Draw me nearer to you. Restore my finances, and please come through for _____ (your entity's name) in the amount of _____.

In Jesus' name, I pray, Amen.

Part 6

MINDSET ACCELERATION

Day 13

RENEW YOUR MIND

Growing up, occasionally we watched *The Beverly Hillbillies*. The sitcom was based on Jed finding oil while hunting rabbits in his backwoods Missouri countryland, which led to his becoming rich. He allowed his family to join and partake in the newly discovered wealth, and they moved to Beverly Hills, CA. They brought their cultural mindset and ways of living that didn't fit in with the upscale lifestyle of those living in their new zip code. Their discomfort with trying to fit in left them feeling out of place and wanting to return to their mountainside Missouri surroundings. Have you ever heard, "You can take the person out the ghetto, but you can't take the ghetto out the person?" Its usage is in black culture's colloquies. It's when someone who grew up in the ghetto takes those mentalities into their new lifestyle or environment.

Likewise, let's look at the Hebrews who spent forty years on an eleven-day journey to the Promised Land. **Deuteronomy 1:2 AMP** says, "It is [only] eleven days' journey from Horeb (Mount Sinai) by way of Mount Seir to Kadesh-Barnea [on Canaan's border; yet Israel wandered in the wilderness for forty years before crossing the border and entering Canaan, the promised land]." Initially, God brought His people the long way because they couldn't fight a war if one broke out (Exodus 13:17). Nevertheless, the long way wasn't supposed to be forty grueling years in the wilderness.

Although God took them a lengthier route, how can it take forty years for such a short journey? The short answer is their minds weren't mature enough or ready to process the blessing and new environment. You can take the Hebrews out of Egypt, but getting Egypt out of them was the actual battle. There wasn't enough faith space for the new way of living to overshadow the old. Without faith, it's impossible to please God. They had an oppression mentality that overrode the new miracle and blessing that God promised them. Their example is a lesson and warning to us all. An old mindset can't go to a new place. We can't "pour new wine into old wineskins" because they'll burst due to elasticity loss (Matthew 9:17). What's in us will spill out—good or bad.

The Hebrews knew the Egyptian lifestyle and wanted what they were familiar with to be a part of their new reality. But for good reasons, they couldn't obtain the success they desired with a double mind, nor can it be feasible for us. Running a flourishing business involves righteous, clear, new thinking and a firm foundation. The old fleshly mind is corrupt, unbeneficial, and crippling. There's nothing noble about it. When God saves us, we don't show up the next day with a mind transformed into Christ's mindset—but it's in us in seed form. Therefore, intentionally and deliberately adapting to the new mind and nature and growing up in our new life like a newborn baby into a mature, responsible adult is the mind renewal journey.

Paul pleads with us to take the gift of renewing our thinking seriously. Since the enemy used our bodies before salvation for many wicked works, sacrificing and giving ourselves entirely to Christ is our reasonable act of worship, and this offering sets the tone for transformation.

> **Accelerated Power – Romans 12:1-2 KJV** I beseech you therefore, brethren, by the mercies of God, that ye present your bodies a living sacrifice, holy, acceptable unto God, which is your reasonable service.
> ² And be not conformed to this world: but be ye transformed by the renewing of your mind, that ye may prove what is that good, and acceptable, and perfect, will of God.

CONFIRMING YOUR FAITH

Before we can move on from the past and understand God's will, we must ensure our calling and election. The Holy Spirit indwells, seals, teaches, and protects those who belong to God (Ephesians 1:13). Thus, I don't want to assume that you're born again and have a mind primed for renewal as faith comes by hearing (the gospel) and hearing by the Word of God (Romans 10:17). Firstly, do you believe you were born a sinner, and Jesus Christ died on the cross for your sins, was buried, and resurrected on the third day (Romans 5:12, John 3:16-17, 1 Corinthians 15:3-5)? Have you ever confessed your conviction out loud? "That if thou shalt confess with thy mouth the Lord Jesus, and shalt believe in thine heart that God hath raised him from the dead, thou shalt be saved. [10] For with the heart man believeth unto righteousness; and with the mouth, confession is made unto salvation" **Romans 10:9-10 KJV**.

As a result of your confession and profession of faith, have you turned from your former ways through repentance? **2 Timothy 2:19 NKJV** says, "Nevertheless the foundation of God standeth sure, having this seal, The Lord knoweth them that are his. And, let every one that nameth the name of Christ depart from iniquity." Have you ever gone public about your conversion by baptism to identify with your new life and the body of Christ? **Matthew 28:18-20 NKJV**, "And Jesus came and spoke to them, saying, 'All authority has been given to Me in heaven and on earth. [19] Go therefore and make disciples of all the nations, baptizing them in the name of the Father and of the Son and of the Holy Spirit, [20] teaching them to observe all things that I have commanded you;'" Have you shared your testimony of redemption with others?

OVERCOMING BARRIERS TO PROGRESS

In agriculture and hauling, two oxen work together side-by-side to plow at the same pace. But before work can occur, the oxen must lower their necks to fit in the yoke. If one oxen is faster or slower than the other, it messes with productivity. If a new ox is uncooperative and stiff-necked, it's no good for the farmer, and it will frustrate the obedient mature ox and accomplish nothing. However, the seasoned ox can bear the whole load if the obstinate one is willing. Like salvation, we can only enter in the one way Jesus opens, and transformation and growth can only occur by cooperating and experiencing it with His methods.

Many of us experience life through our limiting beliefs and are immovable in conforming to God's processes. Likewise, prolonged pursuit of success without refreshing the mind leads to false righteousness, inertia, and failure. Sometimes, when we resist becoming a disciple and learning from others, it can feel like we're stuck in one place. Stagnation keeps us from discovering our true purpose and all the God-ordained things we can do. So, our expedition is more extended than it has to be. Compliance and submission are the keys to unlocking harmonious flow.

A farmer uses a sharp iron stick, a goad, to guide the oxen. But when it kicks back, the goad digs into its flesh. [1]. However, Jesus sinks His neck and welcomes us to take His yoke because His burden is easy and light. Jesus said in **Matthew 11:29-30 KJV**, "Take my yoke upon you, and learn of me; for I am meek and lowly in heart: and ye shall find rest unto your souls. [30] For my yoke is easy, and my burden is light."

Jesus wants to carry the load and give your weary soul rest. Aren't you tired of fighting the world and everyone else who steps on your emotional landmines? Aren't you tired of holding on to baggage restricting you from progress? You can let it go today! Submission—dropping our necks—must arise to allow the Holy Spirit to guide us into all truth to overhaul our minds and give us the freedom and peace we seek.

How much progress can we make with an unrenewed mind? We need only to look at the nation of Israel in the wilderness. We must be open and willing vessels for God's purpose to fully realize our potential. Only then can we embrace what He's laid out for us. Unless something drastic and life-altering like a death or health scare, divorce, getting arrested, loss, hitting rock bottom, or financial ruin forces us to reflect and live upright, we will rarely choose to do it on our own. God has typically brought us all low to humble and transform us in the valley, as people seldom *decide* to change on the mountaintop.

We adapt God's mind through righteousness and guidance, like a recruit trains in the military. Any fruitless views that shaped our yesterday aren't necessarily the ones to keep us in the Promised Land. How you view God and yourself has everything to do with your conceptions. You don't want an identity-blind mind. Your past self is not your present self, and your present self is not your future self. Training in truth and sanctifying in the Spirit is necessary to disengage the carnal mind. "Sanctify them through thy truth: thy word is truth" **John 17:17 KJV.**

Your old way of thinking opposes God's mind, and whichever you choose (old or new) guides your thoughts daily. Those who doubt God find themselves empty-handed regarding His blessings simply because they haven't fully committed to their beliefs. **James** shares in **1:7-8 KJV**, "For let not that man think that he shall receive any thing of the Lord. ⁸ A double minded man is unstable in all his ways." Having a wishy-washy mindset can lead to uncertainty and a lack of trust, making it difficult to seek wisdom from the Lord when we find ourselves torn between worldly desires and deeper truths. However, when we embrace our new heart, we find comfort in submission, making it a more natural and peaceful part of our journey. "I will give them an undivided heart and put a new spirit in them; I will remove from them their heart of stone and give them a heart of flesh" **Ezekiel 11:9 NIV**. Please accept Jesus' offer to renew your mind and cast your cares upon Him instead of kicking against the goads. Restoration transforms us inwardly and outwardly and reflects strength, like a tree planted by the rivers of water.

A MADE-UP MIND

God commands His leaders to strive for excellence; it's essential. Leaders come prepared to serve the Lord and others, regardless of circumstances. People look to those in charge for stability and trust, and God wants us to be secure and adamant visionaries. Our children need consistency in parenting and guidance, too. Whether they are ten or fifty, they always need you. Almighty God desires us to be reliable spouses, friends, and companions. He wants us to make clear, firm decisions and to keep our word whenever possible. When we provide care to those struggling, our steadiness brings calm. A leader's clarity and stability help ease anxieties and turmoil, strengthening those facing difficulties or needing encouragement or support.

We will deeply connect with them as we offer our understanding and assistance with genuine kindness and compassion. Therefore, God wants His children to be unwavering and sure about their decisions and actions and how everything they do affects others. Maintaining control over situations and holding firm to your answers help maintain necessary boundaries. Let your yay be yay so as not to confuse. "But let your communication be, Yea, yea; Nay, nay: for whatsoever is more than these cometh of evil" **Matthew 5:37 KJV**.

An impoverished, doubtful, fearful, traumatized, and unstable mind leads to poor and hazardous businesses and relationships. If one is in the desert when we belong in the Promised Land, we can't help the people we're meant to help. The company will not succeed because the foundation is vulnerable and can break at any time. As Christ's followers, we can commit to changing our beliefs. We can plan ahead for handling situations that occur often and typically throw us off track. That's why Paul encourages us to think about *whatsoever*. "Finally, brethren, whatsoever things are true, whatsoever things are honest, whatsoever things are just, whatsoever things are pure, whatsoever things are lovely, whatsoever things are of good report; if there be any virtue, and if there be any praise, think on these things" **Philippians 4:8 KJV**. We've allowed our thoughts to enslave and hold us captive by invisible chains and mental partitions for too long, but that can shift when meditating on noble things. When we deliberately exercise and pivot to life-giving thoughts, our lives follow.

NEW BIRTH – NEW MIND

Living for the Lord is a privilege, honor, and blessing. That's why glorifying God and maximizing our lives as believers are the goals. We have much work to do for the Lord, and the healthier we are spiritually and mentally, the better. "Jesus said I must work the works of Him who sent Me while it is day; the night is coming when no one can work" **John 9:4 NKJV**. We're unaware of how much time we have to fulfill the commands of our Lord. However, we know it's not long, so when presented with the opportunity to minister to others and articulate the truth with love and clarity, we want to be ready.

Now is not the time to follow everyone on your social feed for advice. Renewal is in the Holy Trinity alone. Therefore, we must invest time and remain dedicated to what leads to seeing change. For starters, we can focus on reading, studying, gathering, and organizing concentrated knowledge on a few subjects. Our main topic must be biblically based—no exceptions. Too many of my fellow brothers and sisters in Christ are misled with false doctrine and follow hireling heretic leaders who speak only about success, wealth, health, and prosperity. Preachers who focus on the doctrine of "self" and what one can gain from God are not true disciples. Engaging with them will continue hindering personal growth and transformation.

God's children are students of Scripture and defend the faith, which starts with allocating time to genuine Bible study and building a library of supporting resources. As you know, I was going down the world's path to success, and God snatched me out! I learned that some of the positive thinking, affirmations, business, and self-help content could contain hints of occult and witchcraft practices to use your mind to manifest what you want. Think about it. These uber-successful people have an energy around them that causes others to be mesmerized, want to be like them, and chase their success. When we aren't grounded in truth, we can unknowingly run off after these uber-rich men and money. The Lord wants us to be followers of His first, which leads to renewed thinking and moving on from the past. Unhindered philosophy from so-called pastors, success and business gurus, leaders, and undisciplined learning give the devil room to play around in the mind. We no longer want random information but focused data.

To remove passive unintentional education, begin organizing your thoughts in a way that helps you become a subject matter authority and strengthens your brain and memory. Start with a few topics you love or need help with, like parenting or prayer, and want to understand more clearly and incorporate repetition into your learning. Then, schedule time in your week to examine the subjects and take notes. Re-read and restudy the same books, notes, and resources, then move on to new ones. And the Holy Spirit will begin showing you new Scriptures and resources that coincide with your discoveries. Your learnings will always lead you to an overall understanding of the Bible.

We can explore so many facets and depths within the Word of God. For instance, my dad loves studying the Bible, but the subjects that light him up and help him to gather reference points are teaching and explaining sound doctrine, prophetic books, and Israel. Yours may be theology, doctrines of the Bible, apologetics, Hebrew or Greek text, Paul's epistles, a specific book of the Bible, archeology, ancient culture, discernment, wisdom literature, or an array of other topics. You'll then begin to see the renewal of the mind and notice how simpler it becomes to build on a topic, articulate your views, and remember things, historical facts, and quotes because you have reference points where you're building your knowledge base.

We struggle to retain things when passively listening to information from many voices on social platforms, podcasts, and friends. When we acquire information absent from implementation, it evades transformation and acceleration because it's not rooted within the foundation. For example, imagine someone starting to explore habits, productivity, and goal-setting topics. They've binge-watched a lot of content on social media and feel incredibly motivated. Eager to share their newfound knowledge, they tell everyone about habits, productivity techniques, and goal-setting strategies. They even launch a YouTube channel to teach others. The problem is that they're acquiring random information from everyone everywhere but aren't seeing change because they've yet to be the person they're attempting to become. They're unaware of the foundation on which these ideas are built, yet they try to teach and lead without first studying and applying the necessary knowledge. However, it's only a matter of time before they're frustrated, as their advice lacks the depth of years of consistency and experience, and it hasn't been adequately tested and firmly rooted. This overflow of unorganized data leads to a myriad of unstructured and incomplete contemplations, distancing them further from articulating value from truth, lived experiences, and the change they so desperately seek. For this reason, I want you to start by building your roots for any topic in truth, then branch out and stack your knowledge base by applying it to your life first.

GUARD YOUR HEART

I love those shepherding pastors and ministers who protect the flock and expose false prophets, apostles, heretics, hirelings, and wolves. The Bible says in **Proverbs 4:23 NIV**, "Above all else, guard your heart, for everything you do flows from it." Our essence streams from our hearts. Do you allow unvetted strangers into your home, risking harm to your family and pets? So, why allow destructive and offensive thoughts to bombard your beautiful mind? Your mind isn't the devil's or anyone's playground or garbage dump. Therefore, the devil and his uninvited guests cannot drop off their junk here and set up puppet strings. If they've already erected forts, evict them! You're responsible for protecting your heart and teaching those you love to defend theirs. Invasive thoughts can no longer divide and conquer partitions in your thinking that keep you from living fully in Christ.

Claim your territory and teach others to do the same by setting boundaries against toxic opinions, manners, mindsets, attitudes, and manipulative behaviors. If your thoughts are unconstructive, refuse to try harmonizing them with an artificial reality; instead, stick to the facts.

Challenge and quarantine every belief to see if they're from God. "The weapons of our warfare are not physical [weapons of flesh and blood]. Our weapons are divinely powerful for the destruction of fortresses. ⁵ *We are* destroying sophisticated arguments and every exalted *and* proud thing that sets itself up against the [true] knowledge of God, and *we are* taking every thought *and* purpose captive to the obedience of Christ" **2 Corinthians 10:4-5 AMP**. Put your thoughts in a lineup like a detective does at a police station! Now, please point out the counterfeits, lock them up without a trial, and throw away the key.

If you get bombarded with questions like, "Why am I doing this?" "This project is never going to work." "I'm a terrible husband/wife." "Nobody cares or likes me." "Who do I think I am to run this business?" "God won't come through financially!" "This is going to fail." "I'm unqualified." "I should quit." "Nobody will buy this or show up." "I can't do this." "I can't remember anything." Henry Ford said, "Whether you think you can, or if you think you can't, you're right either way." We must not make God to be a liar. If He calls you to it, He will see you through it. The Scripture says, "For as he thinketh in his heart, so is he" **Proverbs 23:7 KJV**. Ask Jesus to rebuke the devil for attempting to plant his corrupt seeds. If anything you experience in word or deed doesn't align with God's character and teachings, you'll immediately identify the carnal mind or adversary as the culprit.

RESET

A purpose-driven business is born from a new spirit and renovated attitudes. Life from this level unlocks conviction in the impossible and seeing things we wouldn't ordinarily imagine if we didn't take Jesus' yoke. In submission, your capability is waiting to burst out of you and impact the marketplace. Reset your reasoning today by adopting a biblical worldview and running everything by the Word of God's filter. Your customers, clients, readers, subscribers, and patrons are waiting for you to appear solid. I know it gets tough, but you're resilient and not alone because God sends angels, shepherds, fellow brothers and sisters, and helpers to assist. The body of Christ takes care of itself. Your family in the faith is watchful, vigilant, discerning, and alert, standing firm with the whole armor of God. When you change your thoughts, your life aligns.

Acceleration CURE Actions:

- **Ask** God to rejuvenate your mind each morning so that you clarify your thoughts and commit to the wellness of your soul.
- **Journal** and take inventory of your unsuitable thoughts, focusing on the transformational suitable ones to get unstuck and unshackled from old hindrances. For instance, if you have a dialogue that says, "I can't do this. It's too hard." Replace it with a statement like, "I can accomplish anything God's plans for me."
- **Reclaim** your mindset from the evil one, refuse double-mindedness, rewrite what you want to see according to God's promises, and what reignites you to lower your neck. Ask God to plant seeds of love, faith, and the willingness to change.
- **Effectively** execute a daily reading plan for spiritual growth and other topics you like, which enriches your endurance and helps you to build reference points from the foundation for better learning and memory.

Prayer

Dear Heavenly Father, thank you for blessing me with a sound mind that you're renewing and transforming in every way. Train me to stop giving up mental territory to the evil one. Please help me take every thought captive that doesn't belong here. Show me in your Word where I can begin studying to grow in the knowledge of God, lower my neck, bring about a transformation, and maximize my potential and memory in concentrated areas of study. I want to think more like you and serve with a clear mind and a loving heart. I want to be stable and unmovable, with a solid foundation rooted in truth. Please bless me so I can support others who need strengthening in their decisions and mindsets.

In Jesus' name, I pray, Amen.

Day 14

MOVE FORWARD FROM THE PAST

My mind housed these internal arguments before I started writing *The Acceleration Cure*. Bruisings from my past disabled me from discerning a newfound reality. "Lord, what if I fail—*again*?" "What if I start something new and it doesn't work out—*again*?" "Lord, I didn't always have consistent financial success in business, so why do I think the same collapses won't happen—*again*?" "Yet I have another hidden project people can't discover—*again*?" "Who wants to hear my story—*Lord*?" "But God, many people don't read books or blogs."

"Nonetheless, as I meditated on the famous stories of faith in the Bible, I hid in the All-Knowing God and took Him at His Word! When The Almighty asks us to do a thing, our role as His ambassadors is to obey Him reverently because He's our Sovereign and knows everything. We trust in His omnipotence, supremacy, sufficiency, and wisdom, not our finite power and plans. But God chooses the lowly things that don't make sense to others to humble them. "God chose the weak things of the world to shame the strong" **1 Corinthians 1:27 NIV**. Through obedience and faith, we advance from the former written chapters of our lives into the new unwritten parts and uncharted territories on this journey and gift of life.

Accelerated Power – Isaiah 43:18-19 NIV "Forget the former things; don't dwell on the past. See, I'm doing a new thing! Now it springs up; do you not perceive it? I'm making a way in the wilderness and streams in the wasteland."

During Israel's captivity in Babylon, this passage is one of God's beautiful promises to encourage His people through the prophet Isaiah. The Lord God wanted to do something original when He returned them to their land after exiling them into confinement. Forgetting their former and looking to fresh things is what they had to look forward to. God promised also to cause dead, dry bones to live, as He presented through the prophet Ezekiel. "Then he said to me, 'Prophesy to these bones and say to them, 'Dry bones, hear the word of the LORD!' ⁵ This is what the Sovereign LORD says to these bones: 'I will make breath enter you, and you will come to life. ⁶ I will attach tendons to you and make flesh come upon you and cover you with skin; I will put breath in you, and you will come to life. Then you will know that I am the LORD'" **Ezekiel 37:4-6 NIV.**

Although God hates sin, He kept His Word—His covenant to His chosen people and promised restoration. They got exiled because they needed humbling from their terrible sinful ways and prostituting themselves to other nations, sacrificing their children to Moloch, and idol worship. The Lord Almighty still has a plan for the nation of Israel because His love and covenant are unconditional, and He stands by His unbreakable Word. He didn't throw them away and move on from them to the church permanently, as some believers think with replacement theology. They still have a prophetical place in God's plan, and a remnant is preserved (Zechariah 12:9-11, Psalm 122:6, Romans 11:1-2, 25). The body of Christ and Israel are separate. God loved His people and proclaimed a *new thing*. He still loves and protects them while neighboring enemies block them on every side (see more on *Day 26, Determine Your Location*). Likewise, just as God loves and has a plan for them, He loves you too and gives you a purpose. The Almighty God uses your past losses and faults to establish a brighter future (Romans 8:28).

ANALYSIS

You may have started some personal goals that didn't quite pan out. You may have tried to lose weight, tear down a stronghold of lust, drugs, alcohol, smoking, gambling, anger, even overcome brokenness, childhood or relational trauma, better your marriage, or finish a degree. A natural disaster, illness, injury, divorce, guilt, shame, or unexpected loss may have bound you to your past. There may be a dream God gave you decades ago that's yet to materialize. The COVID-19 crisis might have provoked drastic changes overall and tarnished your growth plans. You may have started multiple unsuccessful organizations that didn't work. Instead of acceleration, you decelerated. You had to shut it down, downsize, rebrand, sell your assets, or run back to living with your parents or sleep on a friend's couch in the basement. When you started and launched your services, you dreamed of being highly successful and making a profit, as nobody ever starts a company with a vision for failure, and now you're swimming in debt.

You prayed, cried, begged, and fasted for your business to work—yet your breakthrough never came. You advertised, marketed, consulted with other business owners, hired a coach, networked, invested in courses, unloaded all your savings, took out lines of credit, and planned for success—but nothing worked in your favor. Ultimately, you had mounting debt, failed/strained relationships, and nothing tangible to show for your efforts. You probably had to beg someone to hire you in a low-paying job to get back on your feet like I did.

Before I restarted my art business in 2017, I had a heartbreak with the company and my first ministry in 2015. I had to shut down and pivot and needed help sorting out my next steps, so I moved in with a Christian family—Richard and Shannon Taylor. She is a sister in ministry who graciously blessed and allowed me to stay with them for a few months. The loss of business and ministry hurt me because I was fighting for what God wanted me to do. I needed all this extra space and room to do the mission, but God wasn't allowing me to do the work.

Like me, now, God is calling you to do something risky—*again*! The Lord will often test our obedience, faith, attitude, and character through a business or relationship that's not intended to make it. He will also use them to hold up a mirror to destroy pride, ungodly character, insecurities, selfish desires, greed, and wrong motives.

Switching income brackets was equally brutal, and my heart was sick. My former employer had a strict non-compete clause, and once my fire dwindled in that industry, it was hard to get back in. I took one job with a three-hour interview process and had to take FBI fingerprints and background checks to make $10 an hour at a compliance company after earning $80k a year in sales.

We must pick up the pieces and move on when the dust settles. It was painful to say goodbye to the dreams I pursued, and watching my businesses and ministry crash fractured me. The experiences felt like an emotionally sickened, broken heart and a bad breakup. When you know that God calls you to higher, there's never a regular job that'll ever fill that void, no matter how much they pay you because you're a purpose-driven believer. Nothing satisfies the heart of an unfulfilled longing.

Sadly, many don't teach that we must still grieve over broken hearts from failed hopes and dreams—this is still sorrow. **Proverbs 13:12 NIV** says, "Hope deferred makes the heat sick, but a longing fulfilled is a tree of life." When what we expect isn't realized, we can feel unworthy. When we don't deal with the wounds from our past, it creates a massive sinkhole and dangerous insecurities. When we're not profitable from our endeavors, it's distressing. Yes, the purpose is more significant than money, but money answers all things. Money expands the mission and provides what we need to maintain a business. That's why so many people ditch their God-given purpose and work jobs due to the level of suffering involved and the stable income they need to live. No wonder many are still stuck, afraid, and unable to accelerate! **Ecclesiastes 10:19 NIV** says, "A feast is made for laughter, wine makes life merry, and money is the answer for everything." Although it may feel like your best life to gain all the material things, it's really a losing and settled life if you never discover your purpose and build the faith to live it out.

After each downfall, you're never the same. But you should *never* be the same after your experiences, good or bad. Without the valleys, we'd have no idea how to appreciate the mountain peaks and our purpose. We must take responsibility for what we can. We can't escape the hardships by being selfish, discontent, bitter, and unhappy with our lives. Because in the valley, we discover beauty we can't see in the mountains. We connect with people we'd never see otherwise. What doesn't break us makes us into what the Father wants us to be—which is more Christlike and represents His glory. Remember that the marriage, relationship, or business failed—not you! God has to destroy, shatter, and fracture your sand-filled foundation to rebuild and grow your faith upon His solid Rock. And He will give you the power to cross the bridge and get to the splendor on the other side. God tests your resilience, integrity, and character to know if you genuinely desire and can handle what you prayed for. Remember, the dream must die for it to live and multiply. Elohim doesn't skip steps to prepare you for your assignment. The rich experiences you gained, the wisdom He deposited, and your leap of faith set you apart from the average person because you kept going. You discover your purpose and identity in the lows of life, not the highs. Sometimes, our plans don't work out even when we do everything right and obey God because we're not the right person at the opportune time. But you're still building a legacy and eternal rewards—true riches. You can use your past wins and losses to plan better. We still have to grow to become the servant leader the Lord sees, and we're not quite there. We're still being metamorphosed from the caterpillar to the butterfly—a spiritually mature us.

PRESS IN

It's dangerous to drive a race car looking backward. Yes, we are individuals of our past to a degree, but what's behind us doesn't have to define us. Living in the past is equally threatening when the Holy Spirit attempts to renew and cure your soul. Can a runner race by looking back? Certainly not! That's why the Apostle Paul compared the Christian life to a race and encouraged us to look ahead and keep pressing towards the mark (1 Corinthians 9:24-25, Philippians 3:14). The angels instructed Lot's wife not to look back when fleeing the destruction of Sodom and Gomorrah. But she turned into a pillar of salt because she stopped and turned around to see the destruction. She disobeyed the command by refusing to listen amid devastation because, in her eyes, looking back was more important than her survival. "As soon as they had brought them out, one of them said, 'Flee for your lives! Don't look back, and don't stop anywhere in the plain! Flee to the mountains or you will be swept away!'" "But Lot's wife looked back, and she became a pillar of salt" **Genesis 19:17, 26 NIV.**

Unfortunately, Lot's wife couldn't help but reminisce and think about all she was fleeing from to her detriment. Unless you want your dreams, relationships, and desires to halt, God commands you to look up and ahead. You're not even the same person you were three, five, ten, or thirty years ago. You did the best you could with what you knew then. You'll have to rest in the God of all compassion to release the horrific trauma from failure, abuse, and the pain of loss. The King calls you a victor. Our life depends on us looking ahead. By taking the accelerated route, you can access everything you need to know about business through Christ's wisdom. We need a new outlook because too many believers are enslaved to their past.

Start fresh with God and your business, and add new learnings, skills, and practices to your memory bank. Become a student of God's Word and sound doctrine. Read new books, grow more profoundly with a few specific topics, minimize TV and social media time, and make time for personal growth. The times and technology are changing drastically, and the Holy Spirit wants you to catch up so that your life and business can survive some things that He can see ahead. The past isn't always bad because it can help you remember the good times and why you love being an entrepreneur. Be delighted with yourself because you went after your dream and did things you have never done before, and that's commendable! You may have lost many *things*, but nobody can ever take away the elevated experience you gained through such a life-changing process. You can always make more money and replace most of what's lost. However, a robust prayer life, obedience, faith, and wisdom are acquired through sacrifice.

SURVIVORS ARE VICTORIOUS

I'm personally attracted to fighters, survivors, and underdogs who got back up to conquer and take what's theirs through God's promises. They walk by faith and not sight. That's another reason I love God's Word; it's full of these victorious stories from our fellow Old and New Testament brothers and sisters. And I love learning about people's courage, survival, and overcoming stories. Even **Revelation** shares in **21:8 NIV**, "But the cowardly, the unbelieving…will be consigned to the fiery lake of burning sulfur." That's why God constantly teaches us to fear not and to live by faith. We don't shrink back ever—regardless of embarrassment or hurtful things we survived in the past. People want to follow great, courageous leaders who inspire and have survived things through the testing of their faith and fiery trials. You're a leader, and God desires you to get up and encourage others to accelerate with your story for His glory.

God's children are the standard; we live up to that identity daily. We should never need to fit in with the world or compare our gifts or success with others because we're a peculiar people. Jesus is coming back for the fighter. We're not victims of our past but overcomers with an eternal, glorious future. We're here to fight through what Satan tried to use to destroy us. We're here to boldly share the good news of Christ's salvation and second return because this world and everything in it will soon pass. John shares, "Then I saw 'a new heaven and a new earth,' for the first heaven and the first earth had passed away, and there was no longer any sea" **Revelation 21:1, 27 NIV**. "Nothing impure will ever enter it, nor will anyone who does what is shameful or deceitful, but only those whose names are written in the Lamb's book of life."

Make sure your name is in the book, and be careful not to let the negative experiences from your past reinforce terrible practices, paralyze you with fear, keep you from trying again, cause anxiety and depression, and block the new next-level vision God wants you to see. The devil is a liar, and he wants to do all in his power to make you discouraged. You can't let him destroy your vision. In Christ, we never lose because we're hidden in the resurrected King. God spared you through your bruised past and temporary scars. Our history is a step up the mountain and toward finishing the race. Everything you survived gave you more wisdom to apply to life and business. Now it's time to go onward and teach the people all you know so they can move others with the truth. Learn your lessons and fight for your dreams.

SOMETHING NEW

Often, we look for God to do things for us the same way He did something in our lives years ago. And He possibly may, but when we think we have it figured out by connecting dots from our past, we put limits on Him and stagnate our faith. Hmmmm, are we forgetting all He made in just six days per the book of Genesis? Limiting our unlimited God means we're not living a purposeful, faith-driven life of acceleration. God is limitless and creative. He can do something different for each of us in a fresh way. Our God will give us a new beginning. He is the God that can part the seas and make paths in the wilderness and wastelands. We can never forget the beginning, as it's the foundation for everything else while also perceiving newness!

No believer should ever live an average life. God didn't save you to fit in because you're in a foreign world that wars against your soul (1 Peter 2:11). He deployed and gave you a light to shine bright for His purposes on top of a hill. The former is gone. You can't bring it back! Last year and last month were not your best days, but today is what you have. So, are you doing the best you can today? Whatever happened or didn't happen years ago, last month, or yesterday—let it go now!

Want better, healthier, loving relationships—be the change you want to see. For God's sake, serve, love, compliment, and support people wholeheartedly. Today is a new day. Do you not perceive it? You have everything in you to succeed, bottled up in faith. If you're not living your life—live now! If you're not connecting with a beautiful family of fellow saints in a local congregation—see how you can get planted. If you haven't pursued your dream or are scared to try again—dream big! Get excited to share the gospel and tell people the truth in love because you love them. Everything you do for the Lord counts, and you're storing rewards in heaven each day you obey God and do His will. Start fresh with God's approval as a fruitful and faithful believer. Be prepared in and out of season to live an abundant life. You'll see restoration from what the locust devoured and grab ahold of your acceleration cure. When you do it this time, do it as a more mature and extensive version of yourself. Press forward! Almighty God is doing *a new thing*.

Acceleration CURE Actions:

- **Take** responsibility and accountability for your contributions to your past. Start fresh today by committing to daily change and clarifying your direction by making new, happy memories.

- **Refuse** to meditate on what's behind you or compare your past to your current situation. Have faith in the Chief Cornerstone—the foundation of Jesus Christ to build your present and future on the Rock to get unshackled and unstuck. Dedicate the rest of your life to your best work.

- **Thank** the Redeemer for delivering, keeping, and giving you a fresh start, survival strength, and the ability to reignite your dreams, discover your purpose, and rewrite the vision. Find hope in knowing that God has new things planned.

- **Enrich** others and endure life graciously. Look deep into your past to see what beautiful gems you can extract from those experiences (good or bad) to glorify God.

Prayer

Dear Heavenly Father, Thank you for my past experiences in life and business. I'm grateful for the mountains and valleys. I had some great victories and moments during those years and some that I do not care to remember. Nonetheless, I've learned so much about you and myself, and I'll use those lessons and memories for the better. Sometimes, I feel that this business is headed for failure because I see some of the same patterns from my past. Seeing old ways makes me anxious and fearful because I don't want to fail again. I know you didn't bring me this far to have history repeat itself similarly. Therefore, please help me focus on what I see ahead and stop comparing my current circumstances to my past. Give me fresh insight, renewed capabilities, deeper relationships, and an excellent business outlook. I want to move forward to bigger and better things. Lord, don't let my prior experiences go to waste. Use the losses to provide me the wisdom to grow and help others. You commanded me to press forward, and I'm asking for your help. Please allow me to trust your plan.

In Jesus' name, I pray, Amen.

Day 15
PRACTICE SELF-DISCIPLINE

Why do some people excel at learning, explaining, and teaching the Bible, leading an accelerated and results-driven prayer life, living boldly and joyfully by faith, managing and growing their finances, and staying fit and active while others struggle for decades in these same areas? Instead of progressing, they find themselves in a cycle of starting and stopping but never reaching their goals. It simply comes down to a lifestyle of self-discipline. Those who have mastered their habits make it look easy because they've developed routines and spiritual disciplines to excel in their non-negotiable areas. They arrange times for daily Bible reading, study, and prayer time. Planning meals, eating well, and prioritizing health, wellness, sleep, and exercise are firm. Saving, investing, delayed gratification, and financial literacy are inflexible. Obeying God and trusting Him by faith is immutable. These habits separate high achievers from low achievers. These individuals go through the same things as everyone else but commit to God and themselves by ditching excuses and doing the hard thing anyway. George Washington Carver says, "Ninety-nine percent of the failures come from people who have the habit of making excuses." [1] Rain or shine, good days and bad, win or lose, they know although you can't change circumstances, self-discipline and self-control can overpower any deficit and override any defense.

Entrepreneurs recognize the immense value and challenges of building a business from the ground up, often sacrificing revenue for months. What distinguishes amateurs from true professionals is their ability to craft organized systems and schedules that seamlessly integrate into their daily lives. On the contrary, some people I've engaged with are excited to leave their jobs to build their dreams full-time. They're ecstatic to work on their custom schedule and terms because of the freedom it offers. However, I found that the excitement wears down after around sixty days. Those individuals normally underestimated the preparation and intense work involved in getting acclimated to building their responsibilities and finances around having more time on their hands. They don't realize that autonomy comes at a high cost. The employer's structure is a valuable asset in preparation for building a successful business. So, when we daydream about starting an endeavor at a day job, we must do our best in that role first. Wherever we find ourselves, we're still accountable to God for our work.

One of the biggest lessons I appreciated from working jobs is how they taught me daily structure and how to show up when I didn't feel like it. My roles taught me effective communication with leadership, peers, customers, and clients. The jobs we dislike are training grounds that stretch us higher because they teach us to keep commitments and honor our word. It teaches us how to push through stresses, illness, complaints, complications, setbacks, and negative emotions because they develop us spiritually and mentally. When believers handle their existing jobs as businesses, they set themselves up for acceleration. Doing the labor the employer hired us to carry out requires clearness of long-term goals, ownership, commitment, and dedication.

The dedicated believers wake up and do things despite not feeling like it, which separates them from the average. And since we're devoted, God wants us to show up to the best of our ability. Focus, persistence, perseverance, endurance, priorities, habits, commitment, and self-discipline carry beyond sickness and health because they're faith-driven actions. When we ask the Holy Spirit for help, He overrides our weaknesses with sufficient grace, and we get the aid we pray for. The Almighty God's power makes self-control readily available for us to progress into our commission because the mission doesn't stop.

Remember, God knows our hearts and everything we're doing (or not doing). Discipline is where our relationship with God accelerates, thus removing laziness and procrastination. Develop grit to eliminate distractions like time and money-wasting activities. Without strong-mindedness, structure, systems, organization, and grind before starting a corporation, it affects all we do. We must be the leaders, coaches, consultants, or managers we want to hire. Based on your disciplines, are you the right person to build a six-figure or million-dollar business, or are you a great idler?

Accelerated Power – Proverbs 18:9 KJV He also that is slothful in his work is brother to him that's a great waster.

Solomon told the sluggard (slothful, lazy, idle, and inactive person) to consider the ways of the ants. They don't have a commander but work hard in unison to reach a unifying goal. "Go to the ant, thou sluggard; consider her ways, and be wise: ⁷ Which having no guide, overseer, or ruler, ⁸ Provideth her meat in the summer, and gathereth her food in the harvest" **Proverbs 6:6-8 KJV.** Self-discipline is continually gathering what's needed to increase and flourish in your purpose. The servant who hid his talent by refusing to put the manager's resources to work was considered wicked and lazy (Matthew 25:26) (see more on *Day 25, Sell It*).

Time and self-control are gifts. But sloth is the companion to procrastination and squandering. Therefore, we steward time and resources like we budget money. For example, planning our habits, routines, activities, priorities, and goals weekly for maximum productivity is budgeting. Likewise, how we manage our money reflects how we value our time. For example, the time I invest in creating income is precious because I can't get it back.

On the contrary, when I spend or give money, I devote it to people, places, things, and ideas that extend value to me and others. When people clock into their jobs, the manager looks at time as a commodity that needs tracking. When we stand before Christ's throne, He will ask for an accounting too. So, I ask, how are you keeping up with your time? Do you know what you did today down to the hour? The Creator's breath keeps us alive to do things He purposed for us before the earth's foundation. Therefore, time is one of our greatest assets because what we do with it matters eternally. When we number our days, we plan effectively and break from the average. "So teach us to number our days, that we may apply our hearts unto wisdom" **Psalm 90:12 KJV.**

FEELINGS LED

Feelings are emotional gauges and barometers that prick the heart and alert the soul. They're beneficial for several reasons because they strengthen discernment. Although emotions are great, and we must pay attention to them, we can't live solely by them as a primary source of decision-making. If we do, they will dictate and rule our lives. As believers, we're fruit inspectors. We qualify people by the type of fruit someone produces—paying attention to what they do, not what they say. Likewise, discipline means taking action and following through on our commitments, regardless of how we feel. It's doing the opposite of what we *feel* like doing. It's taking the long way instead of a shortcut.

Think back to when you accomplished something you didn't want to do. How did you feel? Also, do you remember feeling ecstatic and capable when you achieved something you once struggled with or thought was impossible? You eat the apple instead of the chips. You make the sales call instead of ending the day. You write another chapter instead of binging YouTube. You work out instead of going home to relax. Instead of scrolling on social apps, you prayed and listened to your audio Bible. Victories are won in the mind, one choice at a time.

Inefficient habits won't disappear independently. We must settle to stop them and no longer live solely by our feelings. We must pay the cost to be the boss, starting with reestablishing and solidifying our daily meditations. Righteousness is living in alignment with our words, and we become unstoppable when our actions match our intentions. Intentionality means training ourselves to do what we usually won't and patiently delay gratification for later rewards. Whatever you gain from moving too quickly emotionally, in the short term, you'll have to pay for it long-term.

Our self-discipline ties into every area of our lives. It's a question of who's in control—the new you or your moods and justifications. The Apostle Paul said, "No, I strike a blow to my body and make it my slave so that after I have preached to others, I myself will not be disqualified for the prize" **1 Corinthians 9:27 NIV**. Paul exercised faith and discipline mastery over his feelings and body. We must strengthen our minds by speaking the opposite of negative thoughts with the truth. For example, if I get an idea that says, "Just quit." I'll say, "God didn't tell me to quit!" When the Spirit of God strengthens the inner man, the outpour of controlled power fuels the soul and reinforces the mind. Without complete reliance on the Lord, we cannot overcome excuses, procrastination, gluttony, strongholds, and impatience.

I recommend spiritual fasting, from at least one meal for a few days, to strengthen the spirit. During your fast, pick a book in the Bible, such as Romans, James, Galatians, or Scriptures related to areas you struggle with. If you pick certain verses, I advise you to read the full chapter for context and investigate the cross references highlighted with small letters in the footnotes. Do word studies on those passages by looking up the original meaning in Hebrew or Greek. Then, look at all of the dictionary definitions and synonyms. Then drill down the insight into a summary paragraph. The in-depth studies help strengthen your spiritual disciplines tremendously and gather you closer to your dreams. God is for you and wants you to get understanding. Always consider that God strengthens and tests you but never sets you up to fail. He's doing everything for your good.

DISCIPLINE AND LUST

Nothing can cause stuckness more than sexual sins that burn within. They hinder progress in every area of our lives because it's done inside the body. Its fleshly boldness grieves the Spirit and contaminates our witness. The Bible teaches us to "Flee from sexual immorality. All other sins a person commits are outside the body, but whoever sins sexually, sins against their own body" **1 Corinthians 6:18 NIV**. People think they're self-disciplined because they're strong in fitness, diet, financial provision, and business. They appear successful and charismatic outwardly but are spiritually bankrupt if engaging in adultery and sexual sins, which erode their character, integrity, witness, blessings, and connection with God. Someone who hasn't surrendered their body and mind to God is hazardous and dangerous because their behavior links them to all kinds of depravity and perversion.

If you're facing these things, you must decide if you will continue or choose to surrender fully to God as He will bring you out of bondage. You'll first need genuine repentance, then offensive and defensive spiritual warfare tactics to handle temptations. You then want to submit your urges to the Holy Spirit as pre-determined non-negotiables and set up guard rails for spiritual success through accountability. There are verses and Christian books to help overcome these sexual struggles. For additional resources, visit your local Christian bookstore or online stores like Christianbook.com.

NON-NEGOTIABLES

Now that we've looked at some hindrances to a self-disciplined life, now what? Wearing many hats until the venture grows enough to hire skilled help requires steadfastness, so accounting in advance for how you will keep pushing starts with plans b and c now. At the beginning of your entrepreneurship journey, you work harder for yourself than you'll ever work for anyone. When exhaustion wraps around you like a heavy blanket, and the anticipated influx of revenue fails to materialize as hoped, will you work and find the strength to persevere? How will you navigate those challenging times when setbacks overshadow your efforts? What strategies will you employ during those problematic seasons to keep moving forward? Will you trust God and keep going?

What about your health? When it rains or snows on the day of your outdoor workout, do you have a backup for an indoor plan? What will you do when you can't reach the grocery store for healthy foods and meal prep? Consider your spiritual life. When you miss church or a Bible study day, can you listen to your audio Bible and at least watch a sermon instead?

Despite our most well-laid plans and intentions, there are times when life's unpredictability can lead us astray for extended periods, no matter how self-disciplined we are. Falling off can occur even when we fully commit to our goals and have a solid strategy. It's all too easy to get sidetracked by unforeseen circumstances, daily distractions, or simply the ebb and flow of our Christian walk, resulting in weeks of drifting away from our intended path. So, to soften the blow of living off track in the long term, we can try our best to determine our non-negotiables now. Why? If not, these repeated crashes in the areas we want to thrive and conquer can erode our integrity, self-confidence, and self-image if we're not careful. But knowing that you will fall off sometimes helps you pick back up and move forward quickly instead of nursing your wounds and feeling sorry for not doing your best.

To override identity blindness, we must show up now as the people we want to hire and do business with. God wants you to be dedicated, committed, consistent, diligent, devoted, and stable—and you can do it when you rely on Him. The Lord rewards faith and consistency as they are central to the acceleration cure. Spiritual disciplines are top-tier when navigating through the call of your life. Prayer, fasting, reading, studying, Scripture memory, meditation, and solitude are necessary for every Christian business owner.

The Almighty God wants you to turn to Him for your daily strength and provision. However, whenever you need help, the Holy Spirit will instantly override your inabilities and advance you through the times that will appear impossible, but it starts with discipline.

God is always the Leader! He's from whom we get our commission orders. If you're called to entrepreneurship, He only uses a job as a prerequisite and a training ground to bring us to a place where we can fulfill our life purpose. We can't bypass curriculum, fundamentals, core foundational teachings, principles, laws, sowing, planting, harvesting, and seasons in God's economy.

If you pass the lessons you're to learn in your pre-training—and prioritize discipline and winning habits, God will make room for your business acceleration full-time by His design. Joseph, Moses, Joshua, David, Esther, Paul, Peter, John, and many others underwent divine training, and so must we.

Self-discipline and consistency start with our desire to grow our knowledge and relationship with God. Entry into His presence and commitments eliminates slothfulness, feelings-based living, lustful desires, and unaligned agendas. Reliability with God sets us up for success in every area of our lives and businesses. Imagine self-discipline in spiritual and soul growth, prayer, obligations, workout routines, eating habits, follow-up sales calls, and monthly bookkeeping.

We can accomplish above and beyond when the fruit of the Holy Spirit's self-control and self-discipline is present. We can do nothing unless we remain hidden in Christ. Jesus states, "Remain in me, as I also remain in you. No branch can bear fruit by itself; it must remain in the vine. Neither can you bear fruit unless you remain in me" **John 15:4 NIV**.

God holds His children to higher standards than the world may suppose. Saints depend and rely on the Lord God! If you feel depleted, bounce back into alignment with the Lord for sustenance and restoration. If you're distracted, get back up and restart again. Track the time spent on work and personal tasks and activities. If you're still at a job, dedicate a couple of hours each day to work on your goals to transition into your calling. Hire a coach if necessary and connect with an accountability partner. Jesus Christ rose from the dead with all power in His hands (1 Corinthians 15:4). Surely He can fuel your discipline.

REWRITE AND REINFORCE HABITS

Resolve that God is not causing failure in any area of life. Yes, He's sovereign, and His providence plays a role, but success is how you define it vs. how God does. You don't have to have much money or reach all your well-written goals and plans to succeed. God measures your success by faith and obedience. Additionally, our daily habits, choices, and decisions over the years, months, and days significantly influence the results we experience today and the outcomes we can expect tomorrow. Each small action contributes to a larger pattern that shapes our lives and ultimately determines our future. The new self-disciplined believer must take accountability and make peace with the past. Your future isn't found in the past, so you must embrace the new creation in Christ and move forward. You're never too old to dream. But your new beginning starts with you rewriting and reinforcing your practices today.

- Audit your current habits and see if they're beneficial by tracking your time and daily activities for one week.

- Eliminate all non-productive and corrupt patterns and find a replacement, such as a hobby, to keep you from going backward.

- Write all new habits. For example, write down everything, including, but not limited to, prayer and Bible study time, morning and night routines, exercise, chores, beauty/self-care/grooming, meal planning menus, date nights, time with the family and kids, meetings, appointments, phone calls, free time, and dog walks, etc.

Determine to live up to the best version of yourself by making every effort and attempt to add assurance—goodness—and understanding to your lifestyle. Assurance is confidence. Goodness is beneficial and right actions. And always get understanding. Strive to *OVERstand* and go deep into the things of God. **2 Peter 1:5-10 NIV** says, "For this very reason, make every effort to add to your faith goodness; and to goodness, knowledge; [6] and to knowledge, self-control; and to self-control, perseverance; and to perseverance, godliness; [7] and to godliness, mutual affection; and to mutual affection, love. [8] For if you possess these qualities in increasing measure, they will keep you from being ineffective and unproductive in your knowledge of our Lord Jesus Christ. ⁹But whoever does not have them is nearsighted and blind, forgetting that they have been cleansed from their past sins."

Acceleration CURE Actions:

- **Clarify** your non-negotiables by auditing your prior activities for one week. Highlight the areas where you struggle with self-discipline and control. Then, pray and create new habits based on your goals by committing to freshly structured daily routines you plan weekly.

- **Start** living purposefully and intentionally by writing down and tracking your time spent on routines and goals. Fill in the gaps with something beneficial like reading. Rely on the Spirit to get unstuck and unshackled from patterns contributing to your current situation.

- **Highlight,** rewrite, reignite, and focus on your top three non-negotiable daily priorities. If you do nothing else for the day, what are those three things *you will do*?

- **Dedicate** ten minutes each morning to meditate on one Scripture to help you establish and build enriching and enduring disciplines.

Prayer

Dear Heavenly Father, I need your help. I've struggled with being disciplined and inconsistent for years. I want to succeed in what I set out to do, but I get sidetracked, discouraged, tired, and overwhelmed. I sometimes make excuses and play the blame game because I don't feel energized enough to prioritize my goals and business when things aren't going as planned. I slack on my follow-through and fall short of my goals and commitments because sometimes I'm too tired to accomplish things or don't think I can. I have difficulty sticking to my calendar and plans for the day, week, and month. Old habits and mindsets keep me stuck. I'm better in some areas than I am in others. Lord, I want to be disciplined in my relationship with you and the business you blessed me with. I can't do this work on my own. I need the Holy Spirit to lead me. Please take my hand on this day and lead me to a fresh start with full potential. Protect me from sexual temptation and distractions. Please help me do my work even when I'm not fond of it. I never want to be a weak, wicked, and lazy servant.

In Jesus' name I pray, Amen.

Day 16
COMMIT TO CONSISTENCY

I whisked her from her comfort zone—the only home she'd known. As I drove from Alabama with my friend Cedric Pitts, I placed her in a box for the trip home. I named my 8-week-old blondish Cocker Spaniel, CoCo. I was so delighted to have her in my environment. But I had a demanding job of training and acclimating her to new surroundings. I was also on a medical break from work and about to buy my first home in five months. But since I wanted a dog to love and care for, I got her now so she could be ready for our move. She adapted to training quickly, but things didn't go as planned in successive months. CoCo acted out consistently when I finally returned to work. Although I'd always come home on lunch to care for her, she showed me during the evenings and on weekends how much she hated my schedule by doing bad things.

    I didn't know the enormity of the responsibility I was committing to when I got her, but I had to decide whether to work through the issue or keep her. I was torn and soon to close on my new construction townhome and concluded I couldn't provide the care she needed alone. The new address was a forty-five-minute to hour commute from Lawrenceville to Alpharetta, GA. I tried to work through it, but it wasn't the best for her.

    Regrettably, I didn't count the cost and long-term commitment before bringing her home. I kept my puppy for six months before selling her to my friends and business couple, the Ruffin's—Terrence and Nicole. They had the time as a team to invest in her care. Transferring ownership was for the best because she lived a long life of about fourteen years. Although my experience with wanting a pet as a single woman didn't work out, I loved having her for the time I did. She taught me valuable lessons about love, consistency, discipline, and commitment. Although I love dogs, I know how much you must be dedicated to caring for one alone. Therefore, we must count the cost in all we say *yes* to because constancy and devotion are vital to any undertaking or investment. Stability builds trust. Jesus Christ is the best example of One who counts the cost.

> **Accelerated Power – Hebrews 13:8 NIV** Jesus Christ is the same yesterday and today and forever.

The Lord is the very definition of consistency and commitment. There isn't a promise He doesn't keep. Our Chief Cornerstone is the Rock! Constant is His natural character. He can only be who He is in His perfect nature—immovable, steady, and secure. He's faithful, constant, reliable, dependable, and unfailing. He never changes because He's perfect, holy, and righteous. Yahweh is the forever enduring God.

He's not moody or unpredictable because He doesn't operate on feelings, as He's the same always. He stands by whatever He says and means, regardless of the changing times. His perfect gifts aren't running out of inventory or all over the place. "Every good gift and every perfect gift is from above, and cometh down from the Father of lights, with whom is no variableness, neither shadow of turning" **James 1:17 KJV**. Since the Creator fashioned us in His image, He wants us to be the same, too—authentic, consistent, and committed in character and word.

The Lord God wants our holiness to be associated with our name and business. Good ideas might easily and frequently flow into our minds, like getting a puppy now, but we must prioritize and vet notions to avoid interruptions to our commitments. Since God wants us to commit to whatever we start within His will and finish the task, we should only implement the new ideas if they make sense.

LONG-TERM DEDICATION

Sometimes, we start doing things without a long-term vision, so we commit based on our current evidence and circumstances. We stop building our prayer lives and leaning into the things of God because we don't see immediate results. We stop working on the things we assume aren't working because we don't see instant outcomes. But a purpose-driven business is a long game, and is not for the unattached. It can take years and decades to see the vision, but saying yes to God is a dedication to the journey, no matter how the story ends. It's disciplining our daily habits and routines to synchronize and align with the mandate God placed in our hearts when He deployed us. It looks like sacrificing and doing the hard things today to get to the benefits and rewards of tomorrow. Steadfastness is shifting with the ebbs and flows of life, going through test after trial and pivoting according to the detours. Commitment partners with intention and connects spiritual and personal disciplines to strengthen the inner man, thus letting the Holy Spirit direct thy paths.

Giving up isn't the first line of defense when depleted or worn down when you're loyal to years of what you've set out to do. Sometimes, life happens, and staying down for a few weeks sounds like a lot of downtime in the short term, but when playing a long game, it's not. Like developing any other skill, consistency is measured in years instead of weeks. It takes time and many attempts to get right, but if you don't give up trying, you'll get better as the years progress. Devotion looks like resting spiritually and physically when needed to recover and reenergize for the next season of tests and triumphs. We keep momentum without breaking the pace by reevaluating the plan and reequipping for what's ahead. Still, I discovered you'll always produce your best work when your efforts align with your gifts.

DEVOTION TO GOD AND PURPOSE

Sometimes, the things that we're doing don't appear to be aligned with our dreams, but it doesn't mean that they aren't a part of the experience God wants us to have. My puppy experience helped me to love and care for God's creation. My business losses built my faith and stamina, then led me to my purpose. I also did many jobs over the years that I didn't necessarily care to do, but God used those proficiencies to help me in what I'm doing today. Nothing is wasted if you focus on pleasing God and doing your best with what you have today. Learning to adjust allows a faith-filled life that builds consistency.

However, I want you to think more about your purpose and how it relates to your loyalty to Christ. The author of **1 Kings 8:61 NIV** writes, "And may your hearts be fully committed to the LORD our God, to live by his decrees and obey his commands, as at this time." Today is the day to get honest with yourself and look at your relationship with God. Ask yourself these questions: Is my devotion to God and His will my priority? Are God's standards my values? Do I love what He loves and hate what He hates? Do I stand up for Jesus's name's sake? Is the work I'm doing today purpose-driven and God-honoring? Does my lifestyle and work give God countless opportunities to display His glory? Do I get joy out of the work I do? How does what I'm doing impact others? Can I see myself doing this for the next ten to twenty years? Are my relationships bearing fruit? Am I consistent and committed to being my best?

Once you answer these questions and you've settled that what you're doing now is precisely the work you're supposed to be doing, praise the Lord. But, if not, I encourage you to pray over if the Lord wants you to stick with the business type, job, or career that you're in. By stepping out and living with faith, you can better utilize your time and resources, allowing you to focus on what truly aligns with your goals and values. Also, reevaluate your relationships to see if they align with the person you're becoming and where you're going. Are you the most knowledgeable person in your friend group? What's the unique value you bring to your relationships? Are you here to share and connect or to receive? To accelerate, you must enhance the lives of others and have individuals around you who will challenge, pray, fast, encourage, and inspire you to win long-term.

SLOW AND STEADY

The business world is complex and fast-paced, but operating on purpose balances the tension one typically has while striving to progress. The high-stakes business landscape often changes based on market trends, inflation, the stock market, technology, and whether or not it's an election year. Manufacturers market their new product models with new and improved features on their alluring upgrades annually. One year, something is in, and the next, it's out or better-sized. Trends in home décor, style, and fashion often adjust too. When you're a minor player in the marketplace, keeping up with the pace, race, and range of change is pretty hard. However, to be profitable, we must keep up with everything, right? Or at least that's what I thought.

Our work in the marketplace is an extension of our work for Christ. Although we're in this world and must stay up on our learnings to stay in step with it, God's economy works differently. Hustling until we drop while applying the latest findings is not the formula for the believer's success. That's where taking on the mind of Christ and resting within the Spirit provides endurance and wisdom from above. You gain an edge and stand out from the crowd by staying dependable and definite about the right things, such as remaining faithful in your prayer life, work, and sharing the gospel. Paul expresses it in **1 Corinthians 15:58 NIV** beautifully, "Therefore, my dear brothers and sisters, stand firm. Let nothing move you. Always give yourselves entirely to the work of the Lord, because you know that your labor in the Lord is not in vain." Slow and steady hits the mark, and as long as we're faithful to giving ourselves entirely to the Lord's work, it has rewards attached to us in the land of the living and eternally. My nephew Deontae consistently got straight A's throughout school. I loved rewarding him with gifts to encourage him to keep progressing. Although we can't regulate how God gives favor or gifts, we can choose to trust Him.

We can lean on the Word of God and His promises to persist consistently. Trust, fortitude, importunity, and self-discipline are how we will win in business because our pacing moves at God's speed, not the world's. Daily prayer and Bible study outpaces hustle culture and keeps us from looking back because we're fit for the calling. And due to your deployment, have you considered the impact of stopping or returning? "Jesus replied, 'No one who puts a hand to the plow and looks back is fit for service in the kingdom of God'" **Luke 9:62 NIV**.

Results will follow when we walk by the Spirit to model God's consistency and reliability and keep our hands on the plow. So, what does stick-to-it-ness look like to you? What does it take to break you and make you give up? What does it take to make you get off of your routine? Remember, we're not talking about advancing in just any business. We're talking about acceleration in a profitable, purpose-driven business in the long term.

ACCOUNTABILITY

We often cry about not accomplishing things we set out to do or the plans not working out financially. We stop putting effort into our relationships and expect them to work out. The complaints are valid if there is consistent, reliable action. Nonetheless, this is rarely the case because there weren't any documented or trackable activities we committed to in writing over time. People lie, blame, and make excuses—but numbers don't. Doubt and inconsistency arise when the goal is unclear, and the journey is tiring. Therefore, we must take the time to track our results and get accountability to achieve them. And accountability isn't a dirty word. It's the best thing you can have to keep you focused. Sadly, most give up before establishing a pattern of results because they have no one to help them through the rugged stretches of trials. But when you have someone helping you to stay on course, regardless of how bad you feel, it will give you the strength for long-term endurance.

My parents got us a Doberman Pinscher—Dutchess when I was eight. She was the best addition to our Quinn family of six and a joy within our home. I still think about her. She was beautiful and reddish brown, quick, fun, and protective. However, my father had to train her and commit to her well-being ongoing. Stanchness to the progress was crucial for keeping her feeding schedule and teaching her to potty outdoors. If my dad fed or took her out on the days he felt like it and didn't on other days, he'd confuse Dutchess. She'd think using the bathroom in the house was normal. He couldn't get mad because he'd be accountable for the inconsistent actions. However, the consistency and commitment to outdoor training helped our doggy learn where to go and be responsible to its owner. Thankfully, my dad trained our family pup quickly because she was intelligent. The fundamentals of a good foundation of habits started early and advanced into adult doghood.

CONSISTENCY EQUALS SUCCESS

As an entrepreneur, your consistency, or lack thereof, will start to show after a while. It will show up in your revenue, and your clients and supporters will stop believing you and start complaining about half-hearted products and services. Even when circumstances are rough, honor your commitments to the best of your ability. Failure to maintain your word to yourself means you won't be able to hold it with others. You'll begin to think you're a loser when the problem is your consistency. These issues can be rectified by returning to the Rock of Christ, planning your week, and restructuring and tracking your habits. If you're having trouble with dependability, commit to one big goal you must do daily in three categories without fail.

What is the one big goal you will do daily in your spiritual, health, business, and relationships? For example, I adjusted my schedule to get up at 4:30 am to spend time with God in prayer and Bible study, exercise, and finish one RGA (Revenue Generating Activity) for the business. If I only get a chance to do each for 15 minutes one day, it helps me maintain the habit instead of focusing on the time I spend on it. Consistent effort can break through even the most formidable obstacles, just like persistent pecking in the same spot eventually cracks a rock. If you pray daily at five am for one year, you'll see the power of God move like never before. If you study the Bible daily, you'll discover things you never knew about God, and your life and business will accelerate. Walking for three miles daily will transform your body and strengthen your heart, legs, and core. Therefore, you want to conquer the one big goal daily, even if you can't give it your all.

God wants to bless you in your business, but just like the pup that gets confused if you stop taking it out to potty, God and others are confused by your lack of regularity. Changing old habits is difficult, but you can submit them to Christ. When you get purpose-focused and learn to finish what you start, your confidence will increase, and you'll see considerable tangible financial and creative results in your business. I encourage you to commit your day and abilities to the Lord upon rising. It looks like, "Lord, what would you have me to do, where would you have me to go, and how do you want me to serve today? Please tell me what priorities need focus and bless the work of my hands." Set big goals and challenge yourself to take on life-changing routines. Take one day at a time. Schedule your day and important tasks the night before so you can get more work executed. Check in with an accountability partner or coach weekly. You'll soon see the success you're praying for.

Acceleration CURE Actions:

- **Clarify** your commitments and intentions. Don't rush the process. Instead, track your habits and focus on getting better each month. If you require a tool, my Dream Big Goal-Setting Planner is for daily consistency, habits, and accountability, even on weekends.

- **Combine** your old routines with new habits you want to maintain consistency with. For example, if you're struggling to exercise, walk in place or lift light weights for twenty minutes in front of the TV. If you can't seem to sit and read the Word initially, listen to the audio Bible while cleaning. Trying to build habits together will help you get unshackled and unstuck.

- **Rewrite** your narrative to break away from prior inconsistencies and reignite your vision by remembering why you started. Take spiritual and mental breaks when God tells you to rest.

- **Determine** to enrich and endure the long game because your experiences aren't in vain, and achievements take time.

Prayer

Dear Heavenly Father, I need your help to stay consistent. I have tried to be consistent in the long term but keep falling short horribly. I usually start well, but I always seem to get off course. It's like I lose hope or focus somewhere along the way when something else comes up. Could you help me recognize distractions and the unaligned desires to chase the next best thing? I want to take my purpose, goals, and work assignments you gave me seriously. I realize that I'm weak without the Holy Spirit working through me. Today, I'm calling out to you, Lord, because I want to be committed and consistent. Heavenly Father, you always commit to your Word. I must learn from you if I want to be more like you. I desire to finish the assignments you gave me and do them well. Please help me to get back on course when something takes me off. I ask these things in your name and for your sake.

In Jesus' Name, I pray, Amen.

Day 17

PRODUCTIVELY PRODUCE

As I shared in the introduction, God placed this book in my heart during a struggle in my art business. Writing was an escape that prevented me from worrying about money but also kept me producing—but there hid the blessing. Managing the overhead of building a business without financial support as a single woman has always been my greatest challenge in my creative undertakings. I wasn't thinking that no matter how hard things are for us as believers, our God is giving us His best tests for our good. I wrestled with thinking about joyfully enduring this trial that would make me more Christlike. However, instead of making excuses, I continued to produce in some way. I also acquired a new skill by learning how to build websites and improved my writing.

I kept trying to juggle Paul's encouragement in **Colossians 3:2-3 NIV** which states, "Set your minds on things above, not on earthly things. ³ For you died, and your life is now hidden with Christ in God." However, this book's chapters helped me to look above, strengthen and rededicate myself to living better within God's will, and see where I was stuck. With the Heavenly Father's help and the reality that I'm hidden in Christ, I became more productive when I focused on godly standards of character and integrity that align with the leader and believer I'm called to become. I had to remember that when Jesus asks us to do something, He does it out of love and for a divine reason. None of my writings would have depth if I didn't feel God's love, presence, and grace while navigating every emotion I expound on in these pages. It's easy to be effective when everything is going well, but the real version of who we are as Christ's ambassadors shines through when faced with enduring opposition. Identity blindness can rear its ugly head when we forget who we are. During these hardships, we get to see what we're made of. Only in these times can we experience the potential God placed in us to conquer and move mountains.

> **Accelerated Power – Ephesians 5:15 NIV** Be very careful, then, how you live—not as unwise but as wise,[16] making the most of every opportunity, because the days are evil.[17] Therefore don't be foolish, but understand what the Lord's will is.

We're called to the marketplace to do the will of God. And since we're to wisely use our gifts, skills, and talents to maximize our time and opportunities, what are we producing? See, productivity isn't about *looking* busy. It's about consulting with God for wisdom to be busy doing the right things at the right time. We need His understanding to do everything He's assigned us. If someone called you today to do something related to your industry, such as speak at a conference, take on a large order, jump on the news to commentate about your industry, or give you a free booth at their event to promote your goods, are you prepared to do it?

Making the most of the day is building the best relationship we can create with God. It's ensuring we're sacrificing things in the short term to get to where we're going in the long term. Wisdom causes us to work smarter and more efficiently instead of harder with intense toiling. It's an entrepreneur who knows their busy and slow seasons. Awareness and understanding of your business cycles will help the company run more efficiently and produce results while preparing for future opportunities. When we're blindsided by what season we're in, we'll think we're failing when we may be in a seed planting and cultivating time of thinking, creating, innovating, reevaluating, reassessing, restructuring, and developing for the busy days ahead.

Businesses don't make most of their revenue consistently like a bi-weekly paycheck paid to an employee by an employer. But what's typical for the marketplace is that some months are much more financially lucrative than others. For instance, January to February is slower for some businesses, while some are slower in June to August. Likewise, this busy-to-slow pattern is present in sales careers, as my sales quotas reflected the cycle and season the business was in. Strategizing and completing big projects like launches, writing, and traveling around your industry's downtime will give you an advantage.

RESULT-DRIVEN ENTREPRENEUR

A determined person knows who they are in Christ and looks at their life holistically instead of in fragments. They know one area of life affects the whole. In addition, they understand that there's no success void of God's favor. Clarity of purpose and vision fills leaders with the anointing they need to produce. They also evaluate and take inventory of their existing commitments and remove misalignments that aren't fruit-bearing and adding value. Results-driven husbands and wives don't make excuses. They ensure they excel in loving, respecting, and serving their spouse and carving out quality time to build a bond of trust, faithfulness, friendship, connection, and intimacy. They spend quality time with their children to teach, strengthen their confidence, support, and bring out the best in them. They monitor their stats and know their numbers for their revenue, sales, profit, assets, investment, and monetary goals. Leaders know what they want and the outcome they need to succeed financially.

Top producers know the what, when, where, why, and how of achieving better outcomes, such as what tools they use to achieve their goals. They must have the standard equipment to perform their role optimally, get into the maximum flow zone, and build consistent momentum. For example, I needed a large workspace and desk to study and lay out books, notebooks, and related materials. I need a fast computer processor with good storage, memory, and double monitors to keep up with written, research, and technology-based tasks. Fast internet is also crucial. I need storage, notebooks, colored pens, pencils, highlighters, index cards, and Post-it notes. I need access to a digital and physical personal library for exploration. I access and utilize multiple Bible translations and commentaries, too. Various software or SaaS is vital to my knowledge and information work. Still, I didn't mention all the other things I use for the different departments within my business.

When was the last time you sat down to evaluate your tools of the trade? Ask yourself what you need to produce your best work to get results and what environment suits your production. Did you pray about the need for these supplies and workspace locations? My prayer for a dedicated office space helped me finish this book and provided the clarity to start my publishing, coaching, and consulting business. Why? Because to enter into maximum productive flow, it has to be planned, and you need suitable devices and the ideal atmosphere. You must invest in what's necessary to participate in modern growth and build a purpose-driven business. I thank God for moving me into a new apartment and letting me use His space to do His work. Whenever I go into my home office, I'm inspired and go there to work. I don't get the best results when I work on my laptop in bed, on a sofa, on a table, or in a coffee shop. When I switch to my laptop, tablet, or phone on rare days when I don't feel like sitting upright at my desk—my work isn't as clean. The output results are night and day. I use two monitors in my office to see better and drag things around. That setup helps me to know the lay of the land and strategize. Because of the positioning of my tools, equipment, resources, and everything I need right at my fingertips, I can zone in and work longer beneficial hours.

FLOW STATE

Proverbs 28:19 NIV tells us that "Those who work their land will have abundant food, but those who chase fantasies will have their fill of poverty." Focused and uninterrupted God-honoring work brings results. But wondering, playing around, chatting, and scrolling through apps keeps one impoverished. When we're producing, we're surging. When we're not, we feel down and unworthy. We're made to work, build, grow, cultivate, and flow. Flow is when you hit a sweet, blissful zone within your work that's hard to enter into and challenging to break away from because you're flowing above your average capacity and potential. Flowing is when you're fully immersed and lost in purposeful work generated from the depths of your spirit, which submerses your soul. It's when the Holy Spirit downloads supernatural power and abundance into your workflow. The only things that break a flow are needing to go to the bathroom, get food, answer the phone or door, tend to an urgent matter, or your body screaming to get up and move for a break. Cal Newport wrote a book on the significance of flow called *Deep Work*. [1] It explores and provides case studies about the powerful results of getting into that flow state by removing distractions. He says, "If you don't produce, you won't thrive—no matter how talented you are."

REGULAR WORK VS. PROJECT MODE

There are two modes of work: regular and project-based. Their workflows are vastly different and affect flow state. Regular work is predictable and flexible, allowing for easy adjustments in daily priorities, tasks, and habits. In contrast, project work is intense and requires extended overdrive hours to meet tight deadlines and budgets, often involving additional contractors and an exhilarating race against the clock. In projects, things usually don't go as planned. An assignment you expected to take eight hours can unexpectedly turn into forty. A three-month project can turn into a year. A $20k projected budget can hit $40k. While we can adjust regular assignments easily—projects involve more meetings and checkpoints to ensure progress toward milestones. You'll often set aside routine work to take on the endeavor if you can't afford to pay for help. These differences in work modifications for an entrepreneur can cause stress, fitness inactivity, sleep loss, diet and nutrition changes, and weight gain if we're not careful and develop non-negotiables in our disciplines and commitments.

However, we can prepare for the best productivity and flow state by arranging our projects in a project planning system months in advance and hiring and assigning teams and trackable specific duties. In contrast, we can also organize regular work days, activities, and tasks within a planner and calendar. Making the most of the day also includes scheduling time for family, self-care, physical movement, eating, and supplementing for fuel, which affects our body and brain function.

Visionaries know that when it's time to work, we pray for wisdom and invite God to bless the work of our hands, be our strength, and have His way because He wants us to give our best and desires to be involved in all we do. We want to productively produce stellar, excellent results that we can be proud of, but it requires blocking the time to work in batches to reach the desired outcome. The acceleration principle causes us to live a faith-filled, prolifically aligned life holistically by delivering fruit-bearing results. Even when things don't go as planned, because we're committed to building everything we do on the Rock, rewards will follow if you produce.

Whether your assignment is working, ministering, creating, teaching, coaching, repairing, building, leading, healing, inventing, investing, or implementing—you're doing God's will. **Psalm 128:1-2 NIV** says, "Blessed are all who fear the Lord, who walk in obedience to him. ² You will eat the fruit of your labor; blessings and prosperity will be yours." We're all producers, and God wants us to provide an accounting of what we make with our time. Essential tasks should always take precedence over low-priority ones. Therefore, we must best use the Lord God's time to obey and labor.

The best way to look at this is, when you hire someone to help you, what do you expect them to do? Do you want them searching the internet for fun, shopping, watching reality television, texting all day, talking on the phone, or scrolling through social media? I don't think you'd tolerate such things. So why do we expect God to compensate us when we're not using our best time productively?

And as leaders, are we leading by example? If you're done with the day's work, no worries—you can play hard. If you're unable to focus some days—it happens. If feeling unwell—God understands. But we must ask ourselves why we make excuses for not giving a full day's work when we're not going through anything. All work and no play isn't what God wants, either. The Nation of Israel worked six days and had the sabbath to rest and enjoy one another. Chick-fil-A and Hobby Lobby follow suit. Please know what spiritual rest is for you, your family, and your team. "One person considers one day more sacred than another; another considers every day alike. Each of them should be fully convinced in their own mind" **Romans 14:5 NIV**. Nonetheless, **Philippians 2:12-13 NIV** teaches you to "Continue to work out your salvation with fear and trembling, ¹³ for it is God who works in you to will and to act in order to fulfill his good purpose."

MAXIMIZE TIME AND URGENCY

When Jesus' ministry started at age thirty, He accomplished enormous results within three short years before His crucifixion at thirty-three. He maximized His time and didn't play games with His assignment like we sometimes do. He flowed with urgency and purpose because He knew His time was short, so in those three years, He accelerated. We accelerate like Jesus when we live by faith. Anything unnecessary gets cut out to focus on the mission.

People may not understand your urgency, sternness, and commitment to acceleration, and they may say things like, "You need to get out and have fun." When building a purpose-driven business, we are having fun, but we have so much to do because we don't know when our last day will come. When the Lord God commissions you for work, your goal is to respond and obey because tomorrow isn't promised. When you're finished working for the day and need to rest for the week, there's a time to hang with family and friends, surf the internet and social media sites, and do things you love. There's nothing wrong with this. But when you're dedicated and committed to doing the work you're to do, you must be working during that time. Brian Tracy says it is like this, "Work all the time you're working." God is very serious about us working while we're working. We can't expect to accelerate and get the results we're praying for financially, spiritually, or relationally if we aren't self-disciplined, committed, consistent, or productive. We're productive when profiting financially, building, teaching, learning, producing, generating, or creating systems, products, and resources to work for us and the next generation. Since financial results determine success in our endeavors, we continue feasting off of God's sustainability by abiding in the Vine until we see the fruit and beyond.

As an entrepreneur, it can be easy to get sidetracked when business gets slow, but this is the time to remain diligent and steadfast by knowing the season. If you're a one-person operation, being slow in your company doesn't necessarily mean running off and getting another job. In some cases, that may be what you need to do if that's what God wants for you, but in some cases, He is testing your endurance and trust. Faith without works is dead, and your business is as alive as your confidence level. You can take your slow and down time to practice and perfect your skills and hone your craft, enroll in new training/classes, or complete projects you pushed to the side during your busyness. You can also investigate by reading books or watching videos.

REST TO ACCELERATE

Many of us sometimes struggle with productivity because we're not resting well. To accelerate in our area of anointing, we must rest and renew. We can see things more clearly when we slow down and take breaks. Proper sleep cycling and downtime resets, recharges, refills our spirit, and refreshes the soul. It's valuable for our bodily systems. Rest gives you the stamina to do the things you enjoy. When you run out of fuel, rest gets you to the Almighty God to restock your spiritual tank. We can't fix our productivity issues when unrested simply by setting new ambitious goals. Success follows resting in God and caring for the body He gave us to navigate this earthly life. God is our power source, so don't unplug from Him by not resting. Just like a cell phone needs to sit on the charger to get its juice, we must head back to the charging station in the presence of the Father.

TIME BLOCKS

Although you can't manage time, you can use it wisely by planning and arranging it into time modules. Time blocking is when you schedule a particular task for the day to maximize output but conserve your energy for better flow. I recommend using anywhere from thirty to three-hour increments (with at least a five-minute movement break every thirty minutes if you're sitting all day). I also suggest setting a timer. For example, your schedule might look like this on Tuesdays to concentrate on sales and growth:

- 5:00 – 6:00 am   Bible Study and Prayer
- 6:15 – 7:15 am   Workout
- 7:30 – 8:55 am   Post Workout and Morning Routine
- 9:00 – 10:55 am   Cold Outreach
- 11:00 – 11:55 am   New Sales Leads Research
- 12:00 – 12:55 pm   Lunch, Errands, Personal Calls
- 1:00 – 2:00 pm   Sales Pipeline Review and Follow-up
- 2:15 – 4:55 pm   Cold Outreach
- 5:00 – 5:55 pm   Sales Reading and Objections Review
- 6:00 – 8:25 pm   Family, Friends, Dinner, and Dishes
- 8:30 – 10:00 pm   Nighttime Routine

I used a themed plan to batch and consolidate similar responsibilities. Themed workdays are the best because switching to multiple task types is not the best energy use. For example, Monday can be strategic planning and reviewing your company forecasts, goals, and numbers. Tuesday is for sales, and Wednesday is for website updates, marketing, and promotions. Thursday is writing, proofreading, formatting articles and scripts, and education and learning. Friday is video editing, and Saturday is a catch-all day to complete essential tasks. If your schedule and business allow, themed weeks are more efficient than themed days because you can get work done for a month or two. Thinking and writing down your thoughts and ideas is just as significant as working. Writing them minimizes brain clutter and anxiety that slows you down from producing and affects your rest. Getting those inspirations, feelings, or worries out by putting pen to paper into the open allows you to know what to pray about because we're not to be anxious about anything (Philippians 4:6).

Making lists to organize your processes, workflows, departments, and projects is also an excellent way to systematize and structure your life and business to-dos and build routines. Lists for your tasks may include what's involved in your morning routine, exercise types, meetings and travel days and agendas, sales, marketing, and planning days. What days and times will you focus on what?

In your morning routine, I recommend time blocking your prayer, Bible reading, meditation, and study time. Know what you will study, what books you need, and what specific prayer requests you make on a given day. Yes, always leave room for the Holy Spirit to shift agendas. However, awareness and intentionality of habits and processes will conserve energy, increasing efficiency. Productivity is not a race. It's a marathon. Time blocking will always help you get a lot done because you'll be focused only on these duties at the assigned times. The Dream Big Goal-Setting Planner I offer Christian business owners has a built-in framework to help you plan, set your priorities, set up systems, and track your habits. When partnered with diligence, productivity will get you unstuck and into acceleration. Say goodbye to procrastination and excuses because God has already carved out a way for you to soar.

Acceleration CURE Actions:

- **Clarify** your goals. Then, make lists for your different departments and work processes, organize your work area, and commit to time-blocking your daily habits and tasks in thirty-minute to three-hour increments. Make sure to schedule breaks.

- **Read** and study your Bible above anything else you learn. Then, consider adding books that align with biblical principles to help you get unshackled from procrastination and unstuck from lackluster and unproductive results.

- **Focus** on your purpose-driven assignment and work with all your heart through persistence, diligence, and submission to the Holy Spirit's power. Rewrite your schedule and reignite your passion for your work.

- **Complete** the most complex task first. When you do, you'll strengthen your discipline, ingrain new habits, endure with vigor, and enrich your confidence in relying on Christ for the fortitude to succeed.

Prayer

Dear Heavenly Father, thank you for speaking to my heart about productivity and results. I realize I don't need to fight this working battle alone, but you're right here with me. Please help me be productive, persistent, and diligent whenever I'm scheduled to work on my business and personal commitments. Please show me how to maximize my time, habits, and calendar to produce the results you're expecting. I understand you want me to work when I'm scheduled to work and rest when I'm supposed to relax, recharge, and sleep. Please share more wisdom about planning, developing new ideas, and working when business is slow. I want to maximize opportunities and time to see results in my life and business.

In Jesus' name, I pray, Amen.

Day 18

FOCUS AND PERSIST

Remember when you were on your way to a critical appointment or event, and suddenly, traffic came to a crawl? When you got close enough to see the hold-up, signs directed you to an alternative route. No matter how badly you wanted to remain on the familiar path, the construction signs and barriers veered you in another direction. Yet, though inconvenienced, the detour instructions still got you to your destination safely. Likewise, when you make goals and plans, the way to get there never goes as planned. Because life and business is about solving problems, you'll often need to veer off your perfectly written, detailed, pristine proposal to persist and hit your milestones. Likewise, as you keep living by faith the heavenly Father has pre-established specific alternate diversions to veer you through successfully.

Unfortunately, some of us struggle more than necessary to outlast these roadblocks, barriers, and readjustments because they appear too countless and intense to overcome, so we lose hope and focus. We can't see the light at the end of the tunnel or discern the season. We're focused too much on self-preservation and comfort. We neglect to work when we're to work or continue preparing for the opportunities ahead. Therefore, we overlook that Christ never told us that our road would be easy, but He promised to be with us through everything we face, "Lo, I am with you always, even unto the end of the world" **Matthew 28:20 KJV**. Our propensity to give up is why the Father spends so much time testing and equipping us for maturity. So many times, the Lord God says to fear not! What matters most when detours occur is that they're God's way of warning us to slow down, check in with Him, evaluate what's happening, and press on in the direction He's steering us.

Accelerated Power – Philippians 3:12-14 NIV Not that I have already obtained all this, or have already arrived at my goal, but I press on to take hold of that for which Christ Jesus took hold of me. ¹³ Brothers and sisters, I don't consider myself yet to have taken hold of it. But one thing I do: Forgetting what is behind and straining toward what is ahead, ¹⁴ I press on toward the goal to win the prize for which God has called me heavenward in Christ Jesus.

For Christ's sake, we are in dream big goals mode, bringing His power and purposes to fruition. We haven't achieved the goal yet, but we will one day by faith enter into the revealed hope in our resurrected bodies. In this third chapter of Philippians, Paul spoke of putting no confidence in his flesh. He chose to forget all the deeds and accomplishments done in it before he met Christ. The Apostle Paul could've boasted about his previous achievements but considered them worthless compared to knowing Christ crucified and the power of His resurrection. Instead, he focused on obtaining the eternal crown. Like Paul, we must never forget that anything outside Christ's priorities isn't a success.

The New Testament letters are rich, and the greetings and doxologies found within them are priceless. His life path forever changed once he encountered the risen Lord Jesus on the road to Damascus. He left the religious business of persecuting and killing Christians (as a lawyer and Pharisee) and took on the new call to win the lost to Christ. He became a bondservant, one who utterly surrenders and pledges to the orders of Christ the Lord. **Romans 1:1 NKJV** says, "Paul, a bondservant of Jesus Christ, called *to be* an Apostle, separated to the gospel of God."

Paul knew his Christian identity and his commissioned assignment—to bring the gospel to the Gentiles. He aimed to obtain every blessing connected with knowing the risen Savior—the Lamb of God—and was determined and committed to pressing in. Not only did he share the good news, but he also taught, discipled, and passed God's teachings to other leaders like Timothy and Titus. He loved the church (Christ's body) and trained them to stay focused on the prize by living righteously by faith with reverence and obedience to God, even in jail. In Acts 26, standing in front of King Agrippa and government officials in chains, he shared the testimony of Jesus' death, burial, and resurrection from the dead. His loud profession of Jesus as God and Savior reached anyone who heard. The Apostle focused and persisted in his calling with the power of God sitting on the throne of his heart.

His later and former lives contrast how we can passionately and consistently focus on the wrong mission instead of what God proposed. Passion isn't a sign of righteousness and won't get us to the goal. Sanctification carries a working within surrender, a thirst for holiness, and living as bondslaves to experience God's power in our lives. Only God can lead us discover and activate purpose.

BIG GOALS, BIG FOCUS

On any given day, so many things are competing for our time, and depending on how much we dedicate to unprioritized distractions, we can quickly lose sight of what's crucial. Any goal one sets out to accomplish that isn't scary means God isn't needed to achieve it. We're not dreaming big enough goals if we can reach them without the Holy Spirit's power. When we **dream big goals**, they're God's dreams! Our desires align with His purposes for our lives, so we need reliance and trust in the Lord's power to accomplish what seems impossible. We must dream big goals that knock us off our feet and test our potential and faith to soar. The businesses we start, the children we parent, and the marriage union are more enormous than us—they're gifts from God.

Focusing on your purpose isn't something to take lightly because your family lineage and legacy are affected by what you do or don't do. Your rewards in heaven are tied to what you do for God and how you love others. Like a bone out of its socket, the body of Christ is affected when you're out of alignment. The Lord created you for His glory, which means that whatever you do is to point people to Him—the only hope the world has. When you submit, God wants to use your life and testimony to bring about His work as He advances you. "And I, when I am lifted up from the earth, will draw all people to myself" **John 12:32 NIV**. When people see the beauty of your light, the spirit of excellence, well mannered children, a fruitful marriage, and business success, you'll let them know where it comes from.

The good thing about our Heavenly Father is that He gives us a position to appreciate and prosper because it aligns with how He created us. Our purposefulness involves stuff we love doing and what we've overcome. However, knowing our identity in Christ is vital to acceleration. Therefore, our work and labor shouldn't be dreadful but a blessing. It's delightful to share in the mission of Christ's church and sufferings to share the good news. How lovely are the feet that bring the truth? "And how shall they preach unless they are sent? As it is written: 'How beautiful are the feet of those who preach the gospel of peace, Who bring glad tidings of good things!'" **Romans 10:15 NKJV.**

I'm not saying you're to dump the gospel down every patron's throat, but the Spirit leads you to share it with who He tells you to and still run your business effectively. Our focus is whatever our Lord and Master's focus is, and in it He blesses you with things you love, and once we learn this—fear, worry, and anxiety will ease. Focus takes years of reliance and patience because it requires us to hear God's voice to eliminate distractions and fears. What we focus on expands, so we must be intentional about our concentration. Persistence involves overcoming detours and obstacles, which requires continuous focus on the right things. By establishing our priorities and non-negotiables, we can better persist in our mission.

FEAR AND ASPIRATIONS

Fear is a barrier that often prevents us from concentrating on and realizing our aspirations. This propensity to be afraid is why, throughout Scripture, God repeatedly instructs us to "fear not." The frequency of this implication highlights the need to overcome our worries and fears, often rooted in concerns about others' opinions. We fear rejection, judgment, and criticism, paralyzing us and leading us to hide our thoughts and aspirations. As a result, we may hold back our creativity and potential, stifling the dreams that could lead us to extraordinary achievements and impact the lives of others. By recognizing and addressing these fears, we can free ourselves to focus and pursue our goals with confidence in God. In addition, guilt, shame, and worry about something we've done in the past are causing us to shrink back. Moses killed a man and fled from Egypt for forty years (Exodus 2:11-25). He lived an ordinary life with his wife and family because the word was out about what he did in Egypt. I imagine he was ashamed of his past and believed there was no further God-fulfilling purpose for his life. However, God still called and used Moses and considered him faithful throughout his house. When his siblings Aaron and Moses spoke against him, God disciplined them.

Numbers 12:5-9 NIV says, "...When the two of them stepped forward, ⁶ he said, 'Listen to my words: 'When there is a prophet among you, I, the LORD, reveal myself to them in visions, I speak to them in dreams. ⁷ But this is not true of my servant Moses; he is faithful in all my house. ⁸ With him I speak face to face, clearly and not in riddles; he sees the form of the LORD. Why then were you not afraid to speak against my servant Moses?' ⁹ The anger of the LORD burned against them, and he left them. When the cloud lifted from above the tent, Miriam's skin was leprous—it became as white as snow." I'm not comparing you to Moses, but if you're doing God's will, you'll have to trust that He will always protect His plan against anyone who comes against it, no matter how much someone criticizes your efforts. Financial constraints shouldn't deter your dedication to your purpose work. Exercise faith in God over fear so you can connect with God-aligned opportunities, regardless of your current situation. Remember, work is the best solution for worry, but it's essential to maintain responsibility in managing your finances. Still, I'm encouraging you to walk in the Spirit of God and do whatever He's asking you to do according to your measure of faith. I'm reminding you of **Joshua 1:9 NIV**, "Have I not commanded you? Be strong and courageous. Do not be afraid; do not be discouraged, for the LORD your God will be with you wherever you go."

FOCUS ON THE FINISH LINE

Starting the book writing process was challenging but wasn't nearly as complicated as finishing it. However, I resolved to complete it. I knew it would take determination, but I never imagined the depths of the sanctifying work God injected into this process of authorship. Recalling old emotions, memories, stories, successes, obstacles, struggles, fears, and tears took much time to process on some days. It often felt that I was never going to finish because whenever I thought I was done God would have me to rewrite full chapters. Other times, I felt like I was in the valley of trenches. By the time I'd get to the middle of the book, I'd have to regain a different level of grit and dependency on God to rewrite, restructure, and edit. Writing from my soul often exhausted me. I couldn't find a consistent workflow to continue making videos for my YouTube channel, writing articles and social content, or sending emails. I also forwent things I wanted, removed myself from distractions, and spent hundreds of hours studying, writing, and editing in my office. The labor, stretching, dying to self, loneliness, confessing of sins in my heart, sanctification, tears, highs, lows, and layers involved in the writing, editing, and publishing were enormous. This seemingly minor but gigantic undertaking is one of the most rewarding accomplishments of my life to date. That's why when God commands us to do something, He wants to use that assignment to get some things out of us. We hold a lot of influence as biblical Christians, and everything you contribute matters.

DELAYED GRATIFICATION

Are you willing to pay the cost of delayed gratification and sacrifice to focus and persist in the assignment God placed in your path? If so, what will you give up to follow God by faith? To finish anything for God, you must sacrifice your current desires in the short term for long-term gains. You cannot finish a divine assignment without surrendering, studying the Word, and listening to God's voice. The time you spend on the project will bring you closer to Him. Like Joshua, you must take territory in your mind and overcome your fears. God will allow you to finish and provide for your personal overhead and business expenses, just as He did for me. Soul-transforming products, services, and experiences can only come from our good Father. Although He doesn't need your help, He invites it.

You'll never finish *everything* you desire to do, but you must resolve to die trying. I don't want to sugarcoat anything. Since sin is missing the mark, you'll face many trials if you're determined to reach beyond its blot. Anyone God used in the Bible and life carried a heavy weight on their back for God's glory. You can't get over or around God's divine interrupting and testing. The Father didn't take away the cup of wrath and suffering from His only begotten Son, and He won't remove necessary hardships and testings from you. **Matthew 26:42 NIV** says, "He went away a second time and prayed, 'My Father, if it is not possible for this cup to be taken away unless I drink it, may your will be done." Also, **1 Peter 3:17-18 NIV** teaches, "For it is better, if it is God's will, to suffer for doing good than for doing evil. [18] For Christ also suffered once for sins, the righteous for the unrighteous, to bring you to God. He was put to death in the body but made alive in the Spirit." Know tests and trials are a part of your journey. Consider it pure joy because one day it will produce maturity in you that glorifies Christ. We can't bypass suffering and examinations if Jesus didn't. The only way to accomplish each goal we set and plan is on our knees in the prayer room. For the dream to live, it must first die! Everything we do must start and end with prayer because it ignites faith and fans the flame of worship. Without consistent meetings with God, we can't make it.

Once you've prioritized prayer, ask God to bless the work of your hands and strengthen you to reach the mark. Break down goals by the year, quarters, months, weeks, days, and hours. Build the goals into a group of systems that convert into habits. Then, break them into tiny bite-sized steps by looking at them as projects with many moving parts, components, and deliverables.

PRESS ON

Expect more of yourself than you expect from anyone else. Learning to tame your desires with self-control by waiting on the Lord has rewards. When you find yourself drifting off the path, pray by being honest with the Lord and let Him know what you're feeling. God will listen to your sincere prayer and get you back on track. Remember to look to the things above because your confidence is being tested and refined. Once you're mature and complete, you'll lack nothing. **James 1:2-4 NIV** says, "Consider it pure joy, my brothers and sisters, whenever you face trials of many kinds, [3] because you know that the testing of your faith produces perseverance. [4] Let perseverance finish its work so that you may be mature and complete, not lacking anything." Remember, God's "grace is sufficient" in your greatest weakness (2 Corinthians 12:9).

The purpose-driven, consistent, income-flowing business you dreamed of is nearer than you think. With persistence you'll finally advance from starting, stopping, borrowing, struggling, inconsistency, lacking, and returning to a corporate job to rescue you. God will make it so that you can one day afford the office and warehouse space. Meeting payroll for the contractors' and employees' salaries and benefits is no longer a problem to meet on time. One day, you'll recognize how your focus and persistence are rewarding you. You'll feel the joy of obeying God and experiencing a harmonious acceleration flow. You're finally unstuck, seeing the fruits of your labor, and your gifts are creating new opportunities.

Acceleration CURE Actions:

- **Clarify** what you'll focus on, then determine what biblical books and precepts you'll lean on to readjust as trials, tests, setbacks, and temptations arise.
- **Focus** on long-term goals by regularly reviewing your goals and remembering detours are part of the journey. But you must persist in getting unshackled and unstuck from anything that doesn't align with your mission in the short term.
- **Persist** in your destination through the Holy Spirit's leading. Ask Him to reignite and shine His light on your area of gifting so it's clear enough to rewrite, refocus, and keep with your daily disciplines.
- **Enrich** others with love, wisdom, integrity, and persistence, and be determined to live in your Christian identity to endure what comes your way, for God conforms you into the image of Christ.

Prayer

Dear Heavenly Father, thank you for teaching me about persistence through the life and letters of the Apostle Paul. I'm so grateful to read your written Word, which references your goodness, faithfulness, grace, kindness, and mercy. Sometimes, I struggle to focus and persist on what you placed in my path to do and complete because I get impatient. Can you please clarify what I should prioritize and focus on now? What can I do to finish what I start when I'm exhausted? I sometimes get discouraged because I'm unclear on what you want me to do and when I can't see a way out or through the storms of life. Help me stay on track despite how hard things get. I want to keep my eyes on you, the Author and Finisher of my faith. Could you please strengthen my vision and understanding of my purpose and mission?

In Jesus' name, I pray, Amen.

Day 19
ELIMINATE DISTRACTIONS

When we got a bit older, my mom started working outside the home, and she would keep us on par with to-do checklists to complete after school, on weekends, and in the summer. Taking on responsibilities was a normal part of life and learning in the Quinn household. However, it was easier for my parents to get us to accomplish most tasks when we were younger. When we gained more independence in our teenage years, more things competed for our time and attention. Those *"other things"* caused us to drift from some of our routine priorities. I remember my mama telling me so many times to hang up my clothes (that I'd conveniently put over a chair and let pile up for a few days at a time) in my room and to put the dishes up during my week to wash them. The youngest, Neicy, and I would even get woken up occasionally before we hit a deep sleep to put the dishes away when we kept overlooking this rule. Unfortunately, my stubbornness to these patterns kept me on the hot seat at least every two months.

I often felt my parents were unreasonable and should just let it slide, but they weren't wrong. I enjoyed the blessing and benefits of living at home but wanted to change what was important to household rules to fit my need to be left alone and make my own guidelines. However, I should've paid more attention to my home base and what my parents deemed necessary. They were trying to instill in us that good habits stick with us for years and not to allow temporary adjustments and distractions to deter us from our foundational commitments. We were taught discipline and cleanliness and to care for everything God blesses us with. The Quinn parents were preparing us for what adulting would be like in the real world. Their restraint seemed a bit much then, but the routines I developed at home are still with me (except for putting away the dishes after I wash them).

OUR FIRST PRIORITY

We all have some daily priorities. We also have spiritual disciplines and godly relationships vital to maintaining our spiritual vigor. However, when anything takes our prolonged attention away from caring for what's important to God, He considers it an idol. The nation of Israel couldn't stay on the right track with God for too long after King David's and Solomon's early reigns because they couldn't steer clear of idolatry. Solomon had so much overflow of favor and blessings from God in His life that it became mundane to receive favor. With all his money and wisdom, he turned his attention away from God because he had everything beyond what he could ask or think about and was accustomed to the good life. Consequently, under his leadership, Israel lost track of God Almighty's priorities as King Solomon's interests were whisked further away from the Lord with influence from his foreign wives and concubines.

Ephesians 6:10-20 reminds us to be aware of the devil's schemes because "we wrestle not against flesh and blood." Since Satan is always conspiring to irritate and distract us from prospering, we must stay vigilant and armored up. He sends bait to hook and tempt us to misaligned opportunities, false doctrines and teachers, and selfish desires to get us off course. To break up our relationships and business partnerships, the adversary intends to weigh our hearts with lust, suspicion, irrelevant concerns, quarrels, and conflict. The enemy of our soul plans demonic strategies and tactics to entice us to look at how well something works for others instead of how great our life is in Christ. He wants us to compare our finances, houses, vehicles, spouses, children, influence, subscribers, followers, and comments sections to others and envy what they have.

Like Israel and King Solomon, we can easily fall for Satan's ruses and interferences to lure us into trouble and idolatry. We must be strict about our spiritual, personal, and business priorities and be disciplined enough to avoid pursuing every shiny object or big idea within our non-negotiable habits or annual plans. Instead, let's ask ourselves, "Is this person, place, thing, or idea suitable or distracting me from what God is asking of me?" "Does God want me to have or do this now or wait?" "Is this new idea urgent?" Because if we've yet to implement the other programs and ideas we invested in prior or aren't working on the first thing God asked us to do, we may likely be distracted. The Almighty wants us to accelerate our mission with concentrated actions, but the enemy wants to interfere. But, we must stay vigilant and aware of Satan's counterfeit opportunities that divert, keep us stuck, and hinder our attention.

> **Accelerated Power – Proverbs 4:25 NIV** Let your eyes look straight ahead; fix your gaze directly before you.

When carrying out our assignments, whether serving family members, fellow believers, or working, the only way to win is to keep our eyes on the Author and Finisher of our faith. Christ pressed on to fulfill the will of the Father. No matter how often Satan tried to destroy or tempt the Son of God, He kept His gaze on the joy ahead. "Therefore, since we are surrounded by such a great cloud of witnesses, let us throw off everything that hinders and the sin that so easily entangles. And let us run with perseverance the race marked out for us, [2] fixing our eyes on Jesus, the pioneer and perfecter of faith. For the joy set before him he endured the cross, scorning its shame, and sat down at the right hand of the throne of God" **Hebrews 12:1-2 NIV**.

DIVERSIONS

We can never get back the time we dedicate to distractions, and since we reap what we sow, we must focus on planting and cultivating the right seeds that align with our purpose. We can no longer afford to allow poisonous relationships, pride, jealousy, gossip, gluttony, drugs, gambling, and sexual sins to keep us stuck, unproductive, restless, and going through the same tests and cycles countless times. We must say no to relationships, behaviors, and connections that drain us. Diversions are often sent while we're praying, studying, vulnerable, hungry, emotionally or physically tired, financially strapped, sick, or lonely. They can also appear when you're doing well. Undiscerning distractions can get us caught up in horrible situations. I heard a popular Bible teacher talk about falling for a social media scam despite usually being able to spot it. The scammers took over, locked him out of the social account, and used his credit card linked to the profile. This issue had his mind distorted and preoccupied for weeks, which affected his time with God and his family. Satan is waiting for the best time to creep in and use someone or something to strike a blow to get you off course. So, who is the person, place, or thing moving you away from focusing on your God and goals? Are you a distraction to others?

There's never a shortage of interferences fighting for your attention. I consider a distraction anything that hijacks your purpose and priorities. It also causes you to question or compromise your values and standards. Careless, gullible, seemingly harmless interruptions can quickly divert you from God and other commitments. You can get wrapped up in doing a *good thing* while distracted from the *God thing*. The *God thing* is the proper focus—not a temporary counterfeit. Broken focus keeps you on the struggle bus, and failing to discern the distractions keeps you from progressing. Although you'll spend a lifetime changing, tweaking, and being better at guarding your time, the disciplines and habits you engrain will help you bounce back more quickly.

Interestingly, we can quickly say *no* to allowing one person to persuade us and then turn around and let someone else pull us off track. In Kings 13, the man God sent on a mission to deliver a message to King Jeroboam was given strict orders to obey. He wasn't supposed to eat nor hang out in the town or with anyone after he delivered the Word of judgment from the Lord. "So the prophet said to him, 'Come home with me and eat.' [16] The man of God said, 'I cannot turn back and go with you, nor can I eat bread or drink water with you in this place. [17] I have been told by the word of the LORD: 'You must not eat bread or drink water there or return by the way you came.'" **1 Kings 13:15-17, 23-24 NIV**. So, after delivering the appointed communication, he begins traveling away from the town and meets "an old prophet" who invites him to eat and drink. The man of God disobeyed God and went to dine with the lying old prophet, and it cost him dearly; [23] "When the man of God had finished eating and drinking, the prophet who had brought him back saddled his donkey for him. [24] As he went on his way, a lion met him on the road and killed him, and his body was left lying on the road, with both the donkey and the lion standing beside it."

The man of God's decision to trust the lying prophet over the Lord's orders cost him his life. He steered away from following God's Word—our standard and compass. Distraction seems harmless until it's not! They are the attractive, alluring weapons of Satan. Saying yes to the wrong thing is sometimes deadly. Whether death to one's life, dream, opportunity, marriage, or freedom. The enemy is the master of putting the icing on a poisonous cake. He goes out of his way to create things that allure us from purpose and God's will. He's clever because he will use seemingly innocent things to accomplish his goal. It can appear as something you've been praying for, but it's not real—it's a counterfeit! You can perceive the imitation as good because Satan can make himself appear fitting "And no marvel; for Satan himself is transformed into an angel of light" **2 Corinthians 11:14 KJV**.

But it's not always the devil doing the distracting. Sometimes, it can be your family, friends, and your fleshly desires. It's our choices, decisions, habits, procrastination, excuses, and inconsistencies. We lack insight and willingness to learn more or look into a matter and decipher it. It's also simply rebellion against God's Word! We say, "I just can't...," but it's not that we can't do a thing—we simply won't do it. **James 1:14 AMP** says, "But each one is tempted when he is dragged away, enticed *and* baited [to commit sin] by his own [worldly] desire (lust, passion)." It's so easy to be distracted by our deceitful hearts. The flesh will lead us to stand for things God never approved in His Word. Anything that you put above God's Word and standards and substitute for feelings to lean on your understanding leads to idolatry. Please look for the root of the things that get us off course. There lies the link to our fleshly desires and strings the devil uses to tempt us. We must cry out to the Lord to extract it so the devil can no longer use those things to tempt, bait, lure, and distract.

BUSYNESS

For the last decade, every marketing and business guru has said that you must be busy on your social media profile. They advise you to be consistent with your posting schedule to become influential. However, posting to post and gaining incongruent followers doesn't equal money in your pocket or people who align with your core values or message. These platforms are businesses, too, and they want to use your hard work, gifts, and talents to build their authority. Many of these platforms are nothing but a highway of interruptions. Endless scrolling, posting, creating bottomless content, and responding to comments take a lot of time and require a lot of custom strategies around each platform's uniqueness outside of your everyday business operations. It's a ton of extra work and requires dedication to learning about the algorithms or hiring an expert to get you eyeballs and leads. They want you to jump through hoops to get favored by the algorithm, but are we keeping this same energy and momentum of jumping through hoops to sit at the feet and learn from Jesus as His disciple?

I realize how entertaining and informative the platforms are when you take a work break to scroll. Advanced technology has changed how we do things, and the truth is that you need to be where your clients are hanging out and, most importantly, where God wants you to be. I mainly use social platforms for business, but I don't like the feeling I have when posting tons of content consistently when I could be writing my next book or accelerating my prayer life. I don't want to spend every waking moment building up someone's social platform when there's so much I can do in my areas of gifting. Not to mention, after years of work, they can easily remove your social handle in a day if you post something they disagree with. Busyness doesn't equal productivity, and output doesn't necessarily mean you're pleasing God. Busy can seem productive until you pull back the curtain. We can think we're doing the right things but are focused on the wrong ones. There's nothing wrong with spending time on these platforms if they're reaping a return of some type for you by causing you to accelerate in your marriage, parenting, relationships, attitude, goals, and business. But they're distracting in some seasons, so be aware. Spiritual strength helps us use platforms instead of letting them use us. If you're always busy but stuck in the same place, you'll want to determine if your actions produce acceleration or deceleration. We'll have to take responsibility for anything we're allowing to cause deceleration.

DEDICATED ENTERTAINMENT HOURS

Most mainstream media and entertainment are massive propaganda and indoctrination machines designed to push a narrative and keep you invested in hours of watching their *news and shows*. Consuming endless unplanned hours of programming on Cable Television and streaming services also interferes with what's important. Yes, some shows are really good, but you must mine to find the jewels, as much of the subject matter is dark and is the devil's tool.

Many online activities benefit my business and help me stay with skills and motivation. Still, I need to ensure they don't replace my commitments. As my parents taught me, no matter how many new responsibilities I take on, priorities come first. If I take care of my spiritual life and home first, I can enjoy my time with other interests and activities. The authors in the genres of books I read also have a common theme. Most successful people don't watch TV. However, if they do, some watch very little of it, around five to ten hours a week. However, they love staying on top of critical or political news and current events, reading and learning, training, activities, industry-related events, and educational audio. Again, I'm not telling you to give up anything you love. But you can reserve and save them as a reward on a watch-later playlist to enjoy them without interfering with your productivity. When you weed out the best programs and social content worthy of your mind and attention, you'll find yourself cutting off a lot of unnecessary time wasters.

DEDICATED PEOPLE HOURS

When running a business, most family and friends don't understand your commitment to serving God and may take your work hours personally. In the early years, you will have less time to spend with them like you'd like because you're all the C-Suite executives: CEO, CFO, COO, CMO, promotions, secretary, editor, graphic designer, video editor, customer service, bookkeeper, housekeeper, producer, chef, and everything else. No matter how much people say they know *why you can't go* to the event or take their calls—they don't unless they've sacrificed like you to step out on faith to build a business. The attention to detail it takes to thrive, create a stable income, and lead an organization is challenging. When they don't understand your situation, they'll say things like, "You're always working," "You never go anywhere," "You're no fun," and "Get out and enjoy yourself for a change." Be wary of criticism from those who don't understand your work. Feedback is helpful, but not when concealed in critical critique.

In most instances, they're sincere, but some friends and family aren't concerned about your success. They don't mind if you win or lose. Therefore, you'll have to decide how to manage your relationships and carve out specific times to spend with loved ones and friends. It is a distraction if someone who loves you has difficulty accepting that you're in the building phase and is unwilling to work with your schedule for this season. They don't get your mission, which means they don't get you. Jesus Christ and Paul were unmarried because their missions required consistent focus. And you're married to Christ and His vision. Yes, spend time with loved ones, but prioritize what's important. You're developing a purposeful business, and all your resources are going to care for your household and business expenses.

When a good suggestion comes up in the form of a person, place, thing, or idea, ask yourself if it's a *good or God thing*. Try to arrange the hard stuff first and fulfill your primary responsibilities. Distraction-proof your life, business, and environment by sharpening your discernment and being aware of the devil's schemes and misaligned desires that hinder acceleration. Watch who your spouse, children, and friends are consuming their time with, and pray they aren't getting dragged away into the wrong influence. You can't live a distraction-free life, but you can control your controllables, such as prioritizing, planning, and scheduling leisure, social, and recreational activities. Know that your sacrifices today will pay off and allow you to do more of what you love tomorrow.

Acceleration CURE Actions:

- **Discern**, clarify, and disconnect from what's distracting and robbing you of your productivity (people, places, things, and ideas). Find the root of the things you keep falling for that lure you away from the things of God. Then, recommit to focusing on and completing your more complex task first. Stay alert to scams and schemes, and watch out for your loved ones being wrongfully influenced.

- **Strengthen** your discernment by acknowledging the Lord in all your ways. Get educated on common scams (find them on YouTube). Schedule leisure time for watching TV, scrolling on social media, and attending events as rewards for finishing the central things. Don't allow distractions to keep you shackled and stuck.

- **Nightly** rewrite your priorities, reignite the tasks you didn't complete last year or last week, and add them to tomorrow's or next week's list.
- **Enrich** and endure the problematic days by staying focused on the future outcome. Sacrifice today's pleasures for tomorrow's gains.

Prayer

Thank you, Heavenly Father, for focusing my attention on the distractions in my life. I never looked at them as being an idol. I know I should be dedicating more time to things that are important to you instead of frivolous things. Please remove the people, places, things, and ideas in the way. Please help me to have balanced time for my family, relationships, work, activities, and hobbies. Please help me with self-control when it comes to television and social media. I want to enjoy the same things you want for me. I no longer want to be unfocused. I like to stay alert and beneficial. I won't give the enemy free entry into my life or my business with his distractions. Please help me to identify the root of my desires and anything sent to distract me when they come.

In Jesus' Name, I pray, Amen.

Day 20

OVERCOME OBSTACLES

The housing market crashed in 2008, jobs were scarce, and banks and big corporations needed financial bailouts. During Obama's administration, the economy continued to nose dive. In 2011, I struggled to progress while balancing art, going to school, and searching for work. In 2013, my dad paid a visit from Detroit and helped me to unpack the issue. He had no idea what I was facing because I didn't know how to articulate my hardship. I just learned how to survive. But God used him so I wouldn't have to deal with the decision alone.

After our talk, I decided to file for Chapter 7 bankruptcy and surrender my townhome. Bankruptcy prevented me from avoiding the double whammy of having a foreclosure on my credit report. I was able to put the HOA arrears there, too. I would've worked with my lender and the Fannie Mae program, but my loan servicer had just sold my mortgage, and the package they proposed wanted me to move to a forty-year term to stretch out the back payments while ballooning them every three months for a year. Considering how long I had already been paying for the home, that didn't make financial sense. I had a thirty-year mortgage when I signed my original contract. Forty was too long when considering the interest. My lease for my Cadillac CTS was up a year prior, and I paid cash for an Infiniti I35 that gave me nothing but issues. During the week of my father's visit, he paid for my car repairs, stocked me up with food and essentials, and I found a new job in advertising sales.

I was officially losing everything I had worked hard for while struggling to revive. The foundation I once knew for my life crumbled into a pile of sand. What took years to build was lost within one year. Walking away from my house in January of 2014 was a big part of my losing it all story. The obstacles and trials wouldn't let up. I was still being disciplined by the loving hand of God and struggling in a rough economy.

My valley stretch lasted for a decade (2008-2018). My low point started in 2008 when I met my ex and ended in September 2018 when I walked away from him for good. The Lord God had long-suffered with me enough. I had allowed sin to be my master, and there were consequences for my actions. I had experienced hard times on my faith journey here and there, but nothing compared to this. I had to learn to overcome and rebuild my entire life on the Rock of Christ in a way I'd never known. In 2011, after embarking on a Holy Spirit-led fast that radically changed my life, I felt genuinely born-again when I exited the fast and repentant for sinning against a holy and righteous God. I'm not speaking of me being *sinless*—but of *sinning less*.

I played a role in my loss because, in some compartments, I lived like a pseudo-Christian in a few areas of my life before and during my marriage. But because God is merciful, He granted me repentance and forgiveness. I overcame when Jesus started to cure my soul and restore my faith through my submission to walking by the Spirit. However, living as a Christ-follower hit me hard because life was more brutal when I steadily strived for righteousness. I weathered the drought with God and found joy, peace, and hope in Him. My trust, love, and relationship with the Everlasting Lord grew deeper. Although rough, I overcame that ten-year season when I moved to Dallas. I have a new song in my heart because my lamp kept burning, and God turned my darkness into light. At my worst, He never let me fall. He taught me to depend on Him in ways I never had to lean on Him. Like my mommy loves to say, "There's a message in the music."

Accelerated Power – Psalm 18:28-32 NIV You, Lord, keep my lamp burning; my God turns my darkness into light. [29] With your help I can advance against a troop; with my God I can scale a wall. As for God, his way is perfect: The Lord's word is flawless; he shields all who take refuge in him. [31] For who is God besides the Lord? And who is the Rock except our God? [32] It is God who arms me with strength and keeps my way secure.

David articulated his joy of the Lord when he rescued him in his trials. When he was delivered from Saul's hand, he expressed gratefulness in the eighteenth Psalms through worship and praise. All I know is when God lifts you from the miry clay, you feel like you can advance a wall. But there is still a disconnection from feeling God's presence and navigating His silence in tough times. **Psalm 13:1-2 NIV** says, "How long, LORD? Will you forget me forever? How long will you hide your face from me? ² How long must I wrestle with my thoughts and day after day have sorrow in my heart?"

Think of times when you felt like God was silent or forgot you. How did you have to manage feelings and thoughts of sorrow? The Bible is our instruction manual for getting through every situation, and just because you feel forgotten, it's not factual. David's life is an example of overcoming obstacles and arrows thwarted to destroy him. He couldn't have made it from the shepherd boy to King without his total dependence on God, who answered his prayers and kept his lamp burning—providing him strength, wisdom, and protection. His waiting upon the Lord turned his darkness into light. David *never lost a battle*. He was a type of Christ and a mighty warrior. David knew how to do what seemed impossible with God, like advancing troops and scaling walls. "The LORD is a warrior; the LORD is his name.⁴ Pharaoh's chariots and his army he has hurled into the sea" **Exodus 15:3-4 NIV**. God doesn't play about His children. He always fights for us! Like David, you can overcome trials by placing your faith in the LORD. Although David didn't lead a perfect life, he even had blood on his hands with Uriah's death and conceiving a child that died with Bathsheba, but David knew how to repent and turn from his immoral ways. He had a heart after the Lord because he didn't think living a sinful lifestyle was well with his soul.

DECIDE TO OVERCOME

Defeating hurdles is a part of our identity in Christ. We are overcomers because Christ is victorious. Conquering the very thing that tried to break us is who we are and is a massive part of getting our big idea into the world. If Christians aren't exempt from the guarantee of trials and tribulations, how can they be excluded from the businesses or ministries we founded? We can't escape these obstacles, so we must decide we will overcome them before they arrive. Deciding to win means we shouldn't be surprised when trials come. We must never strive to overcome obstacles *appearing* as giants, alone, or trust in our ways. But, we must decide to face battles in the name of the LORD Almighty. We place our confidence in the Mighty Warrior—The First and the Last—to fight our battles through us like when David slew Goliath. "David said to the Philistine, 'You come against me with sword and spear and javelin, but I come against you in the name of the LORD Almighty, the God of the armies of Israel, whom you have defied.' So David triumphed over the Philistine with a sling and a stone; without a sword in his hand he struck down the Philistine and killed him" **1 Samuel 17:45, 50 NIV.**

Sadly, I believe many Christians are under the impression that they won't have to endure or constantly overcome trials. I get it. None of us want what's hard. Nobody wants to face problematic and uncomfortable times, but we must go through them. King David's story and many others are here to help us know that because we love and are chosen by God, we will still undergo persecution and tribulations for Christ's sake. But we must choose our hard because in or out of God's will, it will be hard, no matter what we decide. Life will present hardships either way, and we must determine which struggles we are willing to embrace. Some have eternal rewards, and others don't. The longer we prolong the obvious, the lengthier we make the test and journey. Therefore, carefully considering our long-term objective of pleasing God, we can trust His outcome and move forward. There's no acceleration cure without overcoming trials. If Jesus went through them, we're not exempt.

Dr. Tony Evans likes to say, "You're either in a storm, coming out of one, or going into one." The great news is that we never have to face our tests alone. No matter their size, they're less significant than the God we serve. Compared to God's massive hand of glory, the size of the prosecutions we face is the equivalent of you dropping a mustard seed into the Universe.

In the CSB (Christian Standard Bible) translation, they translated the measurements of Goliath's height to be 9 feet 9 inches. He was one whom all of Israel's army feared, was intimidated by, and was terrified to fight because he was much taller and stockier than the average-sized man. They didn't see a way out of the situation, and nobody in the camp was brave enough to take him on. But a young David didn't think like everyone else and thought it was blasphemous and insane for one to taunt Israel's God. He also had experience slaying wild animals through God's power, so he approached his problem like his protective shepherding. He operated in God's spiritual armor and power, which gave him physical results with his slingshot and stone. That's why we must co-work with the Spirit of God through obedience in our Christian walk.

VICTORY IN LIFE AND BUSINESS

To embrace a life filled with joy and thanksgiving, you must transform your limiting beliefs regarding obstacles and the meaning of true success in Christ. Instead of perceiving these obstacles and challenges as setbacks, learn to reframe them as valuable divine opportunities for growth and spiritual and personal development. By shifting your perspective and looking at it from another vantage point, you can uncover the potential for the next level of your purpose and resilience that lies within each stumbling block you encounter. These occasions help you grow by leaps and bounds and witness God's supernatural power.

However, it would help if you had a spiritual warfare plan to get through. You'll want to find some books, passages, and people in the Holy Word with whom to identify. Discover what stories and people you resonate with within the text. What about your top ten Scripture passages? For example, Psalms consists of 150 chapters, written mainly by David, but not all. Suppose you haven't read them all multiple times. I highly recommend getting acquainted with them to familiarize yourself with the ebbs and flows of navigating your journey. A solid understanding of the biblical text will help you accelerate through what *appears* gigantic. Do you entrust God to turn any situation around, including but not limited to disease, poor health, financial lack, business failure, lawsuits, judgments, bankruptcy, depression, divorce, abuse, loss, miscarriage, adoption, and loneliness?

It's good to ask yourself, how big is my faith? Do I have faith the size of a grain of mustard seed, and is the Lord calling me into a fast to draw out my belief? Jesus' disciples couldn't cast the demon out of the young boy who was internally and physically tortured. They needed to fast and pray. "And Jesus said unto them, 'Because of your unbelief: for verily I say unto you, If ye have faith as a grain of mustard seed, ye shall say unto this mountain, Remove hence to yonder place; and it shall remove; and nothing shall be impossible unto you. ²¹ Howbeit this kind goeth not out but by prayer and fasting'" **Matthew 17:20-21 KJV**. I'm not saying you need to fast due to having a demon. A demon cannot *possess* a born-again Christian's temple with the Holy Spirit living within. However, outward demonic *oppression* is possible if you've opened the door of your body and soul to anything that isn't in line with God's holiness.

Starting a business is arduous, and making it profitable consistently is equally complicated. It was grueling when I led a team for my magazine because the troubles appeared like mountains and giants. Building a team to produce the vision was intense, but the expenses involved with publishing were distressing when everyone looked to me for results. God blessed me to build and work with talented volunteer writers, a leadership team, and contractors to help me reach my production goals. God surrounded me with a good group of people, and I'm forever grateful to Him for moving their hearts to help me. Without my dad's financial seed to get me to the A and the squad, I would never have seen that dream come to fruition or experience the synergy. That season was one of the highlights of my life, and although I had a ton of fun, what I remember more than the success is how I failed. I couldn't find any funding to get the magazine published again. I tried rebuilding later, but the chemistry of the new team was nothing like the uniqueness and perfect blend God had given me before. I allowed that defeat to define and keep my identity blind for a decade. It extracted something from me, and I let it rob me of my joy. It's no fun when you struggle to bring in the funding to see your baby leap, but you must get up and keep moving with your life.

MEDITATE ON WINNING

Aligning with the Holy Spirit's direction and path for our lives and businesses helps us overcome big or small hardships. God will make something out of nothing when He gives you a vision and your faith aligns with His will. Prayer and seeking wise counsel can also help overcome obstacles and feelings of being stuck. Obedience and faith are the keys to answered prayer, and when you do what the Lord instructs, you'll see acceleration. David's goal aligned perfectly with God's purpose, and they worked in harmonious synchronization to thwart the giant. Therefore, pay attention to your intentions, thoughts, and actions. As a purpose-driven entrepreneur, God wants you to do your part in faith, prayer, fasting, and work to achieve success and overthrow any monster threatening your confidence and trust in God. The LORD Almighty wants you to stand boldly on godly character and integrity. Remember to meditate on the victories God rescued you from and how He provides daily. Look at the birds and animals—God provides for them. Look to the hills where your help comes from. Remember to continually reflect on winning because, in Christ, you are V-I-C-T-O-R-I-O-U-S!

Acceleration CURE Actions:

- **Clarify** why you must overcome your obstacle and commit to God's instructions to get you to the win.
- **Seek** God first for answers in the Bible and prayer to get you unshackled and unstuck before you involve others' opinions. Then you can get the advice of a trustworthy person.
- **Call** to remembrance events of God's faithfulness in your life. Then, reflect on His unchanging power, reignite the joy you felt when God delivered you, and rewrite the things that express gratitude for wins and losses.
- **Endure** obstructions by putting your top ten Scriptures on index cards. Keep them handy to enrich and refresh you when you need strength.

Prayer

Dear Heavenly Father, I pray that you grant me wisdom and endurance in every challenge and obstacle. If you want me to stay in a trial longer than I believe it should take, please allow me to bear it and trust in you. I know I can advance a troop and scale a wall with you. I can rest in your deliverance and salvation. I pray for the deliverance of others undergoing hardships and storms in life and business. Please protect, cover, and turn their darkness into light. The storms can rage so violently, and it seems there's no way to make it out, but I'm faithful that you have already made a way. I also find peace in knowing you will never leave or forsake me. Grant my petition to press ahead for the joy set before me.

In Jesus' name, I pray, Amen.

Day 21
FIND YOUR MOTIVATION

In September 2016, I embarked on a fifteen-day fast to get clarity on a decision and draw closer to God. I ate food the first day because I wanted to partake in a fast with having one meal after six pm. I didn't prefer going without food, but with God's grace, I fasted for the next fourteen days without it. In the mornings, I had 2 ounces of 100% organic apple juice plus 2 ounces of coconut water mixed with 20 ounces of plain water for nausea. I drank a bottle of alkaline water during my work shift. In the evening, before bed, I mix a pinch of cinnamon with 1 cup of chamomile tea to help my body relax for sleep.

In the past, I took on multiple similar one-meal-per-day fasts for seven to ten days, but some were brutal on me spiritually, mentally, and physically. In those fasts, I cried so much, telling God how I wanted to give up. I don't even want to know how I would've felt if I had taken those fasts on in my strength. But, since fasting focuses on humility, spiritual rest, prayer, meditation, denial of self, and time in the Word, the Lord used those disciplines to see me through, but I was so glad when they were over so I could eat.

However, without food, this fast was quite different. I had more energy than I'd typically have compared to consuming daily food. I worked full-time for ten of the fourteen days. I didn't get the detox side effects like headaches, excruciating mouth sores, or body odor that are pretty much a part of a fast when your body's not regularly detoxing from processed foods and chemicals. When it was time to end the fast, I was energized and could have gone longer, but I had lost so much weight I didn't want to go on because I wanted to eat. My pants were so loose and oversized on me. I was already at my ideal weight for my height before starting, so I didn't want to drop down more. What I learned from years of spiritual fasting is that none are the same, and they all serve a different purpose. Therefore, embarking on them requires us to look to Christ Jesus for His sufficient grace and motivation.

> **Accelerated Power – Isaiah 40:28-31 NIV** Do you not know? Have you not heard? The LORD is the everlasting God, the Creator of the ends of the earth. He will not grow tired or weary, and his understanding no one can fathom. [29] He gives strength to the weary and increases the power of the weak. [30] Even youths grow tired and weary, and young men stumble and fall; [31] but those who hope in the LORD will renew their strength. They'll soar on wings like eagles; they'll run and not grow weary, they'll walk and not be faint.

Do you not know and have you not heard how incredible the LORD is? Our eternal Creator of everyone and everything doesn't wear out and tire like we do. Although we search high and low, we can never understand His ways. Jehovah Jireh is the provider of our strength whenever we need it. When it looks like we're out for the count in the twelfth round, He effortlessly renews our strength like an eagle. To wait on the Lord means to serve Him, as in the case of the wait staff at a restaurant. They aren't just sitting around watching people eat. They're actively serving—waiting on the patrons. When we wait on our Lord, He will boost us beyond what our human power produces. He's the power source and doesn't need an external supply. Since motivation is temporal, like an electric charge on a flat iron plugged into the wall, it has no power when unplugged. He's the permanent, perpetual fuel that wakes us up, sustains us, gets us on track, and keeps us moving.

MOTIVATION IN THE WORD

The LORD God is our reason. He's why we can do anything. Without Him, we'd have no purpose, personality, drive, or intelligence to be motivated to accelerate. Therefore, He's given us His thoughts and statues in written form to inspire us. We marvel at His beauty as He blesses us with the glory of His creations, like witnessing the miracle of a woman's pregnancy process and giving birth to a baby. Also, trees, flowers, plants, animals, stars, wind, and seas are glorious wonders. The Word of God is the best motivational resource to live a joyful, prosperous, productive, expansive, and disciplined accelerated life. The Bible is the best book ever pinned. After all, it generates life, power, and fruit in God's children because it's alive and living. **2 Peter 1:3 NIV** says, "His divine power has given us everything we need for a godly life through our knowledge of him who called us by his own glory and goodness." The Bible will incentivize you to see life through the lens of faith in every season you find yourself in. The Bible contains it all if you need enthusiasm, strength, drive, encouragement, wisdom, knowledge, understanding, or a health prescription.

Most pop psychology deals with investigating the soul, but only God alone gets to the hidden parts of the inner man that nobody knows or understands. Therefore, we should never run to the world for solutions to life's problems first. That's why I encourage believers to run to God initially for their issues, pray to see if He wants them to seek biblical counseling for specific matters, and then move into the practical.

Psalm 90:2 NKJV says, "Before the mountains were brought forth, Or ever You had formed the earth and the world, Even from everlasting to everlasting, You *are* God." Before anything was brought forth, our holy, eternal, all-powerful, and full of strength, grace, and truth, God existed. He never has and never will grow weary. You need the LORD's interminable vigor because life can tax your soul if the Bread of Life does not nourish you. "But Jesus replied, 'It is written *and* forever remains written, 'MAN SHALL NOT LIVE BY BREAD ALONE, BUT BY EVERY WORD THAT COMES OUT OF THE MOUTH OF GOD'" **Matthew 4:4 AMP**. Leadership isn't for the weak or easily tempted. Running an organization is a beast all of its own. Most days aren't as exciting as they can appear to others who are looking in from the outside at the highlight reels. The labor and hours invested are substantial. Our only hope is to stay attached to The LORD while doing all of these productive things to minimize the blow of emotional, spiritual, and physical burnout.

FAITH AND HOPE

Without hope, we have nothing to look forward to, and without faith, we have no way to see. As long as we have expectations, we can resonate with the psalmist who wrote in **Psalm 121:1-2 NKJV**, "I will lift up my eyes to the hills—From whence comes my help? ² My help *comes* from the LORD, Who made heaven and earth."

A prayer of immovable confidence gives us hope of seeing things we request become a reality. Jesus tells us in **Matthew 7:7-11 AMP** to "Ask *and* keep on asking and it will be given to you; seek *and* keep on seeking and you will find; knock *and* keep on knocking and the door will be opened to you. ⁸ For everyone who keeps on asking receives, and he who keeps on seeking finds, and to him who keeps on knocking, it will be opened. ⁹ Or what man is there among you who, if his son asks for bread, will [instead] give him a stone? ¹⁰ Or if he asks for a fish, will [instead] give him a snake? ¹¹ If you then, evil (sinful by nature) as you are, know how to give good *and* advantageous gifts to your children, how much more will your Father who is in heaven [perfect as He is] give what is good *and* advantageous to those who keep on asking Him."

Jesus will give us eternal life, kingdom access, and benefits for our asking, seeking, and knocking through faith. However, Jesus still wants us to apply this passage daily to a lifestyle of faith-filled prayer moved by the power and promises of God, highlighted by continuous asking, seeking, and knocking. If a natural parent would give his child a good gift when they ask, how much better would the Father bless His diligent, obedient, and persistent children? The body of Christ has seen the results of many prayers answered by hope-filled, persistent, consistent, faith-driven saints. If you're not already doing it, I encourage you to document your prayer petitions and commit to a thirty-day prayer challenge to get you back motivated and refreshed in your prayer life. **Romans 15:13 NIV** says, "May the God of hope fill you with all joy and peace as you trust in him, so that you may overflow with hope by the power of the Holy Spirit."

Apostles Peter and Paul hoped we'd have increased grace and peace through our familiarity with God. "Grace and peace be multiplied unto you through the knowledge of God, and of Jesus our Lord" **2 Peter 1:2 KJV**. We must daily recognize that there's nothing we can do apart from the Holy Ghost. Our parenting, communication, negotiation, leadership, selling skills, creative marketing abilities, engineering expertise, financial acumen, litigation know-how, computing programming, musicianship, craftsmanship, eye for design, etc., are impossible without the Most High God. That's why the Son of God instructs us to abide in Him—the true Vine.

FAITH OVER FEAR

Fear can be a powerful motivator. Why? Because God repeatedly assures and commands us in His Word to fear not, promising to be there and guide us through any challenges we encounter. The very thing you're anxious about pursuing is the breakthrough that propels you into your true purpose. **Deuteronomy 31:6 NIV** says, "Be strong and courageous. Do not be afraid or terrified because of them, for the LORD your God goes with you; he will never leave you nor forsake you."

Faith is walking into what's unseen and appears crazy to others but is visible to you! Imagine what you can do, where you can go, and what you can accomplish without fear. Will you challenge yourself to surpass your limits and conquer the terror in your path that competes with your potential to live powerfully?

I've watched God lead me through many things I have feared since childhood, and I'm sure you have too. One of the first verses my dad gave me to memorize was **2 Timothy 1:7 KJV**. "For God hath not given us the spirit of fear; but of power, and of love, and a sound mind." God gifts us peace, strength of mind, and a charitable heart. Within them are the dreams and visions to fearlessly bring forth within the Spirit's supernatural power. Never back down in the face of fear; instead, let it be your motivation to boldly call on the name of the Lord to slay the giants in your path through faith.

WHAT MOTIVATES YOU

Once we feast from the Bread of Life, we can venture into other forms of motivation we enjoy. There must be other things that refresh and give you a charge. What kinds of things do you love?

- Working out, being outdoors, hiking, golf, basketball, tennis, fishing, bowling, skating, animals, photography, art, painting, creating or listening to music, dancing, collecting, TV series, movies, documentaries, motivational books, seminars, reading, gaming, working with others, or conversing with like-minded people? Could it be specific restaurants, travel, or a weekend getaway, a favorite food or drink, shopping, building things, woodworking, crafting, sewing, cooking, or baking?

- Maybe you like biographies, leadership content, personal development training, finance education, and productivity hacks. Perhaps it's spending quality time with your spouse, significant other, children, grandchildren, or friends.

Because a purpose-driven business is long-term, and a healthy leader must be happy and not weighed down, finding what motivates and moves you outside of work is essential. Everything I enjoy isn't necessarily spiritual. However, God's presence is near whether enjoying the arts or outdoor activities. When I educate myself with books, documentaries, politics, and religion, I can sharpen my discernment, compare my research with the Word of God, and connect reference points to shape my knowledge bank. However, no compartments in our lives should be hidden from God. He's the best to have near in all we do. We must include and enjoy Him in everything. **Colossians 3:17 NIV** teaches, "And whatever you do in word or deed, *do* all in the name of the Lord Jesus, giving thanks to God the Father through Him." Partaking in what you enjoy makes for a happy lifestyle and expanded experiences.

WHO MOTIVATES YOU

You won't always feel like working to build your business and remain disciplined in your daily success habits. You won't always feel like the best leader, husband/wife, parent, or servant. You'll encounter difficult days, weeks, months, and even years. Some days, you'll be more energetic and enthusiastic than others. On some mornings, you'll feel inspired, and after lunch, you may not feel anything—mainly because outer enthusiasm is temporary and won't last. You'll have to replenish it constantly. Therefore, you'll need to consider additional practical ways to help with inspiration. The good news is that the Lord puts people in your path and allows you to learn from and connect with those faithful, motivating people who stir you to dream big.

Here are some questions to ponder. Who in the Bible inspires you and why? What Christian pastors, teachers, leaders, ministers, authors, creatives, and coaches help you the most? Finding an essential person with whom you resonate to glean lessons in life and business is valuable. You look for goodness in people, not to mimic, put them on pedestals, or copy them, but to learn from them and their spirit of excellence. Why do these people light your fire and motivate you to level up? **Proverbs 27:17 NIV** teaches, "As iron sharpens iron, so one person sharpens another." Whether a preacher or teacher, a content creator or a news anchor, an athlete or a parent, an entrepreneur or a producer, there's someone who inspires you. Again, we're not putting anyone on a pedestal. However, with good examples, we can study their successes, understand their philosophy and work ethic, and learn how they overcome setbacks and adversities.

Rise and live urgently today as if you only have six months to make your dreams happen before the window of opportunity closes. What would you do differently today to accelerate? How would you call on the Lord for wisdom? What prayers would you pray? How will you prepare, train, plan, and seize opportunities? How will you make every day count? Seize the blessing of the day. Remember, **pray + obey + faith + wisdom = accelerate**. Love and serve others. Roll up your sleeves and go after your dreams. Be the best version of yourself to rise into the soul-healthy leader you're born to be. Dig deep into your memory and recall all the times God pulled you up when you were stuck, and know you're already a winner as long as you get up and don't give up.

Acceleration CURE Actions:

- **Find** inspiration in God and the beauty of His creation. Clarify your hobbies and what makes you happy, and commit to experiencing them in some way monthly. You can also challenge yourself to beat your old accomplishments, records, and scores.
- **Locate** a biblical example of someone you can relate to who motivates you. God can use their story, testimony, or work ethic to

release mental shackles and get you unstuck.
- **Reignite** and rewrite your inspiration narrative by identifying why God is the Source of your motivation.
- **Unlock** the best way to enrich and endure through tough times to maintain your connection with the Heavenly Father.

Prayer

Dear Heavenly Father, Before turning to anyone else, I turn my desire towards you for motivation and inspiration. Although I'm thankful for people to learn from, I want to run to you before I run to a person, book, video, or social media for guidance. You're the God that created and purposed me to live a whole and abundant life, and only you know why I feel demotivated at times and how to lift me. Please get to the root of what weighs me down and help me accelerate with more stamina. I look towards the hills which cometh my help. My help comes from the Lord, the Creator of heaven and earth. I pray that I continue to find intimacy in my dependence on you by growing in your Word and connecting with my family in Christ. You're the God who strengthens me to advance my calling. I value the gift of faith and hope. Thank you for placing people and additional resources in my path to help encourage me along the way. Thank you, Lord, for always leading and teaching me.

In Jesus' name, I pray, Amen.

Day 22

CONVEY AN ATTITUDE OF GRATITUDE

I was blessed to work in different industries in my employment journey, as I did contract work over the years. The managers I had the best experiences working for influenced and inspired me to be good at my work. I enjoyed working for them because they had winning attitudes. Equally, the supervisors who gave me the most complex time in my jobs were females. They sometimes didn't even seem to value me or my contributions. Likewise, in business, I also remember the easy clients I worked with over the years and those who were very difficult. When I recall the managers' or clients' names and faces, I reflect on how they made me feel in their presence. In my memory bank, their attitudes (good or bad) and reputation precede them.

Our character, ways, and actions are paramount to our Christian faith. How we behave and present ourselves to people has to reflect the presence of our Father in heaven. The first thing that comes to mind when people think of you is how you make them feel. People's healthy view of you and your company starts with assurance and a humble and gracious attitude because leadership begins at the top and trickles down.

To feel optimistic, confident, and gracious, you must *be* grateful to be alive, serve, grow, and have eternal life. Thanksgiving and gratitude in attitude only come from having the mind of Christ and remembering His grace and mercy when He snatched you from the kingdom of darkness and redeemed your life. Remembering the goodness of the Lord is fundamental to an attitude of kindness. God wants you to lend loving, lasting, and optimistic memories to those you do business with, hire, and encounter. Some good questions are: How do I like to be treated when I do business with or meet someone? How can I shine Jesus' light on this person, situation, or in this environment? What kind of impression do I want to leave with people? How can I lift, bless, and inspire someone today? How can I be expressive and passionate but pleasant while still standing on the truth? Checking the type of attitude we're displaying is vital to spiritual growth, leadership, and maintaining healthy relationships. Unity and deciding to display gratitude as a lifestyle must be the goal of every believer. That's how we glorify our Father and Lord.

Accelerated Power – Romans 15:5-6 NKJV Now may the God of patience and comfort grant you to be like-minded toward one another, according to Christ Jesus, [6] that you may with one mind *and* one mouth glorify the God and Father of our Lord Jesus Christ.

God will give us fortitude and reassurance to unify with our brothers and sisters in love. We don't have to rely on our strength to display harmony. But we'll need to make an effort to walk by the Spirit to experience these benefits. We can learn so much from studying the four Gospels. They get us up close and personal with Jesus's humanity. We know His attitude was consistent and impartial, and He is no respecter of persons. He also had a made-up mind that He would love, encourage, and serve others no matter what. Jesus also demonstrated a Father-pleasing attitude in His obedience at all times. Jesus equips and teaches us in His Word how to act out love in our day-to-day interactions. If you're already doing the right things, there's always room to improve. And if you're struggling with being positive, there's everlasting hope. It doesn't matter if you've lived the prior years of your life with a personality bent toward pessimism and gloom. God's supernatural power can cut right through that downtrodden way of believing if you change your thinking and adopt a fruitful outlook. He can lead you in a like-minded way so that you can set the tone in the environments where you display leadership, such as your home, work, business, church, meetings, etc.

LOVE STARVED

People everywhere are starving for love, validation, affirmation, and to be heard and seen. Many are hurting, lonely, wounded, and stuck. When we look at most of the sins that people have gotten entangled in, most stem from wanting to be loved, accepted, seen, or heard at their core. At least I can speak for myself and other women I've encountered. That's why Satan uses the people closest to us to destroy us. Since relationships are the areas that break and bruise us the most via sexual immorality, abuse, neglect, betrayal, slander, gossip, and downright disrespectful treatment—when we're unhealed and not led by the Spirit of God, we carry and spread the aroma and stench of a bad broken attitude. Some people don't know how their actions hurt us, so the best thing to do is forgive and take accountability for how we show up. Gratefully, we don't have to show up and offer people *our best* in *our strength.*

We know that people want to be championed, supported, and recognized. They want to be loved, respected, and treated kindly. We want people to have good, lasting recollections of us, no matter how uncured their souls may be. As the Father's beloved, be aware of harsh, abrasive, angry, condemning, condescending, complaining, combative, insensitive, and hard-to-talk-to or get-along-with attitudes. Equally, watch the words you speak because they carry weight. **Colossians 4:5-6 NKJV** says, "Walk in wisdom toward those *who are* outside, redeeming the time. *Let* your speech always *be* with grace, seasoned with salt, that you may know how you ought to answer each one." I'm not referring to compromising in situations where we speak truthfully and lovingly with conviction when the recipient refuses to perceive it as such because of the condition of their heart. When possible, seek a good reputation. However, I'd never encourage ditching your personality or dipping into people-pleasing. An excellent way to express a fruit-bearing attitude is to ask how you would want people to speak of you at your funeral, absent of all the accolades and accomplishments. You can change your narrative now. It's up to you how you'd like to be perceived.

God placed us in our circle of influence and type of industry to use as motivators and encouragers. He assigned us unique skills, gifts, and purpose to steward and shine a light on darkness. We're workers of hope and change! Therefore, we must first vow to learn to give ourselves this same love and care and keep our cups full before we can fill someone else's.

THE ENRICHING LEADER

You're here to enrich people's lives through your purpose, calling, products, and services. Your company serves as the hands and feet of our Savior and solves the problems of those needing solutions. It's a privilege and an honor to assist and serve God and others as an intentional business owner, entrepreneur, leader, visionary, teacher, coach, consultant, advisor, or content creator. We get to do the work we're doing regardless of the level of hard. Therefore, we must remember how far we've come. Look at where you were five and ten years ago. You've grown so much since then. God made your blessings possible and put people in your path to help you go from one level to the next. Many prefer not to give others any credit for the spark of ideas, time, and insight they so freely and willingly sown into their lives. Instead, they think they made it all by themselves in life and business. However, God wants us to thank people for their advice, time, generosity, wisdom, tips, and help. In gratitude, we must check any negative attitudes and habits at the door that don't represent the mind of Christ when we arise in the morning and step in to do God's work.

You're a champion leader. Anything you want to change can change. However, make sure to put in the time and work because nothing changes until you do. Lack of self-control and having a bad day will occur because you're human. You're not sinless, but bad days are the exception, not the rule. Multiple bad days are not an excuse to go off on others and belittle anyone. The fruit of the Spirit starts with love and ends with self-control. Therefore, it's in your control to shift perspective.

Years ago, my Editor-in-Chief Christa, gave me a poem about attitude by pastor, author, educator, and radio host Chuck Swindoll. I used to hang the print on the wall in my dining room office and would read it occasionally. It took me years to incorporate its wisdom into my lifestyle. The poem expresses how attitude is more vital than our past, education, money, circumstances, catastrophe, success, and facts. He shared how attitude overrides ability, appearance, and gifts. I also gathered from the poem that a business, life, or church without an attitude and motivation rooted in Christ's goodness is broken and valueless. Swindoll concludes that ninety percent of how we navigate the challenges in life is how we respond and react to them. [1] How we view the simple things determines how much we prosper. Do we respond and react gratefully when we have more or less of what we want? Cheer and gladness shouldn't rest on how much money, health, followers, accolades, awards, or compliments we've achieved. Success is operating in God's abundance within and sharing it with others. **Proverbs 17:20, 22 NIV**, "One whose heart is corrupt does not prosper; one whose tongue is perverse falls into trouble." "A cheerful heart is good medicine, but a crushed spirit dries up the bones." God didn't save us to be grumblers, complainers, and people who always have something to be unhappy about. Joyfulness is contagious, and griping corrupts the heart.

Soulful, our actions are on full display for everyone to see. To accelerate in life and business, we must build attitudes of love and kindness on the great Rock of the Lord Jesus. It's challenging at times to stay focused on the promises of God during the rough times when a way out isn't visible. But if you fold on how you handle things, you'll miss the blessings on the journey and remain stuck. Do your best to persevere and not let your temporary emotional state get the best of you. No matter how tough things may be for you in your current situation, it's all about taking accountability for the right attitude. God hears your concerns and plans something extraordinary for you.

MAINTAINING GOODNESS

The Apostle Paul maintained an attitude of gratitude in his ministry. He endured so much hardship to preach and teach the good news, yet he thanked God and remained steady through the turbulent times and rejection. Paul's beautifully written letters while in prison should inspire us. Furthermore, Paul was challenged and questioned about his authenticity and apostleship by the Corinthians versus the fake ministers. They tolerated the fake bragging men who were going about making it appear like Paul was laying heavy burdens on them and doing too much. Hence, he had to run down his resume and bring up his sufferings, not boastfully but matter of factually. **2 Corinthians 11:16 NIV,** "I repeat: Let no one take me for a fool. But if you do, then tolerate me just as you would a fool, so that I may do a little boasting. [17] In this self-confident boasting I am not talking as the Lord would, but as a fool."

Paul had to overcome and prove his genuineness and love because people were feeding the church of Corinth lies. He was shipwrecked three times, cold, naked, hungry, thirsty, flogged, beaten severely, imprisoned several times, exposed to death multiple times, and in constant danger. He was constantly on the move from Jews and Gentiles, false believers, and bandits, all of whom wanted to take his life. He found no rest in the city, country, or sea. He lived through all of this to spread the gospel. In **verses 30-31,** "If I must boast, I will boast of the things that show my weakness. [31] The God and Father of the Lord Jesus, who is to be praised forever, knows that I am not lying." The Lord Jesus used Paul's life and attitude to help us in every hardship we face. He gave us insight into the mindset and attitude of the adoring Apostle towards God and people. Therefore, I recommend studying the New Testament epistles inductively—precept upon precept—and some good commentaries and books that are invaluable for all believers to grow in their faith.

GOING DEEPER

God encourages us to dig deeper, and that journey requires the right resources and tools. By cultivating consistent study habits, you can create your own curriculum, just like a college experience. Please note, I do not confirm or endorse 100% of anything an imperfect human writer publishes. However, here are some helpful resources to start with:

1. **Commentaries:** *The Bible Exposition Commentary* by Warren W. Wiersbe, *The Believers Bible Commentary* by William McDonald, *Thru the Bible* by J Vernon McGee, *The Tony Evans Bible Commentary* by Tony Evans, and *Living Insights New Testament Commentary* by Charles R. Swindoll.

2. **Books:** *Rightly Dividing the Word* by Clarence Larkin, *Christian Apologetics* by Norman L. Geisler, *Basic Bible Interpretation* by Roy B. Zuck, *Inductive Bible Study* by Richard Alan Fuhr and Andreas J. Köstenberger, *The Essence of the New Testament: A Survey* by Towns and Gutierrez, *Christian Beliefs* by Wayne Grudem, *Vines Complete Expository Dictionary* by W.E. Vine, Merrill F Unger, and William White Jr., *The Spiritual Man* by Watchman Nee, *Life Essentials* by Tony Evans, *Misled* by Allen Parr.

3. **Websites:** gotquestions.org and thebereancall.org.

My shared resources are meaty but designed to align with your biblical worldview. God calls us to step up our knowledge and understanding of Him, His Word, and the world. I especially want my ladies to take notice of these materials because we sometimes think someone is mean or unreasonable when they share truths. Then, we misjudge their attitude and mistake their love. We're also most vulnerable to false teachings and being misled due to our nurturing, sympathetic nature and array of emotional expressions. But as you go deep into your understanding and studies of what you may deem as dull, you'll love it! Trust me. These tools help you dig and mine the Scriptures and become a discerning apologist and a student of the Word. They are substantial and transformative, guiding you to experience the fullness of joy in the Lord, preparing your mind for the journey and harvest ahead, and defending your faith in love and thanksgiving.

The more we know about our God and truth, the more gracious we are in always lifting Him. Constantly give Him praise, appreciation, and honor because He's always giving you His best top-tier excellent and perfect love and blessings. God provides you with beauty in abundance and daily life. He allows you to ask, seek, knock, read, love, work, raise children, care for your pets, run businesses, own homes and vehicles, and enjoy things you love. There is never a shortage of thanksgiving as a child of God. God rewards your ability to keep a good attitude during your testing season and in heaven. Acceleration is a byproduct of an honorable posture toward the King. **Luke 6:31 NIV** teaches, "Do to others as you would have them do to you." But always treat yourself kindly. When you maintain a positive attitude and give thanks (in all things), God can work on your behalf.

Acceleration CURE Actions:

- **Read** 2 Corinthians 11:16-33 to picture and meditate on all the Apostle Paul underwent. Clarify your attitude and motives and commit to serving others with compassion.
- **Decide** on the authentic attitude you want to portray and treat others how you want them to treat you to get unshackled and unstuck.
- **Quarantine** and evaluate your thoughts and attitudes daily. Reignite good thinking and rewrite genuine and helpful compliments and encouragement you can offer others.

- **Immerse** and enrich yourself by studying Jesus' attitude. Endure encounters with those who aren't open to reciprocity of kindness. Decide in advance how you want to respond and react.

Prayer

Dear Heavenly Father, Thank you for all that you do for me, all that you've done, and all that you're going to do. Your word says in all things, give thanks. Thank you for shifting my attention to encouraging others through a gracious and benevolent attitude. I realize that I'm always to represent you with Christlike behavior. I struggle with my attitude being right sometimes, but I'm asking that you help me change it because my request is in your will. Please forgive me for complaining, murmuring, grumbling, and displaying an ungrateful attitude. Thank you for my relational and business successes and for schooling me to stand for you righteously. I can do nothing apart from you.

In Jesus' Name, I pray, Amen.

Part 7

EXECUTION ACCELERATION

Day 23
CREATE AND INNOVATE

My mom cared for and nurtured my sisters Shenetta and Denise and my hair when we were little girls. She regularly shampooed, conditioned, and styled it in ponytails with barrettes and always kept it neat and cute. Occasionally, she pressed and curled our mane with the hot comb at home or took us to her stylist, Nina Fuller. When she needed a break from the regular upkeep of caring for our hair, she took us to get our natural hair braided in cornrows with accent beads due to their cute looks, longevity, and low maintenance. However, I remember getting my hair relaxed at around fourteen by mom. She became a licensed cosmetologist. During my relaxed hair years, I grew accustomed to the *"professional and polished look"* of what society coined as *good*, presentable, straight hair. However, the chemicals of sodium hydroxide in lye relaxers break down the natural bonds, texture, and curl pattern in coily hair to straighten it. I'd continue touching up my new growth for the next twenty-plus years. I didn't know about my hair texture in detail and could only see the new growth since I didn't do my natural textured hair as a youth and never had a reason to learn more about it. I vaguely remember what it felt like outside of my childhood experience or how it reacted without any chemicals on the ends.

Finally, at age thirty-seven, I stopped putting relaxers in my hair in 2014. I big chopped into a TWA (Teeny, Weeny, Afro)! That's when you cut away all the relaxed hair to a low cut and start to grow it out. I went through what we black women call a natural hair journey. At first, I felt like I looked like a boy, and I wasn't comfortable or confident in my skin. Then, over the next few months, I felt freedom in learning to accept myself with short, kinky, coily hair in its regular, God-given state. The big chop led me on a voyage of defeating identity blindness, overcoming societal norms and programmed beauty standards, and growing in confidence. I couldn't keep my hands out of my hair during the first few months. I was in awe by how springy, compact, and shrunken it was and how it coiled and waved up like a slinky. I was amazed at the different patterns in texture and how God created it. I had to learn how to care for my hair in this fresh way—it was a new beginning.

It blows my mind to see how God gave people of African descent this rare kind of hair that doesn't look like anyone else's. Our hairstylists are some of the most creative people I ever met. They style hair into works of art. I wonder about God's thinking when He made it. Its flexibility and strength can transform into all sorts of looks and styles, but at the same time, it's the most delicate of all hair kinds. My mom became a cosmetology instructor and beauty school manager in my teen years. My dad also built a beauty salon for her in our finished basement so she could build her clientele on the side. She told me everyone else has two layers, a cuticle, and a cortex, but we have an additional innermost layer that makes up our strands called the medulla.

Sadly, my black community and peers shunned the kind of hair we have had for many years by calling it nappy, saying it doesn't grow, and most still do. But it does grow long and healthy, just like any other culture, when you have the wisdom to care for it. Many still aren't grateful or accepting of their God-given tresses and don't know how to care for them. Many non-blacks in the corporate or professional environments didn't encourage it as much, and others were unbothered by the expression. Having a fro or what they deemed unprofessional hair wasn't ideal to showcase. Admittedly, I wasn't keen on the look when I saw girls in the 90s and early 2000s rocking their naturalista styles and twists. However, unlocking the confidence to be yourself is rewarding and the surest way to accelerate you into your noncompetitive lane.

In this book, I won't go down the rabbit hole. However, hair with the medulla layer, our crowing glory, shines a light on God's creativity detail. "But if a woman has long hair, it is a glory to her; for *her* hair is given to her for a covering" **1 Corinthians 11:15 NKJV**. We're to be honored by God's signature touch on us, whoever we are, whether it's silky, straight, textured, fine, thick, kinky, coiled, curly, wavy, frizzy, or whatever—thank God for it.

God wants us to be unafraid to be authentic and use our making and creating abilities to prosper. And as children made in His image, we can explore and embrace every angle of creativity He places in us with our renewed minds. Our uniqueness and creations highlight our abilities and capabilities, thus allowing us to grow profitable and purposeful businesses.

> **Accelerated Power – Exodus 35:30-33 NIV** Then Moses said to the Israelites, "See, the LORD has chosen Bezalel son of Uri, the son of Hur, of the tribe of Judah, [31] and he has filled him with the Spirit of God, with wisdom, with understanding, with knowledge and with all kinds of skills— [32] to make artistic designs for work in gold, silver and bronze, [33] to cut and set stones, to work in wood and to engage in all kinds of artistic crafts.

Whatever inspiration you offer the world is a byproduct of God's creativeness if used correctly and isn't perverted. God put the gifts of intelligence, insight, and all kinds of imaginative designs in metal, stones, and wood in Bazalel. Yes, He also planted the purposes, skills, and gifts in you to birth originality through the Holy Spirit's instruction. Recall the details of when God commissioned the Ark of the Covenant, the Tabernacle, and Solomon's Temple. The particulars were specific (Exodus 25-40, 1 Kings 5-9, 2 Chronicles 2). Since the Creator gave each person involved in the building processes exceptional gifts and roles, it speaks to how well He knows and fashioned us.

CREATE

The Creator wants you to highlight your gift of creativity in your calling and mission, just like He used the artisans in the Scriptures. If you get close enough, He will share fresh, innovative ideas that overflow into profitability and a strategy to market the concepts. Over the years, God has already blessed you with many imaginative ideas and thoughts. Since He made you in His image, you have a river of ingenuity in you. God is the Creator of everything beautiful and defines creativeness. The Maker doesn't need a resume to share and explain His track record because His wonders precede Him.

It's impossible to miss His hand upon all we experience, from breathing each breath to seeing the rainbow in the sky after rain. Yet, the Lord tells us all about His wonders in the Holy Scriptures because there are many facets and categories to His originality. For starters, you can find His amazement in the first few chapters of the book of Genesis and all until Revelation. God's mighty and intricate creations don't stop in the Bible—they're eternal. What I find relatively intriguing is how He created us in His image. Out of everything He made, He created us as a close representation of Himself—*Imago Dei*.

"For we are his workmanship, created in Christ Jesus unto good works, which God hath before ordained that we should walk in them" **Ephesians 2:10 KJV**. Some believe we're little gods because we're created in God's image. If God doesn't like us to worship idols (gods), I doubt if He wants little prideful idols running around. God is the One True Living Eternal God, and I'll leave it there.

Please think about the intricacies of your human body for a few minutes. Meditate on your physical frame's structure, DNA, chromosomes, biology, chemistry, and anatomy from your head to your toes. Also, consider the roles of your organs, veins, vessels, and cells. What about your bones, tendons, joints, marrow, limbs, hair, nails, and skin? How about the body's innate repairing and rejuvenation processes? Consider how brilliant and complex your gut, brain, and bodily system are. Ponder about your spirit, heart, and soul. Additionally, God allowed us to touch, hear, smell, see, and taste through our senses.

Imaginativeness fuels our work and helps us to stay focused and motivated to keep going. Everyone should carve out time in life and business to be involved in creative activities. I bet you can develop concepts, creations, songs, drawings, furnishings, décor, clothing, herbal remedies, housing blueprints, engineering renderings, culinary dishes, sales pitches, legal arguments, classic car redesigns, motors, problem-solving inventions, etc. Ideas won't run out if you refresh your mind and generate new things.

USING CREATIVE IDEAS

What do you want to construct? What ideas have you been holding on to? What do you love? What's hindering you from using more of your sharpness? When can you carve out time to create? Sometimes, the Creator can give you an idea to work on in a down season. He will bury the project like a seed for years, reignite the vision, and make it sprout at a pre-determined time. That's why I recommend always running your creative concepts by God first, so you won't get distracted working on something fresh without finishing what you're already working on.

Speaking of inspiration, have you read through the entire Bible from cover to cover? As believers, we should read through the Holy Bible regularly, at least (biennially or triennially). You'll need God's wisdom for originality, as obtaining it is by familiarizing yourself with Him through the Word. Growing in the knowledge of Christ is paramount to being a better creative entrepreneur. Researching, word studies, and efficient note-taking are equally necessary, but it all will make more sense when you first read and become familiar with the Scriptures. If you've yet to take on the challenge of reading the Bible from cover to cover, I encourage you to aim to start within the next quarter and complete it over the next nine to fifteen months. You can start with thirty minutes each day until you finish it. Once you re-read the Bible multiple times, you'll begin to study it and take notes.

ENCOURAGING CREATIVITY

Since God created and assigned your purpose, He built specific tasks into the calling, so you must be intentional about protecting your novelty. Origination keeps us sharp and driven to work even if we don't use any of the concepts. Some are creative in the arts. Others are creative in marketing, teaching, construction design, and arguing the law. Some love writing, colors, the sounds of musical instruments, song lyrics, vocal arrangements, melodies and harmonies, paintings, beautiful interiors, and many other arts-related things. Many people lose interest in their jobs because they can't do anything creative. Although I'm all for systems, I need to live my life and run my business in a way where I can occasionally color outside the lines. Therefore, as a leader, encourage your team to craft more ideas even if they never get utilized. Things like Pinterest boards, puzzles, exploring new genres of books and documentaries, taking a new hobby, classical and jazz music, games, brainstorming, chess, writing, going for a walk without music, talking to kids, waking up before 5 am, and collaborating on ideas can help you flesh out your creative side and spark newness.

You can also be creative in your marriage, relationships, friendships, events, travels, meals, wardrobe, landscaping, studies, etc. Have fun. Please don't stop dreaming or using your imagination. It's not too late to start again if you've stopped innovating. You benefit from products, services, technology, travel experiences, architecture, engineering, literature and films, culture, laws, etc., because great thoughts become pioneering realities. God put conceptions in you to turn the financial trajectory of your life around. He wants to extract the potential in you to bless you and others. The profitable answer is within your reach and is closer than you assume. Exciting yourself to be more ingenious in life and business will lead you to the acceleration cure.

Acceleration CURE Actions:

- **Be** inspired and intentional with creativity. Clarify the ideas God wants you to create and commit to settling on one endeavor you'll work on for personal and business over the next twelve months.
- **Highlight** twenty of God's creations that inspire you. This list will inspire you to get unstuck by drawing you closer to the Creator.
- **Reignite** and rewrite a list of ten things you want to do but have yet to try. Are you interested in exploring the originality of your relationships, rewriting stuff you have always wanted to do, and creating them for fun, like sculpting, memorable travels, photo shoots, local dining experiences, etc?
- **Enrich** and endure the creative process until you see the vision God gave you become a reality.

Prayer

Gracious Creative God, I want to learn more about and appreciate your beauty in creation. I'm in awe just reading and understanding your written Word. There are so many inspiring biblical passages that describe your breathtaking work. Also, when I look outdoors, I see your exquisiteness everywhere. I pray you show me how to use my creativity in life and business to grow financially and add more vibrancy to my life. Inventiveness isn't just for some people. You gave us all the gift in some capacity. I pray for creativity in every area of the assignments you call me to. I'm also asking that you send the right people to share in and appreciate experiencing the imaginative works you bless us with.

In Jesus' name, I pray, Amen.

Day 24
TELL IT

I watched a video some years back that shows strangers calling sheep. Although they're close in proximity, the sheep don't pay them any mind. But when their shepherd calls them, they all stop grazing and run to the fence to greet him. This reality tells us that God's Word is true and His sheep know His voice. **John 10:27 NIV** says, "My sheep listen to my voice; I know them, and they follow me." People think that because others can hear them, they listen and pay attention. This disconnect in the language barrier is where we struggle in the marketplace. Business owners call out to the wrong people who don't recognize them.

Christians believe that because God put a business in their heart, customers will automatically come rushing to buy. Not so. Yes, the Holy Spirit is the One who draws people to purpose-driven entrepreneurs and inclines people to understand their calling code. Therefore, preparing for opportunities and identifying the target audience is crucial for effective marketing communication and business success. Christians who excel in the tell-it phase often outperform others targeting the same group because they relate to their customers and uniquely understand their immediate needs. They speak with them like friends, not distant strangers in the digital world.

Research says that about 85% of business owners make under $100k annually, while a small percentage consistently rack up multi-millions. The Chamber of Commerce cited poor marketing initiatives as the number one reason businesses fail.[1]. Why do the 15% dominate? Because they're masters of advancing their communications skills, leverage, influence, storytelling, crafting irresistible offers, creating systems, and marketing automation. They don't build products and offer services—they build solutions, movements, enthusiasts, and communities. They're also excellent at applying principles like farming multiplication to their business. Although Christians should dominate the business landscape with biblical fundamentals, non-Christians take them and prosper

ASTUTE AND AWARE

After the rich man accused his manager of wasting and mishandling his possessions and affairs, he was to fire him. However, the manager made deals with his employer's debtors to secure his next steps after unemployment. The Bible teaches that unsaved people are more astute in coming up with solutions than believers. "The master commended the dishonest manager because he had acted shrewdly. For the people of this world are more shrewd in dealing with their own kind than are the people of the light" **Luke 16:8 NIV**.

I'm not saying to act dishonestly in your business. On the contrary, you might have a brilliant strategy, product, concept, and idea, but the intended recipients will never discover how good they are if you can't reach them and they can't find you. They can't intercept the business or brand's messaging signal because you aren't on the same wavelength. The goal is to harmonize with your audience. By identifying your target market and constructing impactful messaging, you can ensure your business maximizes its resources and embraces every opportunity that comes your way.

You'll want to understand these questions to increase your astuteness and awareness. **Who** is God calling you to serve? **What** problem are you solving, and what does God want you to offer them as a solution? **Why** are you presenting this, and will they be interested in buying your products or services or attending your events? **How** will you reach them? Your business will survive, thrive, and accelerate by spending time on who, what, why, and how and building a marketing strategy around them with the Holy Spirit's instructions. Constantly ask, "God, can you give me wisdom on how and where I can reach those I'm called to serve? Lord, please teach me what I need to know and where to go."

FARMING (ONE TO MANY)

Entrepreneurship, like farming, is a spiritual journey and lifestyle for the believer. Ancient Israel built its wealth in agriculture and livestock through God's multiplication principle. A farmer's life teaches dependency on God through the laws of working wisely, sowing and reaping, faith, endurance, and prayer. This lifestyle teaches patience, develops character, advances education, a reliable work ethic, rest, consistency, discipline, and seasonal adaptation.

Farming allows one to learn the soil's and crop's various languages, discern threats and enemies, and protect the environment. A farmer won't just throw down any ol' seed, expect anything to spout on certain soils, and then search for buyers. They can't just *hope* for the best void of research. Farmers choose which crops to grow based on market demand, ethics, and conditions. They must know who needs it, what they need it for, and why it solves a problem as they determine the seed and soil condition and consider the distance to markets and specific growing climate requirements for each crop.

Good marketing is like farming, aiming to multiply that one message to reach many with a prepared mind. When prayer, intentionality, biblical principles, and agricultural philosophy harmonize, one good seed planted and cultivated in the fertile soil will spread, reproduce, and significantly increase the yield to a hundredfold or more.

Accelerated Power – Matthew 13:3-8 NIV, "A farmer went out to sow his seed. ⁴ As he was scattering the seed, some fell along the path, and the birds came and ate it up. ⁵ Some fell on rocky places, where it did not have much soil. It sprang up quickly, because the soil was shallow. ⁶ But when the sun came up, the plants were scorched, and they withered because they had no root. ⁷ Other seed fell among thorns, which grew up and choked the plants. ⁸ Still other seed fell on good soil, where it produced a crop—a hundred, sixty or thirty times what was sown."

Although the context of this parable speaks of God's Word as the seed and the message of the good news and what happens in time after sharing it on the soil of people's hearts—its application is valuable holistically in life and business. It helps us understand the four types of soil the farmer contends with for his seed to take root. It also gives us a principle of how our seed (faith) goes through spiritual stages wrapped in prayer for God's increase and the power necessary to break through and grow. When seeds take root in fertile soil, acceleration happens. Therefore, when it comes to marketing, it's all about patiently enduring the trials of tweaking your offering through various stages and seasons until you finally hit lush soil. Also, share a message that can reach and resonate with the soul of your audience in different places at once. **Who/what/why/how + messaging + aligned offer + fertile soil = acceleration multiplication**. **Deuteronomy 32:30 KJV** says, "How should one chase a thousand, and two put ten thousand to flight?"

- Ten entrepreneurs in various cities share the gospel with 100 people: ten souls become converts and later pastors who influence others to share and spread the gospel to thousands more.
- An author writes a book to serve the body of Christ. It sells millions, impacting many to grow in their faith. The book leads to the author's speaking and conference opportunities where new readers buy it. The writer's manuscript can be published in multiple languages and revised and reprinted for years.
- A Christian content creator makes a viral teaching video that leads saints to a desire to grow in Christ.

THE GREATEST PROBLEM SOLVER

We get to learn from the Greatest—the Creator of life, business, and storytelling! God had a redemption plan, so the Father sent His only begotten Son, Jesus, to fulfill the purpose. He devised a life-saving and life-changing call that lost souls could relate to.

Jesus didn't come to earth as a man to wing it, go with the flow, hang out, or play by ear. He had a target audience and deadline; He went right to the lost sheep of Israel (Matthew 15:24, Jeremiah 50:6, Ezekiel 34:23-24). There was a message to spread and a mission to complete during His three-year ministry before His pre-planned appointment as the Sacrificial Lamb (Genesis 3:15). Jesus built relationships, gathered a team of followers, and an inner circle to absorb His teachings, enabling Him to spread and multiply the good news and fulfill His mission. Nevertheless, it's important to note that He envisioned and wrote the plan before He put it into action (who, what, when, where, why, and how).

In John 4, Jesus conversed with the Samaritan woman at the well. He got to the heart of her issues and everything she had ever done. He shared a solution of eternal living water that she couldn't refuse. "The woman said to him, 'Sir, give me this water so that I won't get thirsty and have to keep coming here to draw water'" **John 4:15 NIV**. Regular water or another dead-end relationship couldn't fill the God-sized hole in her heart. Jesus' exchange hit the heart of a soul-striking need in the woman, showing how her sins separated her from God and that the peace she sought through her relationships was in His everlasting water. The woman's soul-transforming encounter led her to tell everyone in her town about the Man who told her all she ever did.

When a message hits home, it multiplies and spreads quickly through word of mouth. God's redemption plan to reconcile the unconverted to the Father continues to bear fruit, and new converts daily! Jesus' short ministry continues to outlast and outperform that time frame thousands of years after His death, burial, and resurrection. The world stole His method and called it marketing. But Jesus is God, which means He's the Creator and innovator of every business, marketing, or success principle and gives the believer access to His divine wisdom.

A BIBLICAL FRAMEWORK

I'm sharing this with you as brothers and sisters in the faith. However, before we go further, it's crucial to understand that I would never compare the sacrifice and finished work of Jesus Christ with a marketing message. No! We never sell or profit from the message of the cross, but I will use this example to help you see a framework for organizing your message. I honor our Lord and Savior and don't make merchandise of Him in any way.

- **WHO has a problem?** Jews and Gentiles (mankind).
- **WHAT is the problem?** People suffer from a deadly condition and plague called sin (which makes them sinners) with an eternal

judgment, consequence, and penalty of hell as a sentence. This sickness separates them from fellowship with God. **Romans 5:12 NKJV**, "Therefore, just as through one man sin entered the world, and death through sin, and thus death spread to all men, because all sinned." "And anyone not found written in the Book of Life was cast into the lake of fire" **Revelation 20:15 NKJV**.

- **WHY is there pain?** Sin resides in mankind—everyone born under Adam. **Romans 3:23 NKJV** teaches, "For all have sinned and fall short of the glory of God." All sinners are enslaved to depravity and unrighteousness. They've tried everything to overcome and cover up the sting of death—but it's impossible.

- **HOW is it solved?** The Father sent a Sufficient Sacrifice—His Son (the innocent Lamb). The Messiah, Savior Jesus Christ, came to rescue sinners from their guilt of sin and pay their judgment penalty fine of death with His own death and blood. We're in the wrong, but Jesus paid the penalty for us. Gratefully, we have a cure for this sickness and fellowship and a home with God by accepting His grace and placing our faith in Christ's finished work (death, burial, resurrection) for the payment of sins' debt. **John 3:16-17 NKJV**, "For God so loved the world that He gave His only begotten Son, that whoever believes in Him should not perish but have everlasting life. ¹⁷ For God did not send His Son into the world to condemn the world, but that the world through Him might be saved." **1 John 1:8-9 NKJV** says, "If we say that we have no sin, we deceive ourselves, and the truth is not in us. ⁹ If we confess our sins, He is faithful and just to forgive us *our* sins and to cleanse us from all unrighteousness." **Romans 10:13 NKJV** says, "For 'whoever calls on the name of the Lord shall be saved." There is no other solution, substitution, or resolution.

There you have a framework that should draw you closer to the precious bleeding side of our Savior and the cross and fuel you to go forward in power on your mission to spread the good news.

HEART WAR

Now, let's switch gears and look back at the business. Like farming, there's a tug of war in the heart of the individual you share the good news with, and it will be that way for those you want to do business with. Although you know and see the problem and pain, have the solution to help them get unshackled and unstuck—Satan has them blind, deaf, and bound. Some of the people you're called to serve are numb, while others have learned to live with the pain. And if they're already in Christ, the devil knows that if they do business with you, they'll eventually understand the truth about living abundantly in Jesus and the power of faith. But you know better! There is a spiritual battle for their soul, and you have to fight it on your knees in prayer.

That's where you come in with the aligned messaging to help them see the truth, life, and light. Because God gave you the purpose to reach those of a particular background, you know they're captive to something preventing them from connecting with you. For instance, several factors contribute to seeds falling on fertile soil. **Mark 4:17 NIV** says, "But since they have no root, they last only a short time. When trouble or persecution comes because of the word, they quickly fall away." They need prepared hearts to receive your message. Can you see why your calling into entrepreneurship as Christ's deployed ambassador is a mandate to live a life of fellowship, humility, study, Scripture memory, meditation, fasting, and prayer? God is preparing you for the heart and soul war people are battling.

BRAND IDENTITY AND TEAMWORK

Many people pour their hearts into starting companies, services, and YouTube channels, yet often overlook the importance of consistency in their messaging and details. This can lead to confusion and uncertainty for the very audience they wish to connect with. I've also observed that many individuals don't have a reliable online business hub that they can fully control, separate from third-party platforms. It's essential for every business to have access to knowledgeable support in various areas to truly thrive. For those in the Christian community, having a professionally designed website as a central business hub and a few targeted landing pages is crucial. These tools can help effectively share our messages and promote events and offerings, making a meaningful impact in our communities.

We also need the help of good people who specialize in things to help us grow and expand in areas specific to our business needs to share our message. Similarly, receiving unaligned, unsuitable, or unskilled help can be a significant obstacle because you'll wind up doing their job and yours. In my magazine days, I needed qualified, proactive people to help the vision materialize. God blessed me with a gift early on related to identifying the rarity of synergetic work. The right mix of help is a blessing and reward from God and is hard to replace.

A DREAM TEAM

Before I stepped foot in Atlanta, I had a plan and knew who I was targeting, and I had no issues building the dream team. By the time it finally went to print, the word had been getting out and into the hands of everyone from New York, Miami, and LA. My team was phenomenal; they all spread the brand message, and many people wanted to join us. So imagine the devastation I felt as a young woman under thirty making power moves, seeing a dream crumble before it could take off.

Artist Michael Demby designed the logo. Derek Blanks, a celebrity photographer and artist, built my first website and took my headshot. I also worked with photographers Shawn Dowdell, Brian L. Christian, Adrian Jackson, and Donna Permell. Designers Sante White, Les Randall, and Yakka Murphy demonstrated creative and professional graphic layouts and magazine design. Jai Stone, a brand coach, coached me on the importance of branding and consistency in the new magazine layouts moving forward. My Marketing Director, Kimberly S. Webster, and Operations Director, Sean M. Rush, taught me more about marketing and messaging than I had already been using in the past. Angela Watts, Antonio Maddox, Franco Summerour, Venus Clarke, Quincy S. Young, Monica Brown, and Melanie Williams assisted with marketing and promotions. My Fashion Editor, celebrity stylist, Kim Maxwell, showed me the importance of wardrobe and personal image presentation and fashion editorial shoots.

Copy Chief Billye Cox highlighted the need for editing copy and the technique used. Editor-in-Chief Christa E. Jackson assigned and helped the writers stay on topic with word counts, deadlines, and building alliances. Senior and Contributing Writers Rahiem Shabazz, Vicki Gray, and Frank

Rivera had more significant assignments. Dee Dee Cocheta handled all PR. My assistant, Jeanise Chaplin, enabled me to stay organized and build out the administrative side. The majority of contributors had their own businesses. There were many other talented contributors and assistants as things began to flourish, and I can't name them all. All these departments and contributions were in place to help us in the tell-it phase and stay on brand. I'm forever grateful to everyone who lent a hand to help my business. Words can't express my gratitude.

LONGEVITY

Nowadays, many Christian entrepreneurs lack help from a team, coach, brand, or online presence, but every enduring company here for the long haul has them. What do McDonald's, Wendy's, Subway, Starbucks, Coca-Cola, Nike, Adidas, Gucci, Tiffany's, Macy's, Costco, Walmart, Target, Cadillac, Lincoln, Audi, etc have in common? They're brands!

A brand has an easily identifiable stand-out logo, color scheme, and aesthetic. However, though important, a brand isn't just about the website, logo, design consistency, photography, typography, fonts, and colors. The colors are essential, but the branding reflects the origin story that drives the name, essence, and mission. It embodies and attracts a particular community and supporters of like minds, culture, status, and energy. Movements share their offerings in a way that ignites feelings, such as excitement, cravings, motivation, success, luxury, happiness, peace, rest, productivity, etc.

Brands are in the business for the long haul. The message tells who to target, where to focus efforts, and why the products and services offerings solve a problem. You want to be authentic to who your brand represents and how you communicate with them. What is your USP? A brand sets the Unique Selling Proposition apart from everyone else in the marketplace. That's the brand's story and image. Consumers are very savvy and picky, and they buy from or invest in those they trust, resonate with, and will be around for a while. People love great products, but long-term repeat connections like to resound with stories hidden within the brand message.

What is your personal and company story? How can it connect with your people? How will you serve them? Where are they going for this now? How can you test this concept? What's your go-to-market strategy? Will they pay for this, and how much? How will you reach them? What value will this add to their life or business? How will this help them to improve their lives? The brand isn't for you, but it's about how your customers view the problem and how you want them to feel during and after the solution.

Sometimes, what we say doesn't resonate because it's the messenger, not the message, so we need to become the right person in Christ to whom people want to listen and relate. The key is to spend more time personally cultivating yourself spiritually and listening to others. When you become a person of service, everything else will align to reproduce the seed on lush soil.

THE GATHERING

People are looking for root pain cure, not just symptom relief. Once they discover it, they'll pay whatever it costs to alleviate it. Your gathering and tribe are looking for a place they belong. They want to be in the company and culture of like-minded people and someone who understands their needs, struggles, and desires. Again, this concept originates with God and is native to how the body of Christ assembles to fellowship at a local church to worship God, learn and be fed the Bread of Life, and connect with our fellow brothers and sisters.

Your ideal audience is hemorrhaging and drowning in problems, unprofitable habits, patterns, and blind spots that aren't fixing their issues. The community is also looking for speed and convenience. Not necessarily quickness for the sake of being quick, but for the shortest time frame to get them closer to their desires. They need help and results, but they can't find you. Instead, they've settled for someone who lacks the anointing to fulfill their needs or because they don't know where else to turn. They are either stuck and sitting in the same place they were five years ago because the person they hired or took a chance with is the best they could locate at the time. That's why God is preparing you to show up to serve them.

GAP MARKETING

It's erroneous to think Christians don't need a marketing plan. Everything we do needs one because we serve the God of all planning. Although what we offer isn't about mimicking, gimmicks, and fancy strategies, we must realize that God had us to live in this technologically advanced age for a reason and to acquire skills to keep up with it. We shouldn't shun using the resources available to reach the people God wants us to connect with. If I were fishing for salmon, I wouldn't fish at my local pond. Just as a fisherman needs the proper body of water and bait to hook his catch, we need a targeted strategy to accompany our prayers for our offerings. Russell Brunson uses the hook, story, offer, and call to action framework. And the thing about frameworks is that they work when we apply them.

Your plan should focus on the gap between people's current positions and their desired goals. For instance, a hair stylist specializing in hair restoration for women with scalp or health conditions may call out to those dealing with female pattern androgenetic alopecia, alopecia areata, traction alopecia, postpartum shedding, etc. You do this by thoroughly unpacking and researching the pain and disruption they're experiencing. What's robbing their peace and keeping them up at night? They may be coping with embarrassment, shame, confusion, etc. What's hindering them from accomplishing their goal of hair restoration and growth? How will they feel when they get unstuck? How long is the results process? You may find them through referrals from other stylists, dermatologists, beauty and women's church events, braiding salons, or by making educational videos they'll find online. Those who align with your call and solutions will respond.

Ever notice how people light up in conversations when you unlock an answer to an issue they're facing? Wouldn't you like to experience that reaction from people regularly buying your products and services and seeking your advice for their problems? You are the person they're seeking because God carved out a territory in the marketplace for your purpose and unique capability. God wants to use your exclusive triumphs and achievement stories to serve others. You're the qualified teacher because your faith in Christ as His ambassador already qualifies you. And you have the answers because you submit yourself to the Holy Spirit and apply the Word. Therefore, trust that God equipped *you* to grow a business and be someone's answer to their prayer and pain.

The last step in this process is implementation, which is executing your findings and research with a beta test. A good reason to test is to help you uncover flaws. This process allows you to tweak and refine things. Entrepreneurs are risk-takers, and having everything right at the start is impossible. Many companies test their products first. Based on the test results, they decide whether to produce them full-scale or eliminate them. The execution plan will help you measure your campaigns and allow you to see what's working and what's not. You can test your ideas by conducting market research calls, offering sample sizes, digital products, webinars, trials, pamphlets, T-shirts, etc. Faith-driven action, prayer, messaging, uncovering their pain, branding, and multiplication will advance you sooner than you imagine.

Acceleration CURE Actions:

- **Clarify** who God's calling you to reach and commit to seeing how you can serve them.
- **Apply** wisdom from the Bible to expand confident communications to help you get unshackled and unstuck in your marketing efforts.
- **Reignite** your brand's mission and rewrite its story to better align with the people God assigns to you.
- **Include** a gap strategy and framework in your plan to enrich, endure, and help people get to the root of their problems.

Prayer

Dear Heavenly Father, Forgive me for shunning things I didn't know I needed. I can't plan, market, and execute this mission without you. I want to ask who you want me to reach and by what means. I don't want to toil all night without a catch, as the venture can't survive without knowing where to throw out my net. I've tried to do it my way and have experienced little success. I want to enjoy the work you called me to do, and my prayer is for you to help me and the other kingdom builders find where we fit in the marketplace so we can bring glory to your name. Please lead us in talking to the right people and using the right messaging and strategies. Teach us how to study your Word and learn from you.

Please help us to market and execute effectively.

In Jesus' name, I pray, Amen.

Day 25
SELL IT

I remember when we had annual candy drives during the elementary school year. Netta, Neicy, Franco, and I used to win the big prizes because once my dad got a hold of those forms, He'd take them to his job, and his friends and co-workers would buy so much stuff from their middle-income salaries. The people wanted to support us, and they wanted those annual goodies. My dad was our sell-it representative who went out to exceed the quota. Without his front-line efforts and diligence, my brother, sisters, and I wouldn't have won any prizes for our solo efforts. Many believers struggle with the sell-it aspect of their business. Most new Christian start-ups fail to allocate time to develop an outbound strategy that effectively reaches their ideal consumers. They say they're waiting on the Lord, pray for customers to pour in, and are terrified to ask people to do business with them. Instead, they say, "I don't like sales." The Chamber of Commerce estimates that around 590,000 businesses shut down annually. [1] Most of these closings fail because revenue doesn't exceed operating expenses and costs.

FISCALLY RESPONSIBLE

God desires fiscally responsible leaders and profitability. We're accountable for producing fruit in all God gives us. Failure to use or misuse what the good Lord gives is a form of disobedience, discontentment, and grumbling. While the devil works to keep us stuck by incapacitating fear, we can choose to activate our faith instead. God helps us overcome our worries and maximize the impact of our gifts and skills. When an honest businessperson takes risks, the rewards outweigh the threats. We can get ahead by producing results, introducing our business to someone new, or following up on a prior interaction. We can speak to strangers at a store, online, church, park, etc, and leave a gospel tract, brochure, or business card with them.

> **Accelerated Power – Matthew 25:14-18 KJV** For the kingdom of heaven is as a man travelling into a far country, who called his own servants, and delivered unto them his goods. And unto one he gave five talents, to another two, and to another one; to every man according to his several ability; and straightway took his journey. Then he that had received the five talents went and traded with the same, and made them other five talents. [17] And likewise he that had received two, he also gained other two. [18] But he that had received one went and digged in the earth, and hid his lord's money.

In context, Jesus is explaining this parable to share what the Kingdom of Heaven is like and teach us how to steward our gifts and talents. In the story, the manager took a trip and entrusted three men with talents based on their capacity. He expected the servants to do something with and multiply them in their territories based on their knowledge and understanding. When the leader returned, he asked for an accounting. The men he gave five and two doubled what they were given, but the person who received one hid his in the ground.

Here's what he told the men who did well with what they received. "His lord said unto him, 'Well done, thou good and faithful servant: thou hast been faithful over a few things, I will make thee ruler over many things: enter thou into the joy of thy lord'" **(verses 21, 23)**. The third servant didn't believe he could do anything with what he was given. He was afraid to lose and take risks with his gift. So he lived fearfully, did nothing productive, and heaped up an accusation to his leader. "I knew thee that thou art an hard man, reaping where thou hast not sown, and gathering where thou hast not strawed:" **(verse 24)**. "His lord answered and said unto him, 'Thou wicked and slothful servant, thou knewest that I reap where I sowed not, and gather where I have not strawed. Thou oughtest therefore to have put my money to the exchangers, and then at my coming I should have received mine own with usury'" (**verses 26-27**).

Displeasure and slothfulness are enemies of faith and hide resentment, bitterness, and jealousy. And if given a handout free of effort, it stagnates the acceleration potential. The wicked, lazy servant was operating in pride and excuses as opposed to faith. **Habakkuk 2:4 NIV** expresses. "See, the enemy is puffed up; his desires are not upright—but the righteous person will live by his faithfulness."

The invested men were praised, counted as faithful, and given blessings and future rewards. In contrast, the uninvested man's effort to preserve his manager's goods didn't work out. He didn't even put it somewhere to gain interest. Consequently, his gift was taken from him and handed to the man with the most. "Take therefore the talent from him, and give it unto him which hath ten talents" (**verse 28**). This parable reminds me of how a sales manager hands a territory to their representative. That rep is responsible for growing sales in that region and reporting to them with gain. The better they do, the manager will give them more monetary rewards, responsibilities, and areas to cover. William MacDonald shares in *Believers Bible Commentary*, "The test of their service was not how much they earned, but how hard they tried." [2] This passage also shows how wealthy people acquire more wealth through leverage, negotiating, and ongoing investing. Since God desires us to maximize and increase what He gives us, how can we do this when we lack confidence? To build faith, ask, "God, how do I do this?" and step outside your comfort zone. MacDonald continues, "Those who desire to be used for God's glory are given the means. The more they do, the more they are enabled to do for Him." [2] Everyone has something valuable to multiply, but people tend to make excuses for their shortcomings and focus on what they don't have instead of using the good things and abilities given to them by God.

SELLING STARTS SOMEWHERE

Since my fellowship with the Lord started early, God prepared me through many opportunities to overcome my shyness and fear of speaking in front of crowds throughout school, church, and my jobs. When I got my first salon job, all those years of building my confidence conditioned me to step into offering, selling, and building relationships. Salon Managers at

Hudson's Department Store at Eastland Mall in Harper Woods taught me that no matter how much business I have on the books, I can do outreach to fill unbooked slots. I was booked for the first few weeks because I took over from my mom's friend and seasoned nail technician, Brenda Ferguson, who had established a solid client base before leaving. Then, I had some space to test out their advice. I learned most shoppers didn't even know a salon existed. So, I'd share what we offered and give them my card with a list of our services. This strategy worked because their brand backed me! After I left Hudson's for self-employment, I realized that I wouldn't build a clientele if I didn't do a combination of walk-ins and outreach to get people in my chair to try my services. So, I prayed and asked God to show me how to do it with my new conditions. His wisdom helped me to build my clientele, taught me what marketing books to buy, and sustained me in business when others were waiting for the phone to ring.

Years later, I needed to learn how to sell and close large-ticket offers for my magazine. I prayed and asked God for wisdom to sell. I purchased *The Sales Bible* by Jeffery Gitomer. As a result of my desire to learn and grow, I closed a $6500 three-issue ad from a referral from my Fashion Editor, Kim Maxwell. Then, I acquired *Think Like Your Customer* by Bill Stinnett while learning to sell in the B2B (business to business) space in corporate jobs.

The lesson is that God enables you to do everything under your calling. If you're teachable and patient, you can learn whatever you want. There's no shortage of prayers, faith, Bible verses, wisdom, books, courses, videos, mentors, and coaches. Like Paul, who experienced brushes with death and imprisonment while finding contentment in the Lord, he shared that "I can do all this through him who gives me strength" **Philippians 4:13 NIV.**

SHARING IS CARING

Caring and sharing something to serve and better people's lives is a natural part of our Christian living. For instance, if a man desires a wife, he believes he can love, provide, care for, and share his life with her. First, he has to pique her interest by saying something she cares about and inviting her to the next phase of their connection by asking for her number. She also has to like his personality, looks, and style. Then, if they're on the same page, she'll say yes to his invitation. Now, they talk on the phone and back and forth, dialoguing. They vet one another by asking questions and listening intently to specific answers and other indicators to determine alignment. They're looking for qualifying criteria such as authenticity, character, integrity, confidence, personality, communication style, shared morals and values, and long-term goals to see if they want to advance to the next stage.

If the first few conversations go well, they move into the next phase, a meeting, and the subsequent—courtship, engagement, and marriage. The movement along the process requires both parties to desire the same outcome and value, making the connection a win-win. What started with hello and the intent to serve became a continuous value flow of benefits.

It's helpful to change how you look at selling. See it as serving and building a long-term relationship lasting for years. Also, know that everyone you meet and greet is valuable and must be treated and respected as such. Before initiating that first conversation, make sure you understand where your confidence comes from. Never make it about you by prioritizing your quota or coming off as uneducated about the person you're helping. Ask them questions about things that may interest them, then see if there is alignment in what you offer.

SOLUTION OR SYMPTOMS

Presenting solutions is an honorable skill. You're like an herbalist who never deals with the symptoms. They consult by diagnosing the root cause of the malady. In the detecting questions, they uncover multiple contributors the patient never knew they had. When they discover the trouble, they'll share an herbal protocol the patient didn't know they needed until the herbalist unlocked it. Like an herb doctor, being an expert in your call is about dependency on the Holy Spirit to highlight what you're best at. The servants doubled their money because they were confident in what they offered, had no issue sharing it, and wanted to please their master. Presenting an offer is about glorifying God. It's connecting and transferring value to the people you're here to serve and build with. If you don't believe in your calling, you'll stay stuck and blame your losses on God.

DISCOVER A LOVE FOR SELLING

Getting back to the "I don't like sales" statement. It's an oxymoron unless you're in this for a hobby. From my experience, nobody starts a business they don't want anyone to know about. Selling is an organized and systematic way of sharing valuable transformational evidence that helps someone meet a need and solve their problems. A purposeful business serves people through products, services, experiences, events, training, opportunities, resources, or programs. In sales, we're told to **ABC**—Always Be Closing, and I conclude we're here to be **AAV**—Always Add Value. But when people don't know your hidden value, you must present opportunities to share it.

For instance, if you're not getting the traffic you need through the *tell-it* phase of marketing and know you have a good offering, you'll have to go to where the people you want to work with are hanging out to test it further. That's where outreach comes in. Sometimes, the people you contact won't know they need your solution until you educate them and identify with their desires or struggles. You know they need it, but they don't. You must message, call, or see them in person or online. When we don't train and explore something, it's easy to say we don't want a particular thing, especially if it takes us out of our comfort zone. Selling isn't harmful, unethical, or complicated—it's a learned, invaluable skill. The more you practice it, the better you get. Whether you call it a product or service, everyone who owns a business is part of the sales business.

GOD'S GOSPEL SOLUTION

Let's explore an example of outreach offering through a spiritual example—the Gospel of Jesus Christ. Before you read further, please hear me. As I mentioned on *Day 24, Tell It*, I don't believe the gospel is sales or marketing and would never compare my Savior's blood to making money. Let me not confuse you by saying you sell the gospel—we know it's free to the recipient! The blood of Christ and God's grace are invaluable; no one should make merchandise of salvation because it can't be bought or sold.

Matthew 28:19 KJV says, "Go ye therefore, and teach all nations, baptizing them in the name of the Father, and of the Son, and of the Holy Ghost." First, the boldness to share the message of the cross comes from God! If a fellow believer doesn't share the good news, you'll want to question if they believe and have been changed by it. When someone believes it, it's engrained into their conversation and lifestyle, and they can't keep quiet about it. Christians don't just express boldness in the company of other believers. They reach out to those who need Christ's rescuing power and lifeline.

To start a conversation with a stranger, you must be easy to talk to, know your subject, and handle objections, criticisms, arguments, and doubts people express. That's why we study to show ourselves approved. **2 Timothy 2:15 KJV** says, "Study to shew thyself approved unto God, a workman that needeth not to be ashamed, rightly dividing the word of truth." We also memorize the Word of God to be ready to give a defense and an answer for the hope within us. "But in your hearts revere Christ as Lord. Always be prepared to give an answer to everyone who asks you to give the reason for the hope that you have" **1 Peter 3:15 NIV**.

When you're prepared, you don't have to rely solely on your memory or perfection. You'll proactively start conversations because you know the Holy Spirit is with you, and you're not dependent on yourself. However, God wants us to prepare for opportunities.

Too many of God's children are stuck because they refuse to invest in learning and studying anything outside of the mandatory curriculum from an institution. But God's education is ongoing, and we can no longer shy away from and hide in fear of things that challenge us to dig deeper. Here are some biblical examples of outreach.

- God *sent* His only begotten Son, Jesus Christ.
- Jesus *came to seek* and save the lost.
- Jesus *came for* the lost sheep of Israel.
- Jesus *sent out* the disciples.
- The king's servant *invited* guests to his son's wedding feast.
- Esther *presented* herself before King Ahasuerus to be chosen as queen and later to save her people from destruction.
- Abraham *conversed and reasoned* with God on behalf of Lot, other family members, and righteous people before He destroyed Sodom and Gomorrah.
- Joseph *conversed with Pharaoh* about letting his family acquire

land and settle in Egypt during the famine.

Where would we be if someone didn't share the good news with us when we were about to perish in our sins? Someone loved God and us enough to obey His will and share the good news of Jesus Christ's redemption. Also, *telling strangers that Jesus loves them* is not the same as sharing the Gospel of Jesus Christ. The other loving and truthful part of that message is they were born sinners, will die in their sins, and go to hell if they don't seek forgiveness and repent and turn from their wicked ways. An invite shares loving details, reasoning is a back-and-forth conversation, and going out to seek involves reaching the people's hearts. Telling someone the whole truth in love is the most loving and valuable thing you can do. When we become a child of God, it's important to remember that we're not our own. Just like Jesus sent out the twelve and the seventy—He's sending us out. Lost souls need the Lord; your message will help them discover His call. **Matthew 9:37-38 NKJV** says, "Then He said to His disciples, 'The harvest truly *is* plentiful, but the laborers *are* few. ^{38} Therefore pray the Lord of the harvest to send out laborers into His harvest.'" We're always adding value because God is with us, and we come bearing the truth and cure from above.

REJECTION IS NECESSARY

Rejection is not personal but a part of the process. Once you realize there's no way around it, the faster you get them out of the way. You're only one *no* away from a *yes*. People say *no* and reject Jesus Christ daily, and His eternal life solution is the only way to be saved from sin. Since rejection happens to our perfect God, why wouldn't it happen to you? In my business and work journey, I learned to navigate a ton of nos, and I want to share a win on my career timeline for encouragement.

- One of the clients (a well-known clothing brand) I served at Grainger only spent $97 annually when I acquired the account. The purchaser rejected me on calls for close to two years. However, I'd always add value and offer a way to help regardless of how often I was told NO! A year later, the customer needed my expertise on an expansion project. I was the first person she called for this kind of help. I researched and provided a proposal and quote against the competitors she considered. By the end of that next year, the account had grown to $90k in revenue.

It's exciting to partner with God to win and close deals. I have many wins to share, none of which would have been possible without prayer and reliance on the Holy Spirit. While in account relationship management (farming), I accomplished, met, and reached my goals for six out of eight and a half years and met over $8M in total revenue goal attainment. Why? Because God gave me wisdom and taught me that rejection is necessary for all we do. Even when it comes to prayer petitions, God's answers are yes, no, or not now. No will accelerate your growth and keep you hungry and preparing for opportunities. When you practice, sharpen, train, and continue advancing your education, you'll learn to see rejections as necessary to reach your destination.

The acceleration cure is possible when we change how we see sales because the skill is a great tool to add to your competencies. It's an actual walk of faith, and it helps you identify with Christ and others in a new way. You don't have to love it, but you'll want to embrace it. Be intentional about setting RGA's (Revenue Generating Activities) and continuous education goals. We're here to offer customers and clients the best solutions as specialists. When God is in charge of the selling process, it will go smoothly, and the rewards will be greater than you ever imagined. God has sent you out with your talents and offerings according to your skills, and it's time to sell it!

Acceleration CURE Actions:

- **Clarify** the value and benefits you offer. Study selling to reinforce how your offers can help people. Then, commit to consistently presenting them to potential consumers or businesses. Identify any Scriptures you can use to help you look at selling in a better way. Grab some new books and watch some free online selling content.
- **Focus** on God's will to get you unshackled and unstuck by studying the passage in this chapter about how the good servants pleased their master by doubling their money.
- **Refocus**, reevaluate, reignite, and rewrite your RGA (Revenue

Generating Activities) goals and intentionally and consistently plan outreach activities into your weekly planning.

- **Enrich** and endure rejections because *no* is how you get to *yes*.

Prayer

Dear Heavenly Father, please help me boldly communicate with people. Please help me improve at solving people's problems by confidently sharing my offerings. Shyness, fear, anxiety, and doubt are not a part of my service to you. Please provide the wisdom in your Word to help me apply biblical principles for my presentation. May I not give up and realize that rejection is a part of the process, so help me not take it personally. I recognize that selling is like training as an athlete. I'll have to practice it to get better. Please help me to talk to people, send messages and emails, and make calls when I don't feel like it. God, when I bring in the revenue from my sales effort, teach me where to place the funds for future growth. I want to run a business that's fiscally responsible and thriving consistently where revenue exceeds expenses and costs.

In Jesus' name, I pray, Amen.

Day 26

DETERMINE YOUR LOCATION

Hamas attacked Israel on October 7, 2023, the sabbath, and carried away some of its citizens as hostages. Israel defended itself by fighting back and recovering some of its civilians. The sneak attack claimed the lives of nearly 1200 citizens. Additionally, the Israeli military located and killed Hezbollah's leader a year later, on September 27, 2024. These factions are terrorist organizations disguised as Palestinian political and military groups that operate in the Gaza Strip. To the natural mind, one would wonder why so much hostility and world news come from such a small location. Furthermore, one question we should ask is if this land is so tiny—why has it yet to be conquered in modern times with all of the sophisticated military weaponry and the billions of aid funding attacks?

According to *Britannica*, the land of Israel occupies about 290 miles north to south and 85 miles east to west. [1] The warfare is between Abraham's children—the Jewish people descend from Isaac's lineage, and the Arab nations from Ishmael's. The Muslim countries that box them in believe the land belongs to Palestine, so they want to take it over and for the Jewish nation to cease existing. Israel's enemies have access to more sophisticated weapons of destruction now compared to any time in history. And when the land was conquered twice in ancient times, did God not allow it to be seized to discipline His covenant people (see the books of Isaiah, Jeremiah, Ezekiel)? Though forcibly exiled and surviving many annihilation attempts like the satanic and nefarious Nazi Holocaust. Satan hates God and His Jewish nation. The covenant people never gave up hope in God's guarantees, and He always preserves a remnant.

What we're witnessing consistently in the Middle East has everything to do with spiritual warfare against God's prophetic plan and promises to His beloved Israel. We must first note that the existence of the Nation of Israel is supernatural. The land is God's holy place on earth. It's the territory He promised Abraham and his descendants—the Promised Land. From 70 AD to May 14, 1948, God prevented *anyone* from declaring their land as an official state. [2] Nor did He allow *anyone* to wipe them off the face of the earth when He scattered them in judgment. Instead, God allowed them to return to their original country from the earth's four corners. The Mighty God still has a unique plan for them now and upon His return. As modest of a community as they are, the viciousness surrounding them shows the hand of God's shield in protecting and sustaining them.

No believer is ever to be anti-Semitic because doing so opposes Jesus Christ because He is a Jew (the Lion from the Tribe of Judah). There would be no Christian faith or redemption of our sins had it not been for God's supernatural creation of Israel. And if the Church replaced Israel and God is finished with them, why are they still victorious over the jealous nations? We who love the God of Abraham, Isaac, and Jacob must know why Israel's occupying and standing firm on their land is biblical, prophetic, and their right because God marks it off for His special needs. We're to pray for and bless them. "And I will bless (do good for, benefit) those who bless you, And I will curse [that is, subject to My wrath and judgment] the one who curses (despises, dishonors, has contempt for) you. And in you all the families (nations) of the earth will be blessed" **Genesis 12:3 AMP**.

They aren't the *fake* Israel (though some people are), as some naively belt off. The Jews have the right to defend themselves because God placed wisdom into them and their leadership, so we must keep them in our regular prayers. As believers, we must be sensitive to these warfare and invasion tragedies because there will never be lasting peace in the Middle East until Christ returns to set up His kingdom. **Revelation 21:2 NKJV**, "Then I, John, saw the holy city, New Jerusalem, coming down out of heaven from God."

The Israeli military is the most remarkable military force around. King David never lost a battle—no one could and still can't fight against the Lord of Armies. There's no mystery why Satan fuels the Muslim nations to desire the holy land—because it's God's. He wants to destroy their inheritance and constantly comes up empty. These perpetual wars are the adversary's attempt at winning against God and obliterating anyone preventing him from his goal. The serpent has been trying to terminate God's people and plans since he swayed Eve to eat the fruit in the Garden of Eden and the first prophecy (Genesis 3:15). No plan will ever flourish against God—ever! He never loses a battle.

THE COVENANT

The church and the Jewish nation are not the same. Reading and interpreting the Scriptures through a dispensational hermeneutical framework clarifies the distinction. In *Jews, Gentiles, and the Church*, Dave Hunt writes, "After the Cross a new entity came into existence—the *church* that Jesus Christ promised He would build. As a result, there are now three divisions of mankind: *Jews, Gentiles* and the *church*." [3] An absence of understanding of the two leads to mishandling of the Scriptures, which leads to false doctrines, prophecies, application, and contempt against Israel. Some biblical promises are universal for the body of Christ, while others are just for Israel. Understanding how both groups fit into God's plan is vital.

Bible prophecy enables you to trust God's plans for where He positions anyone at a given time. When reading and studying the Bible, pay close attention to the many specifics related to people groups, demographics, regions, national boundaries, and locations. Also, the maps and charts help you better understand the Scriptures from an ancient and spiritual geographical perspective.

God made a covenant with Abraham, a promise and a guarantee. Yahweh made a nation out of him and gave his descendants the land from Egypt's river and the Euphrates. God chose the seed of Abraham to bring about His chosen nation—Israel, from the agreement (Genesis 12:2-3, 15:1-6). God predestined the land for *them—not anyone else*. The land God gave to the descendants of Abraham—Canaan—was first Palestine. (Genesis 12:7, 17:8, Joshua 1:4). God made the land His own and for His people. Without historical context, we can't see the complete story.

Accelerated Power – Genesis 15:18 KJV In the same day the Lord made a covenant with Abram, saying, "Unto thy seed have

I given this land, from the river of Egypt unto the great river, the river Euphrates:"

CONTEXT MATTERS

When Abraham and Sarah were past childbearing age, God promised them they would have a child named Isaac. "Is any thing too hard for the LORD? At the time appointed I will return unto thee, according to the time of life, and Sarah shall have a son" **Genesis 18:14 KJV**.

God's promise caused Sarah to chuckle! Therefore, Sarah laughed within herself, saying, After I am waxed old shall I have pleasure, my lord being old also? **Verse 12.** God told Abraham that his descendants would be as numerous as the stars and the sand (Genesis 5:5, 22:17, 26:4).

God created a new nation through the father of faith and Sarah's womb. The child of the covenant, Isaac, had twin sons Jacob and Esau. Jacob, whose name God changed to Israel, was heir to the promise as the twelve nations of Israel came through him. The tribes of Israel laying claim to the Promised Land was the key to unlocking God's promises in Canaan. Note—*God didn't modify the location* or the people He promised it to because the territory was and still is reserved for a particular nation (Israel) and God's holy place on earth. Therefore, no matter how bad—*you*—may want something, if it's *not for you*—you won't have it. And if anyone is after what God assigned you, they can't have it either. No matter what they try to do to obtain it.

I wish these enemies got the memo. But again, how can they get the message when it's spiritually discerned? **Joshua 1:3 KJV** says, "Every place that the sole of your foot shall tread upon, that have I given unto you, as I said unto Moses." Soulful, I hope you're picking up what I'm putting down. The Almighty is intentional about every boundary He marks. Therefore, we can always trust His province mapping. When we know where we belong, we can cultivate and accelerate.

Acts 17:26 NIV says, "From one man he made all the nations, that they should inhabit the whole earth; and he marked out their appointed times in history and the boundaries of their lands." God made all the nations from Adam and moved them about the earth. The Holy Spirit connects us with people He wants us to encounter on our journey and places us in appointed destinations and geographies for His will to unfold. Therefore, there's no such thing as a coincidence in our life and purpose. When Yahweh has a plan, He's precise about the details, the execution of the strategy, and the people, places, and things involved. But, God works through our faith—someone who's surrendered—a person willing to believe and serve the Lord God with all their heart.

TERRITORY

Where are you supposed to be living now? Jacob had to leave his homeland for God to bring about the twelve tribes. If you love the Lord and are willing to follow His plan for your life and business, are you also committed to following His leading you to a new place? The *details' where, when, and who* are essential to future outcomes. When you love the Lord and seek His wisdom and guidance on further data, you discern His voice more clearly. But you won't hear His voice tell you to move or go if history shows you've already said no. But when your faith is rooted in the Rock, and you're maneuvering as a living stone and abiding within the Vine, you'll say yes! The **acceleration principle** synchronizes prayer with obedience, faith-driven action, and God's wisdom for acceleration.

If the LORD God wants you in Atlanta, you shouldn't be in Detroit. If He wants your business located in a downtown Chicago retail store, you shouldn't be in an industrial office park in the suburbs of Mississippi. If He needs you in Japan, and you're working remotely in Brazil, that isn't it! Although He will and can use you anywhere. However, sometimes, you'll need access to the appointed location for specific things He wants to transpire. Location, location, location leads to acceleration because zone matters.

Sometimes, we can look at location-based life and business decisions as small. But we shouldn't, as the right location aligns, intersects, and appoints purpose with destiny. You can't establish some blessings, ideas, and relationships because you're in the wrong environment. Say you have two keys. The **first key** fits in the lock but *cannot* unlock the door. The **second key** fits in the lock but *can* unlock *and open the door*. Like the first key, you can be in a functional place that *seems* accommodating, but you're unfilled and unmotivated because you don't fit in the setting and something is missing. So, ensure you're in the right place at the right time and be willing to relocate if God says move. Many goals and plans fail due to the attempt to fulfill them in the wrong place. However, the accurate destination and boundary markers will bring about the acceleration cure. The Holy Spirit causes the key to fit, unlocking and opening the door of promise.

DECISIONS AND SUPPORT

It's possible to believe you're making the right choices when you're not. When you have a good idea, you're so juiced up and sometimes make decisions based on emotions instead of consulting with God to ensure this is what He wants. As always, confirm decisions with God and be patient with His answer. Also, running good ideas by your spouse, a team of leaders, friends, or networks is helpful. *A good idea* isn't necessarily a *God idea*; a God idea isn't always a *right now plan*. Sometimes, options feel and appear perfect, but upon further inspection, they can be wrong and not God's best for you. When Samuel went to anoint one of Jesse's sons as king, he felt the first few sons he met were *the one*. However, God affirmed that he doesn't look at the outside appearance like men but looks at the heart (1 Samuel 16:7). Frequently, the Holy Spirit will confirm a decision with only you, and you'll feel peace in your spirit when you get an answer.

However, you want to trust the people you connect with because they often become an extension of your family. You enjoy a network of people you believe in and feel safe enough to share ideas and wins. The people you entrust will also tell you when you're right or wrong. Surrounding yourself with the right circle of supporters will accelerate your success and quality of life.

Territory and national, state, and city borders matter to your quality of life because God is particular about the boundary markers for your family, relationships, purpose, spiritual growth, business headquarters, neighborhood, and subdivision or apartment community. When you're praying for connection to meet your spouse, new friends, team members, network, contractors, freelancers, associations, or groups to join, I encourage you to pray for insight and fast for clarity. Also, pray about discovering aligned clients, customers, and partners. The choice might seem obvious, but you want to ensure you're yoking up with people who share your values and vision and are heading in the same direction. Avoid feeling stuck by gaining clarity and ensuring you're building in the right area.

Additionally, don't give up your territory if someone is trying to force you out and God is telling you to stay. The enemy can only take what you allow him to access. If he's stolen your land, dreams, or finances, submit to The Lord and ask Him to reclaim them. God wants inclusion in everything you do. He desires to be first in your life and the business. If God told you something is yours, never give up on that house, apartment, office, building, land, or farm you believe in. Like Israel's homeland, The Lord has a destination for you. If God knows the amount of hair you have on your head and cares very much about everything you do, where you go, and where you're planted to do His will. He wants to surround you with suitable people in your life and business to advance your spiritual growth and accelerate your business.

Acceleration CURE Actions:

- **Clarify** where you should reside if you're uncertain in anyway. Study a city, state, or country you love, and investigate why you're drawn to those surroundings. Research the business communities and schools in those areas to see if there is growth potential for your calling and gifts. Once God has confirmed that you're in the right place or to relocate, commit to obeying and serving God there.
- **Obey** God and follow the Holy Spirit's compass to get unshackled and unstuck.
- **Refresh**, reignite, and rewrite what God shows you about Israel, and pray for and support them. Those who have not placed their faith in Jesus Christ still need salvation.
- **Enrich** and endure the ups and downs of your location, maintain your territory, and maximize your capabilities.

Prayer

Dear Heavenly Father, I pray your kingdom comes, and you continue to stand as a guard and protector over Israel and Jerusalem. May you also redeem those Israelites who don't call upon the name of Jesus Christ as Savior and Lord of all. Through how you set up the Jewish nation, I thank you for teaching me about the power of your covenant, promises, love, protection, and boundaries. Thank you for reminding me of how intentional you are with every area of my life down to where I reside. Teach me to guard against all you give me and never surrender territory to the enemy. You care about my location and the circle of people around me. I pray for the right relationships in every area of my life. I pray that I become the person you created me to be in the destination you saw fit to plant me. May you lead me to produce fruit from your fertile soil and abide within the Vine. If I'm in the wrong boundary marker, please show me where you need me to be. God, I pray that you share with me any sins I'm guilty of so I can confess them and keep a clear line of communication between you and the friends, family, and circle of influence in my life. I pray that the people assigned to connect with me in life and business can locate me and I can discover them.

In Jesus' name, I pray, Amen.

Day 27
ROOT FOR THEIR SUCCESS

In one season, Saul of Tarsus intensely persecutes, captures, screams murderous threats, and destroys followers *of* The Way. In the next, he's a missionary bondservant, dedicated to God our Father and the Lord Jesus Christ, rescuing and converting followers *to* The Way. The Apostle's ministry placed him in the center of intense persecution and spiritual warfare for Christ's sake. In the New Testament epistles, we learn that he was an immensely loving leader who excelled at encouraging and building others up. His writings openly displayed his passion for the saints in the churches through teaching, correction, discipline, admonishment, patience, and support. Paul wanted nothing but the best and success for the body of Christ. Some of his affirming and enriching displays are in the letters he wrote to his spiritual son in the faith, Timothy. **2 Timothy 2:22 NIV** says, "Flee the evil desires of youth and pursue righteousness, faith, love, and peace, along with those who call on the Lord out of a pure heart."

During His earthly ministry, Jesus demonstrated His love through actions, bringing out the best in people. However, it was always a personal choice whether to accept His love, truth, and wisdom. Our new identity is deeply rooted in our ability to build up people and show Christ's love. As we interact with people daily, they remember our impact on them.

Accelerated Power – 1 Thessalonians 5:11 NIV Therefore encourage one another and build each other up, just as in fact you are doing.

It's so easy to think only about ourselves and what exists in our own space, mind, and emotions—but being concerned about the needs of others and their success in life and Christ is essential, too. We fail to remember there's no competition. There's enough pasture land for sheep to feed and overflowing waters for us to drink. God made room for us all to accelerate. As we grow our understanding of this, let's allow God's command to love our neighbors and selflessly value and serve others to dominate our thoughts. **Philippians 2:3-4 NIV** says, "Do nothing out of selfish ambition or vain conceit. Rather, in humility value others above yourselves, ⁴ not looking to your own interests but each of you to the interests of the others."

LEAD WITH LOVE

When leading and working with others, it's essential to respect others and hear them out. Keep your mind on the outcome of pleasing God. As the one in charge, leading without selfish ambition, pride, or conceit is important. The dream works when there's teamwork. When building and running your organization, you spend many hours growing, cultivating, maintaining, and managing it weekly. If you fail to rest and walk in the Spirit, the long hours can deplete you and lead to irritable reactions. When the focus is always on *your* needs, growth, agenda, and goals, when do you have time to consider the needs of others? Similarly, in your relationships, if the conversation is about you and how great your life is, when do you have the compassion or concern to see how the person you're speaking to is doing in their happy or trial season? Checking on, praying, and having regard for others is a sign of spiritual maturity.

If we look at the life of Christ, remember all He sacrificed to meet our needs and serve? He left His throne in heaven and laid down His life because of love. **Philippians 2:5-8 NIV** says, "In your relationships with one another, have the same mindset as Christ Jesus: ⁶ Who, being in very nature God, did not consider equality with God something to be used to his own advantage; ⁷ rather, he made himself nothing by taking the very nature of a servant, being made in human likeness. ⁸ And being found in appearance as a man, he humbled himself by becoming obedient to death—even death on a cross!"

Yes, God—Jesus Christ—didn't consider equality in His co-equality in the Godhead but humbled Himself and came as a servant to redeem us from sin out of love. God wants us in His family. And anyone in His family who follows His teachings are His disciples indeed. God gave us new life, built us up, and equipped us to be more than conquerors. He doesn't talk to or treat us badly, even when disciplining us. He gives us unconditional love, mercy, and grace. **Ephesians 4:29-32 NIV** says, "Do not let any unwholesome talk come out of your mouths, but only what is helpful for building others up according to their needs, that it may benefit those who listen. [30] And do not grieve the Holy Spirit of God, with whom you were sealed for the day of redemption. [31] Get rid of all bitterness, rage and anger, brawling and slander, along with every form of malice. [32] Be kind and compassionate to one another, forgiving each other, just as in Christ God forgave you."

To pray for the success of others, we have to care for their needs and have interest and consideration for them. If we're filled with unwholesome talk and choose to operate in the flesh, we grieve the Spirit when we harbor unforgiveness, bitterness, and envy. Jesus has already shown us how to love and serve others, providing us with a powerful blueprint. We can pray for our fellow believers' needs, protection, and spiritual growth. Focusing on their outstanding qualities is possible because we're all made in God's image. Christians desire to see others win—not just ourselves.

CHEER THEM ON

As a business owner, you'll be doing business with many other companies, partners, affiliates, and vendors, some of whom are Christians and others are not. Some organizations may be young and starting, while others may be more seasoned. No matter what—the Scripture says you're to encourage and build up one another. You can build up others by supporting their business or content, complementing them, or leaving a glowing review. Sending an encouraging text or email and leaving a detailed comment under their video or social posts is another way to bless someone. Purchasing one of their products, signing up for their services, or referring someone to their organization can go far. You can also foster inspiration by praying for the success of their mission, sending a lovely gift/card, joining their email list or group, and even listening to their sales pitch when they contact you. Kindness, humbleness, and gratitude never go out of style. "Therefore, as God's chosen people, holy and dearly loved, clothe yourselves with compassion, kindness, humility, gentleness and patience" **Colossians 3:12 NIV.**

Every part of the body of Christ is essential to the others. Each individual is needed (1 Corinthians 12:12-27). God commissions you for the greater good when He calls you to the marketplace. Therefore, everyone needs hope and support to keep going in their lives, relationships, and work. Other business owners need motivation and the confirmation of someone who wants to see them win and succeed. Even if you both are in the same industry, build them up with reinforcement because there is no competition in Christ. If you met people through networking or in some alternate capacity, it would be nice if they would hear from you now and then. Encourage them even if their offerings don't fit your mission, style, or taste. Yes, I know it's impossible to do this with everyone you know, receive a sales call, offer, or a business card from, but the Holy Spirit will let you know whom He'd like you to cheer on.

During Jesus' ministry, He built up others and brought out the best in them. He spoke to them from their potential and not what they were at that moment. You can occasionally look at others and not see their value. Your assumptions of them can be skewed because you don't know them or understand their story in a spiritual sense. Therefore, you judge them based on where they are now and their small beginnings. Consequently, the Bible instructs us to reject attitudes of partiality, criticism, unrighteous judgment, pride, and self-righteousness.

It's essential to recognize that even those who seem or present more stable, prosperous, and successful might appear to have everything figured out, but that doesn't mean they don't need your support, contribution, or compliment. In fact, everyone can benefit from inspiration and assistance, especially those who project and give the appearance of strength on the outside. A little encouragement can go a long way for anyone, regardless of your perception of their needs. Life's circumstances and trials caused them to be strong enough to survive and overcome adversities. But they experience and process emotions like you. There are just other ways they filter difficulties. Jesus always discerned His audience and their individualistic needs—your ability to ascertain who needs whatever leads to acceleration. The key is to be sensitive to the assurances of the Holy Spirit. Be open to whom He'd like you to minister or check on.

ACCELERATION

God doesn't only want to accelerate your mission. He desires to bless other business's big dreams, too. You may be the help someone is praying for, that one contact that could aid them in growing their business. Your network, advice, and referral may be what their company has been missing. When people give us their business cards, we don't always look twice at their business or what they offer. We may take the card and stuff it in our purse or wallet and write it off as them having nothing to offer. Remember, stepping out on faith takes a lot of courage to start anything. Humble beginnings or not, we're not to frown on others.

Refuse to acquiesce to the enemy's plan to destroy and tear down people. Never collaborate with the ops. You enter the wrong territory once you criticize, talk bad about, or dash people's dreams, whether verbally or in your heart. At least they have aspirations and ambitions, and they'll learn how to pivot along the way as they walk their path and are willing to be taught.

Also, someone's young or older age doesn't mean they don't have what it takes to be successful in business. Their lack of experience doesn't disqualify them either. Nor does their people group, geographic location, or status. If you lived in ancient times and looked at young David, you would think he couldn't defeat Goliath or be a future King, but God did! When Jesus went into His ministry, many questioned it. "'Nazareth! Can anything good come from there?' Nathanael asked. 'Come and see,' said Philip" **John 1:46 NIV**.

Like the Apostle Paul, God equipped you with tenderness and awe-inspiring qualities in your born-again spirit. Be the person people get excited to share their dreams and accomplishments with. The more you avail yourself to support others, the happier you'll be. You'll immediately see a change in your life, and the mission thrive and accelerate. When you serve others, you infuse good into their purpose. When you read, study, and apply the Word of God, you advance in the kind of warmth and charity to assist. Resolve to benefit the brethren in getting what they need. When you encourage others, it also makes you feel inspired in Christ. When you're of a healthy mindset, you can see that it's necessary to stand in the gap in prayer for the fruit-bearing success of others because you want them to accelerate.

Acceleration CURE Actions:

- **Clarify** how your purpose connects with your faith and charitable attitude, and commit to being an encourager.
- **Study** Jesus's life and how He met the individual needs of others to help them get unstuck and break free from the shackles of only helping themselves.
- **Rewrite** and send three people an email or text with encouraging Scriptures and a personalized message to reignite their belief in God's faithfulness and humanity.
- **Enrich,** endure, and be determined to build others up with support when it's righteously aligned.

Prayer

Dear Gracious Father, I'm grateful that you gave me a business to start so that it can help the needs of others. Please recall any unkind behavior I've exhibited to shun and criticize anyone's progress or dreams.

You also gave your other children a mission. I want to be a vessel to encourage them. Please help me to see fresh opportunities for promoting, praying, or ministering to the needs of others. I pray believers will draw closer to you as they operate their businesses and that you'll bless them with the success and the right subscribers, readers, customers, patrons, and clients they need to be profitable. I pray that the doors of their businesses will remain open and that you'll grow their businesses and ministries through all the ups and downs of our economic climate. I pray they survive spiritual attacks from the enemy. Grant me a charitable heart of humility, compassion, and kindness to serve people. Allow me to be a haven for others to share their dreams and aspirations. Grace me to operate in the Holy Spirit to glorify your name.

In Jesus' name, I pray, Amen.

Day 28

FINISH STRONG

I learned to create consistently with my first ministry by writing weekly for two years. I wrote all of 2013 and 2014 between losing my house and renting the worst condo ever. Although I didn't see it then, God was preparing me for going back into print publishing. He taught me how writers write when they don't feel inspired because it's a craft, skill, and discipline. Additionally, you're strengthening your character traits of endurance, perseverance, patience, discipline, consistency, and faithfulness. Many people don't finish reading books, but you made it to the closing lap, and now you're accelerating. You're growing in your faith, drawing closer to Christ, advancing your studies, setting new goals, and reigniting your dreams, no matter the challenges or obstacles.

You laughed, cried, got some ah-ha moments, and asked God to increase your capacity to finish strong. You've tackled your fears, weaknesses, and identity blindness. You recalibrated your habits and disciplines, called out unfruitful habits, confessed your sins, and took ownership of your choices. You allowed God to identify your strongholds and hindrances to success and submit to the Spirit for the spiritual and soul work of sanctification. Most of all, you got honest with God about your aspirations and difficulties. You didn't walk away from the Holy Spirit's conviction but allowed Him to show you what needs overcoming in your heart. Your anguish and trials produce perseverance. You're now more aware of your spiritual tools and equipped with more of what it takes to finish strong. Your steadfastness should assure you that you're firm and dedicated to living the accelerated life destined by God the Father in Christ Jesus by the power of the Holy Spirit. He claimed you as His own because you're a living stone.

Noah finished what He started. Joshua obeyed God and conquered the Promised Land. Nehemiah stood firm in leadership and faithfully completed rebuilding Jerusalem's wall. The prophet Ezekiel finished strong and lay on his left side for 390 days and 40 days on the right as a sign to the Israelites to return to God. Peter denied Christ three times but returned and became one of the boldest of His Apostles. Most importantly, through Jesus Christ's life on earth, He finished what He started, and we're recipients of eternal life due to His finished work.

God rewarded those He called for their fidelity and endurance. Your reward is on the way, too. You're not among the many believers who start commitments, projects, courses, programs, books, businesses, employment, hobbies, and activities and never finish faithfully. You don't abandon significant responsibilities.

WHY NOT FINISH

Many Christ followers don't finish what they start for reasons such as health, marital, and financial setbacks, providing for the family, death of a loved one, loss, grief, enslavement to the past, and unforeseen obstacles that halt the ability to complete commitments. Outside of those dramatic life changes, they mainly neglect to count the cost and the amount of dedication it takes to advance. They take on too much and aren't willing to follow through due to the sacrifice and monetary commitment. They forget the long-term mission and quit because they didn't see instant results. Some don't know their season or purpose, so they throw in the towel before seeing the promise. Others are in unaligned environments, living situations, jobs, and relationships that hinder their spiritual and personal development.

Many Christians struggle to break free from their past, fears, habits, excuses, and comfort zones without accountability. They often blame others and avoid taking responsibility for their circumstances. Incessantly stuck in a rut, creating a faux reality, and living off of a diet of justifications makes it impossible to move forward. Avoiding accountability and seeking help is unwise. God's people should not regularly withdraw from or avoid their tasks. When we do, it creates a culture, lifestyle, and pattern. What we must do is pivot, not quit. It's a matter of recalibrating and readjusting. It looks like keeping your dream or big idea in your heart but putting it aside for a year or three if necessary. It seems like rewriting, researching, rebranding, restarting, rebuilding, and retweaking. It could be moving your expertise from the previous plan into a new purpose-driven business based on new information from the Father.

For example, all my work history, business pursuits, gifts, skills, and experiences rolled into what I'm doing today. Therefore, you must be able to shift as your mind renews. Faithfulness links to accountability, consistency, dependability, and reliability. Even Jesus was accountable to the Father. A determined, diligent, and trustworthy believer will always find a way to pull through and seek help at the throne of God.

The Christ follower's way of life is about progressing, fighting the good fight of faith, and finishing strong. Finishing our race and running in the lane God placed us in gets us rewards and the crown of victory. We push on because purpose is more significant than us, as souls are attached to our mission. God will use our obedience to snatch someone out of the fire. He wants to use your testimony to build His church. He wants you to share the business solutions written in your notebook with the marketplace. An audience awaits your knowledge bank, unique teaching style, book, service, course, training, and concepts. Someone is desperately stuck, looking for you to pass the torch, and you have the solution to help them win their race. God didn't ask you to decide whether or not you're the person for the job or add up how much money you have in the bank. He's already determined that you are qualified.

RUN FOR THE PRIZE

The Apostle Paul encouraged Timothy by sharing how he had fought his good fight and finished his race. He persevered in faith to the end and was now preparing to pass the torch. In this passage, we're to think of how our influence and obedience affect the call of those who come behind us to do the work of God. Our faith links to the next generation.

Accelerated Power – 2 Timothy 4:7-8 NIV I have fought the good fight, I have finished the race, I have kept the faith. [8] Now there's in store for me the crown of righteousness, which the Lord, the righteous Judge, will award to me on that day—and not only to me, but also to all who have longed for his appearing.

I believe you're fighting the good fight and keeping the faith. You get up daily, giving it your all, even when you don't *feel* like it. You realize that your crown and more excellent awards await you due to your faithful living. The Spirit fuels you to run the race and accelerate like competing for the prize. Runners train year-round and maintain a proper, strict diet. "Do you not know that in a race all the runners run, but only one gets the prize? Run in such a way as to get the prize. ²⁵ Everyone who competes in the games goes into strict training. They do it to get a crown that will not last, but we do it to get a crown that will last forever" **1 Corinthians 9:24-25 NIV**. No track and field athlete competes in a race, believing they will lose. A good coach instructs them to win and give their best to finish the race no matter what. We all must have a mentor, coach, disciple, or teacher because we're in it for the crown.

When it appears you're failing, redirect your mindset. You lose whenever you make excuses, give up, and try winning alone! You can't finish strong as a lone ranger Christian. There's no acceleration cure for individualism. Call in for some help. No matter how talented you are, you cannot finish effectively solo. Yes, God may consecrate you in sanctifying solitude in seasons for things like finishing big projects, testing, pruning, and restoration. Still, He wants you to join your fellow believers and people to make a difference in the world so He can use you when that season ends.

Since our home is here for now and in heavenly places, we cannot receive proper spiritual nourishment without our daily manna and filling up on the Bread of Life (Matthew 4:4, 2 Timothy 2:15). Additionally, we must stand determined in our responsibilities as leaders. Don't just take whatever opportunity comes your way. Instead, evaluate all proposals, projects, promises, and commitments. It's okay to reprioritize to meet obligations or even put them aside for a time. Effective leading is about learning how to manage priorities and produce results.

THE ACCELERATED SEASON

Some keys to succeeding are dependency on God, the wisdom and application of God's Word, and humility. If you apply the biblical principles in this book, you will enter a winning season. To start, produce a list of unfinished projects. Review the top three you'll want to finish before leaving this earth and three you'll want to finish in the next eighteen months. Decide how much time you need to complete them. Ask God to give you the wisdom to prioritize and finish what needs finishing first. Most of your ideas can't be implemented immediately. However, in the meantime, start building your resource bank by writing down every idea or concept the Holy Spirit thrusts into your spirit. Collect concepts and begin shaping your purpose-driven products or services. For example, the inspiration for Dream Big Goals originated as a free goal-setting guide through my art business in 2017. It evolved into a biblical principles-based lead magnet with my ministry and business. Then, it grew into a two-book print version of the Dream Big Goal-Setting Guide & Planner system and multiple programs for Christian visionaries. God used that original seed idea to build upon. The puzzle pieces wouldn't have connected if I had published this book before doing those assignments.

Friend, it's not too late for you to accelerate. A season remains yet for your appointed vision, but you must plant the seed. "While the earth remaineth, seedtime and harvest, and cold and heat, and summer and winter, and day and night shall not cease" **Genesis 8:22 KJV**. If you prioritize building everything you do on the Lord's unmovable foundation, you'll eventually see the harvest from your diligence. He wants to give you fresh ideas that keep you busy, making good use of your time to finish what you start. He wants to get you unstuck so you can prosper and help others. God will provide the time, money, resources, people, environment, and answers you seek for completion.

DID GOD SAY

We often say, "God told me to do this or that," if this is the case, make sure that you finish what *He told you* to complete. When God speaks, you must obey what He tells you. Please don't make Him out to be a liar. God speaks to us primarily with alignment in His Word. "I will worship toward thy holy temple, and praise thy name for thy lovingkindness and for thy truth: for thou hast magnified thy word above all thy name" **Psalm 138:2 KJV**. You don't want to keep starting things *you think* or believe you heard God say to begin because when it doesn't work, you're angry at God, upset, and ready to give up. I'd also caution you not to use a lack of clarity for not moving ahead. Sometimes, we use that defense not to do something. The Lord may ask you to start something, but use it as a testing rehearsal before He moves you to the real deal because you'll need that experience for the next level.

Additionally, He can use fragments of what He told you to do and roll them into multiple income streams if you allow God to push and accelerate you as far as possible. Those assignments you focused on can advance you into new business ventures, financially lucrative products, another city, or partnering with a new investor or collaborator. There is no such thing as waste in God's economy. Whether or not the business you start, the book you write, the class you take, or the invention you have will turn into what you want it to be.

THE JOURNEY

Can you imagine how Noah felt through his lengthy ark-building journey? Although I can only use my spiritual imagination, he probably felt weathered along the way. It's estimated to have taken at least fifty-five years to construct. Researchers with The Ark Encounter share the likely view of about seventy-five years. [1] Meanwhile, Answers in Genesis are estimated to be between fifty-five and seventy-five. [2] Although the time frame varies, my question is, do you have faith like Noah? Can you work without fail on the dream for ten, twenty, or thirty years until it turns a profit? We often miss out on what God wants to do in our lives because we lack the steadfastness to see them bear fruit. We give up too soon and move on to the next money-making thing that *seemingly offers* us faster results. Misaligned opportunities are distractions. Pursuing your dream will often feel as though your vision is failing. You'll question yourself frequently along the faith-filled journey. You'll question your purpose when the dream dies and doubt whether God asked you to start. It's like when the serpent asked Eve, "Did God really say?" The truth is, there are no shortcuts. Please don't get upset or impatient with how long it takes. A sprouting seed perished first. Similarly, for a vision to thrive, it must undergo a renovation.

An intentional shortcut violates God's laws. **Proverbs 16:25 NIV** says, "There is a way that appears to be right, but in the end it leads to death." Therefore, you must refuse to view temporary loss as permanent. What we perceive as a failure connects us to the blessing of gain in the pain.

I'm reminding you of the **The Acceleration Cure** as it involves living purposefully and trusting God to guide your steps toward succeeding in what truly matters and counts for eternity. Your acceleration cure is nearer than you think when you live by faith and obey God consistently for many years—not just days and weeks. God has more planned for you than you can expect through His radiating supernatural power within you. **Ephesians 3:20 NIV** shares, "Now to him who is able to do immeasurably more than all we ask or imagine, according to his power that is at work within us." He wants you to draw near to teach you and share more of the abundant life He promised. Hold fast, and don't doubt. Before you know it, the things you've been praying for will be part of your new reality, and one day, we will be with the King—our ultimate reward for finishing strong. **Jude 1:24-25 NKJV** reassures, "Now to Him who is able to keep you from stumbling, And to present *you* faultless Before the presence of His glory with exceeding joy, [25] To God our Savior, Who alone is wise, *Be* glory and majesty, Dominion and power, Both now and forever. Amen."

Acceleration CURE Actions:

- **Commit** to a twelve-week deep dive to organize your life and business so you can accelerate with new goals, priorities, habits, focused energy, and accountability. Write down your spiritual, relational, health, and financial goals. Then, connect them with weekly habits and an updated daily schedule. The Dream Big Goal-Setting Guide & Planner walks you through this.

- **Consider** what will happen if you do NOT live in your purpose. How long will you be stuck and shackled? Who else will be affected by your lack of progress? How will God view any absence of faith?

- **Fight** the good fight of faith for the crown by reigniting your trust in the Lord and rewriting your narrative from a biblical worldview to make the rest of your days the best.

- **Build** on the Rock and abide in the Vine. Enrich and endure life's good, bad, and ugly seasons through dedicated prayer and the armor of God to accelerate and finish strong.

Prayer

Dear Sovereign Lord, I want to thank and praise you. I want to lift you high and worship your Holy name. I glorify and honor you for who you are, all you've done, and all you will do. You've taught me how to tackle things that hinder me in areas I didn't think about. Thank you for your unsearchable wisdom, purpose, and prevailing will. I'm excited to finish strong because I'm not alone. I want to obey your instructions and run in a way to win the prize. Help me to share the gospel of salvation with the lost, support and encourage my brothers and sisters, and become the leader and visionary you created me to become. Please help me see what it looks like to get unstuck and see the transformation. Please help me to endure and enjoy the journey and process. I need the grace to stay in the race. I desire to please you and accomplish things that bear good fruit. May you continuously strengthen me and help me focus on your purposes for my life and business to finish strong.

In Jesus' name, I pray, Amen.

NOTES

Chapter One – The Acceleration Shift – My Story

[1] GotQuestions.org, "What is biblical typology?," 1 2022. [Online]. Available: https://www.gotquestions.org/typology-Biblical.html. [Accessed 15 1 2024].

Chapter Two – Why Christians Are Stuck

[1] Carsons Scholarship, "Carsons Scholarship Fund," 2024. [Online]. Available: https://carsonscholars.org/reading-rooms/. [Accessed 27 9 2024].

[2] HeartCry Missionary Society, "Tour of Paul Washer's Library," 5 1 2021. [Online]. Available: https://www.youtube.com/watch?v=KWGhe01BTLI. [Accessed 16 4 2024].

[3] GotQuestions.org, "What does it mean that Jesus Christ is the Cornerstone," 4 1 2022. [Online]. Available: https://www.gotquestions.org/Jesus-Christ-cornerstone.html. [Accessed 15 1 2024].

[4] W. MacDonald, Believer's Bible Commentary Ephesians 19-22, Second Edition ed., A. Farstad, Ed., Nashville, TN: Thomas Nelson Harper Collins Christian Publishing, 2016, pp. 1956-1958.

[5] Bible Study Verse by Verse, "How is Christ the Chief Cornerstone? 1 Peter 2:6. (#136) YouTube," 2 4 2022. [Online]. Available: https://www.youtube.com/watch?v=PHEbr9ucrZw. [Accessed 10 4 2024].

[6] Oxford University Press, "Accelerate," Oxford Learner's Dictionary, [Online]. Available: https://www.oxfordlearnersdictionaries.com/us/definition/english/accelerate. [Accessed 15 10 2023].

Chapter Three – Identity Blindness

[1] Oxford University Press, "Purpose Google Search," 2024. [Online]. [Accessed 20 April 2024]

[2] Merriam Webster, "deployment and employment," Merriam Webster, 2024. [Online]. [Accessed 2024].

Day 1 – Put Off Anger

[1] KCAL News, "Man who killed 6-year-old in road rage shooting sentenced to 40 years to life in prison," CBS, 2024. [Online]. Available: https://www.youtube.com/watch?v=KQAhoBRwqVI. [Accessed 20 April 2024].

[2] A. Strauch, If You Bite & Devour One Another, Littleton: Lewis and Roth Publishers, 2011.

Day 4 – Conquer Depression

[1] Forum of Christian Leaders, "A Thorn in the Flesh: Is Depression Relevant to Artists?," [Online]. Available: https://foclonline.org/talk/thorn-flesh-depression-relevant-artists. [Accessed 23 4 2024].

[2] Bite-sized Philosophy, "Jordan Peterson - The Curse of Creativity," [Online]. Available: https://www.youtube.com/watch?v=ocDli45faiw. [Accessed 23 4 2024].

[3] D. G. Barnhouse, "Man's RuinThe Trinity," in Romans Expositions of Bible Doctrines Chapters 1:1-5:11, 2nd ed., Peabody, MA: Hendrickson Publishers Marketing LLC, 1952, pp. 69-70.

[4] S. Walling, "Entrepreneurs Could Be at a Higher Risk for Suicide. A Psychologist Explains Why.," Entrepreneur.com, 4 9 2022. [Online]. Available: https://www.entrepreneur.com/living/why-entrepreneurs-could-be-at-a-higher-risk-for-suicide/432083. [Accessed 14 9 2024].

Day 6 –Unlock the Vision

[1] S. M. Houdmann, "What is the story of Scripture?," GotQuestions.blog, 15 3 2023. [Online].

Available: https://www.gotquestions.blog/The-Story-of-Scripture.html#. [Accessed 3 2024].

Day 7 – Use Wisdom and Discernment

[1] ETWN Youtube, "Why the Most Dangerous Place for African Americans is the Womb," 20 7 2018. [Online]. Available: https://www.youtube.com/watch?v=ZWNFUmBbam4. [Accessed 2023].

[2] B. Little, "History.com," A&E Television Networks, LLC, 8 2023. [Online]. Available: https://www.history.com/news/how-the-nazis-were-inspired-by-jim-crow. [Accessed 17 9 2024].

[3] V. E. Ellison, 25 Lies: Exposing Democrats Most Dangerous, Seductive, Damnable, Destructive Lies and How to Refute Them, New York/Nashville: Bombardier Books/Post Hill Press, 2022.

Day 12 – Navigate Financial Emergencies

[1] Merriam Webster, "Entrepreneur," [Online]. Available: https://www.merriam-webster.com/dictionary/entrepreneur. [Accessed 2024].

Day 15 – Practice Self-Discipline

[1] "Brainy Quote," 2024. [Online]. Available: https://www.brainyquote.com/quotes/george_washington_carver_158549.

Day 17 – Productively Produce

[1] C. Newport, "Deep Work Is Valuable," in Deep Work (Rules for Focused Success in a Distracted World), New York, Hachette Book Group/Grand Central Publishing, 2016, p. 232.

Day 22 – Convey and Attitude of Gratitude

[1] C. Swindoll, Zondervan, 1 October 1995. [Online]. [Accessed 2024].

Day 24 – Tell It

[1] Chamber of Commerce, "Small Business Statistics," 24 7 2024. [Online]. Available: https://www.chamberofcommerce.org/small-business-statistics [Accessed 7 9 2024].

Day 25 – Sell It

[1] Chamber of Commerce, "Small Business Statistics," 24 7 2024. [Online]. Available: https://www.chamberofcommerce.org/small-business-statistics [Accessed 7 9 2024].

[2] W. MacDonald, Believer's Bible Commentary Matthew 25:14-18 Parable of the Talents, Second ed., F. Art, Ed., Nashville, TN: Tomas Nelson Harper Collins Christian Publishing, 2016, pp. 1222-1223.

Day 26 – Determine Your Location

[1] "Israel - Land," Britannica, [Online]. Available: https://www.britannica.com/place/Israel#ref23066. [Accessed 2024].

[2] Britannica, "Israel War of 1948," [Online]. Available: https://www.britannica.com/place/Israel/Establishment-of-Israel. [Accessed 2024].

[3] D. Hunt, "Jews, Gentiles, and the Church," The Berean Call, 1 9 1989. [Online]. Available: https://www.thebereancall.org/content/jews-gentiles-and-church?. [Accessed 10 2024].

Day 28 – Finish Strong

[1] Ark Encounter, "Ark Encounter," 2023 10 2023. [Online]. Available: https://arkencounter.com/blog/2023/11/02/how-long-did-it-take-to-build-ark/. [Accessed 12 2023].

[2] B. Hodge, "Answers in Genesis," [Online]. Available: https://answersingenesis.org/bible-timeline/how-long-did-it-take-for-noah-to-build-the-ark/. [Accessed 12 2023].

ABOUT THE AUTHOR

LaTanya R. Quinn – The Soul Coach, is a Christ-follower, author, artist, coach, and publisher. She placed her faith in Jesus Christ at seven when her father, George Quinn, shared the gospel. She discovered her gift for speaking and ministering by delivering two impactful Women's Day messages at her home church, Bible Community Baptist, in Detroit, MI, under Pastor George Gooden, at nineteen and twenty. She founded Cure for Bare Walls in 2011 and Cure 4 the Soul Ministries in 2018. LaTanya has over 12 years of high-achieving consultative selling experience and has been in business in various seasons. She's passionate about conserving God's standards and sound doctrine, teaching the Bible, sharing the gospel with the lost, encouraging singles, and assisting believers to break free from stagnation and live soul-transforming and purpose-driven lives fueled by faith.

To connect with or book LaTanya for coaching, consulting, interviews, or speaking, please email us at info@cure4thesoul.com.

CURE 4 THE SOUL MINISTRIES

Cure 4 the Soul Ministries was founded in 2018. We equip believers with soul-transforming teachings for spiritual growth and purposeful living to be bold, stand for righteousness, and defend the faith through media and resources. We focus on encouragement, discernment, current events, commentary, and sanctifying soul work.

For more info visit https://cure4thesoul.org/
https://www.youtube.com/@Cure4theSoulMin

ABOUT CURE 4 THE SOUL

Cure 4 the Soul, Inc. is a soul-transforming company that provides coaching, consulting, and published resources for purpose-driven Christian entrepreneurs, business owners, creatives, visionaries, leaders, big dreamers, and goal-getters. Here, we prioritize the ultimate soul cure—Jesus Christ as the Author and Finisher of our faith, dreams, visions, and success. Utilizing biblical principles, soul work, goal setting, planning, and practical teachings, we equip leaders to grow spiritually and live soul-healthy lives.

Our mission is to assist and empower 10k purpose-driven believers called to business and leadership to grow spiritually, fulfill their mission, and profitably succeed in the marketplace for God's glory.

For more info visit https://cure4thesoul.com/
info@cure4thesoul.com
https://www.youtube.com/@Cure4theSoulInc
Socials @cure4thesoul

DREAM BIG GOALS

Dream Big Goals is a Cure 4 the Soul program and community geared towards goals and planning acceleration for life and business. Through our challenges, events, accountability programs, goal-setting guides, planners, and group coaching, we serve Christians called to the marketplace from infancy to the early start-up stages of their purpose-driven venture. Join the

challenge, masterclass, or event.
For more info, visit https://dreambiggoals.com/

DREAM BIG GOALS ACCELERATOR

Dream Big Goals Accelerator is a one-to-one coaching program designed for Christians looking build a profitable, purpose-driven business. This program helps you clarify, refine, and discover your purpose, deal with the soul/mind issues keeping you stuck, reignite your dreams, set new goals, and execute your plan with guidance through our CURE framework. This program is perfect for anyone needing to clarify their purpose, start or restart a business with a refined vision and fresh branding, struggling in the early phases of a current concept, or want accountability to get results in their life and business.

For more info, please visit https://dreambiggoals.com/call/

CURE 4 HER SOUL

Cure 4 Her Soul is a one-to-one and group coaching program for women of faith. It is customized to help you navigate areas of your life that keep you stuck. Our focus areas are *Her life, Her soul, and Her time*. These can be defined but not limited to overcoming fear and depression, growing in faith, living a successful single life, time management, productivity, well-being, organization, and accountability.

LaTanya is equipped and available to consult with your church's singles ministries.

For more info visit https://cure4hersoul.com/
https://www.youtube.com/@cure4hersoul

PURCHASE COPIES OF THIS BOOK

To purchase additional copies of The Acceleration Cure please visit:

https://dreambiggoals.com/theaccelerationcure/
https://cure4thesoul.com/shop/

DREAM BIG GOAL-SETTING GUIDE & PLANNER

THE ULTIMATE 2 PART PLANNER FOR EVERY CHRISTIAN VISIONARY

Join our Challenge or Events

www.ingramcontent.com/pod-product-compliance
Lightning Source LLC
Chambersburg PA
CBHW070632160426
43194CB00009B/1443